INDIAN ASTROLOGY

INDIAN ASTROLOGY

A Western Approach
to the Ancient Hindu Art

by

Ronnie Gale Dreyer

THE AQUARIAN PRESS

First published 1990

British Library Cataloguing in Publication Data

Dreyer, Ronnie Gale
Indian Astrology: a Western interpretation
of the ancient Hindu art.
1. Hindu astrology
I. Title
133.5'0954

ISBN 0-85030-738-4

The Aquarian Press is part of the Thorsons Publishing Group, Wellingborough, Northamptonshire, NN8 2RQ, England.

Printed in Great Britain by Mackays of Chatham, Kent

1 3 5 7 9 10 8 6 4 2

CONTENTS

DEDICATION

*This book is dedicated to my parents,
Frances and Herbert Dreyer,
for their encouragement, support
and unconditional love;
and who, after all these years,
finally know how everything came to pass.*

LIST OF ILLUSTRATIONS

ACKNOWLEDGEMENTS

There are so many people without whose help this book could never have been conceived and written and to whom I would like to express my gratitude: first to Dr Muralil Sharma, Professor at Jyotish of Sanskrit University, who taught me about Hindu astrology because I had travelled so far in search of knowledge; and to my second teacher, Deoki Nandan Shastri, who chanted the slokas (stanzas) of the *Phaladeepika* in Sanskrit and entrusted me with his only translated copy; to Richard Lamm, whose astro-psychology classes propelled my interest in horoscope interpretation; to Ellen Perchonock and the staff of De Kosmos Meditation Center, who gave me my first opportunity to teach what I had learned; to Rachel Pollack and Edith Katz, who always encouraged me to write a book and then had to convince me that I could actually do it; and to Coen Cornelisen, a loyal student and wonderful friend, who let me use his computer and borrow his books in the early stages of writing; and Diana Blok for her detailed recollections and generosity. I would also like to thank my students, clients, family and friends for volunteering their horoscopes to me over the years and especially 'Annemarie' and 'Barbara', who graciously donated their charts for this book.

I never would have been able to complete this book had it not been for the remarkable collections, research facilities and services offered by the New York Public Library. The uninterrupted hours that I spent in the Library's Frederick Allen Memorial Room—a private oasis for writers—proved invaluable, as did the Inter-Library Loan Service which tracked down the Report of the Calendar Reform Committee for me. I would also like to cite Dr Alex

Wayman, Professor of Middle East Languages and Cultures at Columbia University, who informed me about the existence of the Calendar Reform Committee's Report, the best source of data on the history of astrology; and Elizabeth Dorjee for referring me to Dr Wayman. I am grateful to everyone at Thorsons who worked on the manuscript and especially to my editors — Michael Cox, who initiated the project, and Eileen Campbell and Iain Rodger, who took over the project and put up with my irregular schedule and transatlantic correspondence.

On a personal note, I want to express my thanks to friends and relatives who helped me adjust to being back in America and who had to accept a lack of quality time. To my aunt, Sylvia Crystal, who gave me a place to live where I could set up my computer, and to Joe and Bea Segal who allowed me the use of their home office, to Herbert Dreyer, for simply being nearby, and to Randi and Rene Jurgens, Karen Dreyer, Lieblein and Dan Lieblein for their contributions. I am especially indebted to Frances Dreyer, my mother, friend, and the best editor I know, who took the extra time to read, re-read and correct this manuscript. Her intuitive feeling for words and command of the English language enabled her to offer invaluable insights into the book's form and content. To Dani Roth, whose love, support and belief in me eased my adjustment to a strange way of life and who made the writing of this book a joyous task. And, finally, to my friends from Benares, India — Roger, Henry, Tott, Todd, Monty, Hughes, Vina, Alain, Maureen, Marilyn, Carol and Guru Prasad Shrivastava – may we all meet again someday for another group picture.

Ronnie Gale Dreyer
February 1990

INTRODUCTION

In the autumn of 1976, I was fortunate enough to travel overland to India where I had the rare opportunity to study Hindu astrology in Benares, first with Dr Muralil Sharma, a Professor of Jyotish at Sanskrit University, and later with Pandit Deoki Nandan Shastri, a practising astrologer. It was an exceptional time, as many Westerners — both young and old — had, like me, embarked on the same quest for Eastern knowledge and culture to bring back home to Europe and America.

Starting out from Athens, our tour bus with its 22 passengers journeyed through eastern Greece, Turkey, Iran, Afghanistan, and Pakistan before reaching its final destination: India. My memories of the mosques of Istanbul, the city of Teheran torn between the Shah of Iran's modernization and its traditional Islamic culture, the expansive barren deserts and wild-eyed nomads of Afghanistan, and the Golden Temple of the Sikhs in Amritsar, India (later used as a fortress during their internal strife with the Hindus) bring back images that seem as vivid and clear today as they were when I first encountered them. Looking back, I feel lucky that I was able to travel through Asia during this historically unique period when there was still the chance to view Iran and Afghanistan first-hand — countries that have since been transformed and will probably never be the way they once were again.

When we finally arrived in India, my first reaction to this strange land was, to say the least, one of total disorientation and complete cultural shock. While I had expected India to be consummately different from both Europe and America, never in my wildest dreams could I envision the overwhelming pandemonium which I encountered there. Everywhere I looked I saw cows — deemed holy by the Hindus — freely roaming the streets, seeming, at times, more human than the homeless beggars whose frail bodies dotted every street corner. The cyclists and rickshaw drivers added to the chaos by obstructing and tying up traffic not unlike the motorists and taxi drivers of any Western metropolitan city. To add to the confusion, tea shops, clothing stores and perfume stands were all wedged together waiting to be patronized by the crowds of exotic Indian men and women dressed in their kortas and saris. The styles and materials of these garments have not been altered by the passage of time and seem to parallel Hindu astrology whose basic principles can be found in ancient definitive texts written as far back as AD 500. The application of the rules of Hindu astrology to the lives of contemporary Indians evinces their adherence to the tenets of Hinduism — a centuries-old religion — and contributes to the cohesiveness of a society virtually untouched by modern life.

In the capital city of New Delhi — the end point of the bus ride — I enquired as to where I could learn Hindu astrology to supplement my knowledge of Occidental astrology. I was told to go to Benares,* a city in the north-central province of Uttar Pradesh, which houses Benares Hindu University, one of the largest and most diverse centres of learning in India. In addition to the University's matriculated Indian population, its enrolment boasts a huge cross-section of international students whose education is also conducted in English. In Benares, where I lived for the next six months, I met many Europeans and Americans who were studying subjects such as religion, philosophy, Indian music, Hindi and Sanskrit both at the University and/or with a private tutor. None of them, however, were familiar with anybody studying or teaching Jyotish, the term for the mathematical and astronomical principles which are the foundation of Hindu astrology. By querying professors at Benares Hindu University I learned that Jyotish was taught at Sanskrit University located at the opposite end of the city.

---

* Benares is also called Varanasi by religious Hindus, who come from all over India just to swim in the blessed waters of the Ganges River which runs through the city.

However, there was one drawback. Instruction at Sanskrit University was conducted using Sanskrit texts, the ancient written language of India.

By chance (if there is such a thing), Dr Muralil Sharma, a Professor of Jyotish, was in the Mathematics Department office at Sanskrit University at the precise moment of my enquiry and promptly offered to tutor me for one hour every day. Furthermore, his English was impeccable. When I brought up the question of payment, his reply was simple. Because I had travelled such a long distance in search of knowledge, it was his professional obligation to teach me whatever he could for the duration of my stay. This attitude exemplifies the Hindu conviction of predestination to fulfil a particular task. Dr Sharma was grateful that the gods had entrusted him with their wisdom and, by passing it on to others, he was repaying them for granting him that knowledge.

In order to take notes from Dr Sharma for one hour each morning, I bicycled cross-town faithfully each day to the Sanskrit University campus braving the intense heat, the freely roaming cows and the aggressive rickshaw drivers. Dr Sharma instructed me to wear a traditional Indian sari so as not to distract the young Indian men on campus and it was imperative that I be prepared for my daily lesson by reciting what I learnt the previous day. Because Dr Sharma knew that the length of my stay in India was limited to six months, he gave me a crash course in Hindu astrology by enlightening me about the ancient scriptural writings most relevant to modern life. He defined the nature of the Sidereal Zodiac, tithis, nakshatras and other astronomical principles unique to Hindu astrology and explained the fundamental interpretive techniques which required the least complicated mathematical calculations. In order to illustrate the intrinsic relationship between astrology and Hinduism, Dr Sharma also pointed out the horoscopic indications of an individual's patron god or goddess, caste, previous incarnations and other religious principles which could affect him/her.

About two months later, I met my second astrology teacher, Pandit Deoki Nandan Shastri, whose impressive reading of a friend's horoscope led to our introduction. From his commercial storefront practice located in the heart of the bazaar — a myriad of tourist shops, boutiques, temples and tea shops best described as an Indian shopping mall — he had become quite well-versed in interpreting charts for a foreign clientele. Whereas Dr Sharma excelled in teaching theory and astronomical principles, Pandit Shastri's forté was the art of interpretation. He introduced me to the complicated numerical system used by Hindu astrologers to evaluate character traits and to determine whether the ensuing periods will be 'good' or 'bad'. He also taught me how to calculate the different types of charts which are constructed for every aspect of life — marriage, journeys, illness, etc. — many of which require hour-long mathematical calculations. I spent my morning hour with Dr Sharma and my afternoon hour with 'Guru-ji' (as I referred to Pandit Shastri) who recited to me in Sanskrit the verses of the ancient text, *Phaladeepika*, followed by their English translations. I left India with English-language books about Indian astrology, notebooks containing a wealth of information but, most of all, with a heart filled with gratitude for all the kindness shown me not only by my teachers but by all the Indian families and other friends I met along the way.

When I returned to America during the summer of 1977, I considered writing an astrology book which would combine ancient Hindu principles with modern Western methods of interpretation. The United States and England were at the height of the 'Me Generation' and the popular mode of the day was the Human Potential Movement which expounded theories such as 'we have total control over everything that happens — past, present and future' and 'nothing is ever left to chance'. Humanistic Astrology — whose philosophy was adapted from Humanistic Psychology as pioneered by Alfred Adler, Abraham Maslow and Fritz Perls, was in vogue and there was no interest in publishing an astrology book pertaining to ancient fatalistic principles translated into a modern context. The tide has since turned and people have begun to accept that, in addition to the 'awareness' or control they have developed over their lives, there are always certain elements from their past or in their environment which are beyond their grasp. It is in this contemporary mode that the idea of transforming ancient beliefs into contemporary philosophy could begin to be embraced.

In 1986, nine years after returning from India, I was approached to write a book about Hindu astrology and decided that the key would be to address the Westerner who wishes to apply Hindu astrology to his/her own study of Occidental astrology. Although I use many Hindu astrological principles in my own practice, quite some time had elapsed since I reviewed my notes and the English language texts I brought back from the East. In writing this book, however, I have once again been able to relive those six months in India and recall quite vividly my two Indian astrology teachers — the academic Dr Sharma and the professional Pandit Shastri.

What follows, therefore, is a compilation of what I learned from my teachers, from books written in English by Hindu astrologers, and from translations of *Brihat Jataka*, *Saravali* and *Phaladeepika* — ancient astrological texts. Most importantly, I have incorporated both Eastern and Western techniques which I have utilized in my own astrological practice over the years. Because the astrological scriptures were written by Indians who were practising Hindus attempting to understand their stations in life from the perspective of Hindu life cycles, the term 'Indian astrology' can be misleading. Throughout the book, therefore, I more often use the words 'Hindu astrology'. In this regard, it is important to distinguish between an Indian (belonging to the nation of India) and a Hindu (belonging to the religion) since there are so many religious groups in India.

Since this book is merely an introduction to the basic principles of Hindu astrology, I have extracted from the scriptures practical and non-religious concepts which can be used to enhance Western methods of horoscopy. Although I have omitted references to past and future lives or classifications by caste, I have inserted non-secular Hindu principles for the insight they provide into Indian lifestyles. On many occasions, I have transposed archaic expressions into modern Western terminology and have condensed complicated methods of interpretation into concise easy-to-use formulas. In other instances, I have quoted directly from the scriptures to illustrate the authenticity of the language that was used.

I do not attempt to prove the complete accuracy of Hindu astrology, and I do not recommend that Western astrologers or students of astrology replace their present systems with it. While Jyotish may be a feasible means of prediction for the follower of Hinduism who does not have complete autonomy over life, its formulas are not always applicable to Westerners who have so many available choices. To this end, I have consciously omitted scriptural methods of foretelling illness and death, and I advise anyone researching Hindu astrology to ignore these aspects of it, since they are not pertinent to modern life and can be dangerous and misleading.

Because these pages contain new and strange-sounding material, I recommend that this book not be devoured but instead be digested, chapter by chapter, over an extended period of time. I hope that in addition to providing a methodical means for understanding and, perhaps, using Hindu astrology, this book will convey the significant role that astrology plays in uniting the Hindu community whose religion still dictates most of their activities. Finally, my wish is for this work to serve as one more link between East and West — if only because the roots of both our astrological systems lie in ancient Babylonia and Greece — and as one more way of saying that despite cultural, religious and national identity, we are all synchronized with the universal rhythm of life.

PART I
STRUCTURE

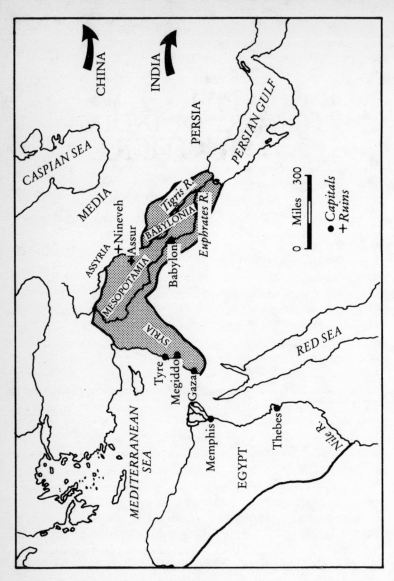

Fig 1.1. A map of the Ancient Middle East.

1
HISTORY OF INDIAN ASTROLOGY

Astrology in the Ancient World

To trace the roots of astrology in India, we must first go back to the period between 4000 and 2000 BC (also called the Age of Taurus) when there were four major Eastern civilizations whose communities centred around fertile river valleys. The locations of these thriving cultures were the Nile valley in Egypt, the valley between the Tigris and Euphrates rivers in Sumer (southern Mesopotamia and present-day southern Iraq), the Hwang Ho valley in China and the Indus valley in India (Fig 1.1). Due to advanced irrigation techniques, agriculture flourished and food was abundant. Sailors and merchants traded profitably with one another, and each area was introduced to the other's natural resources. What these agrarian cultures ultimately had in common was their commitment to self-sufficiency, maximum productivity and economic stability: qualities of the sign of Taurus from which this era derives its name.

These early farming communities depended upon seasonal changes and meteorological conditions to stimulate vegetative growth and they adjusted their planting methods accordingly. By directly observing the patterns in the sky, they came to know how planetary movements affected weather conditions and, in turn, their harvest. They were soon able to predict auspicious times for planting based not only on the seasonal changes but on the prominence of certain stars — later identified as planets — and the phases of the Moon. In Sumer, China, and India, the Moon was revered as a creative power, while the Sun, due to its intense heat, was viewed as a destructive entity which scorched the earth and left the land parched. The Moon, on the other hand, brought the cool night air and promoted growth. Planting during the waxing phase of the Moon was common among the farmers of these cultures and is practised even today. In fact, it is still said that one should begin a project during the waxing moon but never during a waning moon.

Up until approximately 2000 BC, the Mesopotamian peninsula (present-day Iraq) was divided into two distinct settlements, Sumer in the south and Assyria in the north. The Sumerian people came from the East and were Oriental in appearance, while Assyria was occupied by a variety of nomadic Semitic tribes originally from southern Arabia. Between 2000 and 1750 BC, the Akkadians (named for their Semitic dialect) who lived in northern Mesopotamia slowly inhabited the southern part of the peninsula. Initially the area was renamed Sumer-Akkad to designate the cohabitation and co-operation between these two cultures which nevertheless maintained separate identities. The Akkadians proved to be the stronger power, however, and they eventually took over the region. In c.1750 BC the great civilization of Babylonia was born with Babylon as its capital replacing Nippur, the former capital of Sumer-Akkad.

The Babylonian empire became known throughout the ancient world for its agricultural, intellectual and scientific advances, including astrology. In their function as soothsayers, the Babylonian priests had already developed an extensive method of divination linking certain events and growing patterns to earthquakes, floods, wind directions, thunder, lightning and other meteorological phenomena which they thought to be manifestations of the divine will. These conditions guided the Babylonian farmers in the timing of their harvest, the king as to when he could travel, and the merchants and sailors in planning their voyages. Precision and attention to detail made the priests impeccable record keepers and most of their omens were recorded on clay tablets between 1750 and 1500 BC. By studying the heavenly bodies, however, the Babylonian priests soon found the luminaries to be superior omens from which they could efficiently anticipate natural phenomena and their accompanying significant events.

Within the hierarchy of Babylonian society, the priests were the scientists and, as such, the most educated class. They were given access to the libraries and observatories where they spent countless solitary hours watching the sky with the most advanced instruments of their day. In Babylonia, as well as in Greece, India and China, these early observations of the Sun, Moon and the planets were made with the gnomon, a vertical stick used to measure astronomical distances by the length and directions of the shadow it cast. By methodically studying planetary configurations they were able to time planetary cycles and to determine astronomical distances and relationships. This led them to the development of a more advanced method of prediction by which they charted recurring configurations such as eclipses, phases of the Moon and the positions of the most prominent 'stars' — the Moon, the Sun, Jupiter, Venus, Saturn, Mercury and Mars.[1] This was coupled with what seemed to be a coinciding event, growing pattern, or meteorological condition. With the knowledge they acquired, they were soon able to predict, with amazing regularity, weather patterns, auspicious planting times and whether the ensuing period would bring peace or hostility. Though all ancient civilizations were aware of the correlations between the timing of celestial movements and mundane conditions, the Babylonians methodically logged this information and are thus credited with creating the first recorded astrological system.

It was about 721 BC during the reign of Sargon II of Nineveh that the astronomical data along with their accompanying effects were recorded onto thousands of cuneiform tablets. Cuneiform writing entailed pressing wedge-shaped leaves incised with marks and symbols into wet clay tablets. By uncovering and translating these tablets which lay buried for thousands of years, archaeologists in the nineteenth century were able not only to decipher astronomical and astrological data, but to learn about life in Mesopotamia itself.

The desire to know beforehand when to expect certain climatic conditions, holidays and other phenomena brought about the creation of a calendar and accurate scientific data to back up the calendrical listings. Since approximately 3000 BC, the Egyptians had been using a completely solar calendar which based the year on 365 days, the time it took for the annual floods of the Nile to reach that same point each year. In the eighth century BC, the Babylonians constructed a soli-lunar calendar which fitted lunar days and months into the Egyptian solar year of 365 days. The Egyptians had been dividing their year into three seasons of four months each marked by distinct climatic changes; by contrast, the Babylonians divided their year — the way we still do today — by the spring equinox, autumn equinox, winter solstice, and summer solstice, the four cardinal points. The months were marked off by the cycle of the phases of the Moon and the days were divided by the appearance and disappearance of the Moon rather than by the rising and the setting of the Sun. The calendar also included planetary placements and conjunctions, phases of the Moon, and lunar and solar eclipses. It was with the gnomon that the equinoctial and solstitial points, along with other lunar measurements included on the calendar, were discovered.[2]

In the eyes of the priests, the celestial bodies were manifestations of their gods and goddesses. To this end, many religious holidays held in their honour were celebrated in accordance with the New Moon or Full Moon whereas other pagan festivities occurred on one of the equinoxes or solstices. The Babylonians celebrated their New Year at the autumn equinox, the time of sowing the crop, whereas the Sumerians before them had celebrated the New Year on the spring equinox, the time of reaping the harvest. By marking off the holidays on their lunar calendar, the Babylonians knew in advance when to make the necessary preparations for these rites which were such a vital part of the religious and social life of the community.

From the time of the Persian conquest in 539 BC and up until the final Greek take-over in c.330 BC, the Babylonians continued to make great strides in both the fields of astronomy and astrology. These advances included the discovery of the astrolabe (an instrument used to measure altitudes), the perfection of lunar measurements, and the early use of the zodiac. From records of the period, it appears that it was not until the fifth or sixth century that the first individual horoscopes were calculated. These earliest horoscopes were most probably the charts of their kings whose destinies as supreme rulers represented the fate of their nation. Until this time the Babylonians had primarily been concerned with agricultural planning and with political and economic forecasting.

The philosopher Herodotus and the mathematician Pythagoras were among the Greek intellectuals who visited Babylonia in the sixth century BC and brought back impressive astronomical data which included lunar measurements, the equinoctial and solstitial points, the constellations of the zodiac, and the construction of individual horoscopes. When Babylonia was finally annexed by the Greek empire in 330 BC, this information was fully transmitted to Greek scientists who combined Babylonian findings with their own astronomical theories. Unlike the combined field of Babylonian astronomy and astrology, Greek astronomy was, up until this time, neither mathematically sophisticated nor religious. It was only when Babylonian astronomy was introduced into Greek culture that the planets took on qualities similar to those of the Greek gods and goddesses of Mount Olympus. Gradually, as it did in our own culture, two sciences developed side by side — astronomy and astrology. While *astronomers* map out the positions of the Sun, the Moon, and the planets which determine, among other things, length of the year and timing of the seasons, it is *astrologers* who raise these physical bodies to the level of religious deities or other influential symbols.

The Greek astronomers Hipparchus and Ptolemy went even further than their Babylonian counterparts, and their advanced techniques calculated the rate of the movement of the equinoxes and divided the stars into the twelve constellations of the zodiac. But it was Greek astrologers — whose philosophy emphasized the inherent dignity and self-determination of man — who lifted the horoscope beyond its religious and mundane aspects in order to view

TABLE 1.1 CHRONOLOGY OF ERAS OF THE ANCIENT WORLD

Approx. Years BC	Southern Mesopotamia	Egypt	Greece	Rome	India
3000	3000 BC–1750 BC				Pre-2500 BC Indus River Valley settlements
2500	Sumer				2500–1500 BC Aryan Afghani Tribes who wrote Vedas
2000	1750–1500 BC Sumer-Akkad				
1500					
1000	1500–537 BC Babylonia				1300–400 BC Vedanga Jyotish Calendar
500	539-330 BC Persian Empire				
	330 BC- Annexed by Alexander the Great as part of Greek Empire		330 BC Rise of Alexander the Great		400 BC–AD 0 Buddhist rule
0		44 BC Conquered by Caesar and Roman Empire			323 BC Greek empire extends to India
AD		Egypt and Greece and Italy under auspices of Roman Empire AD 0–500			
500					AD 400–1200 Siddhantic Calendar
1000					AD 1200–1757 Moslem Rule
1500					AD 1757 –1948 British Rule

the fate of the individual, and greatly influenced the way we approach astrological interpretation today.

As the Euphrates River changed direction, the canals which supplied the large cities no longer received water and the once fertile Mesopotamian valley became dry and barren. With the water supply practically cut off, the great agrarian communities of the Middle East slowly disappeared and the region became uninhabitable. Egypt was conquered by Caesar in 44 BC and by the time the Christian era was finally heralded, the Roman Empire ruled the ancient world. The Julian calendar, implemented throughout the Roman Empire, was not initially calculated according to Christian dates. Later on, the Christians introduced their own holidays, however, which were Hebrew in origin. Most of the astrological tablets of the era were either destroyed or buried when Babylon was finally pillaged by the Romans in the first century AD.

During the Christian era, astrology was rejected as heresy by the Church, and did not resurface in the Western world until the Renaissance, when it was once again taught in universities and revered as a science. Only since these tablets were recovered during the nineteenth-century excavations in Iraq have we learned that it was not the Greeks who originated the astrology we use today — though they did indeed perfect it — but the Babylonians.

It is the consensus of most archaeologists and historians that astronomical and astrological knowledge was disseminated throughout the ancient world by sailors, merchants, and, most importantly, by conquering peoples. The Babylonian system of star-gazing and measuring of time was the forerunner of most modern astrological systems and it especially influenced the lunar-based systems of China and India which are still used today. Though each culture used its own particular observations to develop an astrological system which best suited its religious and cultural needs, the origins of astrology, as we know it today, lie in ancient Babylonia.

TABLE 1.2 OVERVIEW OF INDIAN ERAS[4]

Pre-2500 BC	Cities of Harappa and Mohenjodaro along the Indus River Valley, contemporaneous with the civilizations of Egypt and Sumer.
2500-1500 BC	Settled by Indo-Aryan tribes from Afghanistan, who conquered Indus River Valley and settled Ganges River Valley. Responsible for writing of Vedas and the beginnings of Hinduism.
1300 BC–AD 300	Dominated by the calendaric and astronomical principles of the *Vedanga Jyotish*.
500 BC	Germination of the teachings of Gauthama Buddha.
323 BC	Alexander the Great extends his empire to India, bringing Greek astronomical principles such as Precession of the Equinoxes and zodiacal signs.
273–200 BC	Buddhist domination especially strong under Emperor Asoka (273–236 BC).
100 BC–AD 200	Saka and Kusana Era.
AD 400–1200	Dominated by the Siddhantic Calendar, Rise of Astrology as an interpretive art and emergence of first astrologers.
AD 1200–1757	Islamic domination under Hejira Calendar while Hindus still use religious calendar.
AD 1757–1948	British rule and use of the Gregorian Calendar, with Hindus still using their own religious calendar.
AD 1948 –present	India is an independent state with the decision to retain the two calendars — the Gregorian Calendar for official purposes and their own lunar calendar based on the Siddhantic calendar.

Development of Astrology in India

Pre-2500 BC

The earliest settlements in India, contemporaneous with Egypt and Sumer, were the two cities of Harappa and Mohenjodaro, which flourished before 2500 BC. These settlements of the Indus River valley were among the largest and most progressive of their time.

Not much is known about these people except that their sailors and merchants most probably travelled to the Near and Middle East. Like the Egyptians and the Sumerians, Indians were adept at working with metals and bronze and were also great innovators in the arts and sciences. On the symmetrical avenues and streets of their well-planned cities stood architecturally advanced buildings used for living quarters, government offices, and temples. There were courtyards, facilities for bathing and even advanced drainage systems.[5] Their irrigation techniques made them successful farmers, and their cities prospered and became great commercial centres. Due to their peace-loving ethos, however, these Indians were easily defeated by nomadic Afghani tribes who ultimately conquered the region.

2500-1500 BC

Between 2500 BC and 1500 BC, India was inhabited and ruled by Indo-Aryan tribes from Afghanistan who resettled the Indus River valley and formed their own communities in the Ganges River valley. These Afghani tribes also settled parts of Mesopotamia and some of the royal families of Asia Minor were thought to belong to this group of people. In the same way that the Akkadians overran the Sumerians and conquered southern Mesopotamia, the Afghanis, more adventurous and aggressive than the early Indian farmers, easily took possession of the land and inherited their cities.

This period is famous for its Epics, great stories of the earliest heroes of Hinduism.

> The Epics were passed on by word of mouth . . . The longest of the two Epics is the *Mahabharata*, . . . the longest poem in the world . . . It is the story of a great

civil war in the region where now is located the city of Delhi. Its most famous portion is the *Bhagavadgita*. The second of the two great Epics, the *Ramayana*, tells the story of Rama, a heroic Aryan king of Vedic times. It relates the adventures of Rama as he undertakes to rescue his wife Sita, who had been kidnapped by a devil-king of Ceylon . . . Originally the tales in the Epics were told to preserve the memory of the deeds of famous Aryan warriors. However, as the stories were passed down from generation to generation they began to take on religious significance. Many of the basic beliefs of modern Hinduism became embodied in the tales.[6]

These Indo-Aryans are also credited with writing a series of religious books called the Vedas. Considered to be the 'Hindu Bible', the Vedas are a rich body of literature comprised of sacred hymns and poems which map out basic creation myths and legends of the people. The Vedic hymns were said to have been revealed by the seven stars or planets called rishis, literally meaning 'to shine'.[7] The priests who wrote the Vedas were called Brahmins and they dedicated the Vedas to their god, Brahma, the source of life. The Vedas, as well as other religious and astrological scriptures that followed, were written in Sanskrit, the original language of the Hindu people. But most importantly, these scriptures outlined the original tenets of Hinduism, the religion of four-fifths of today's Indian population. The following passages from the Vedas illustrate some of these ideas which form the doctrine of Hinduism.

1) The essence of all things is one supreme energy which permeates every aspect of the universe. It is an impersonal, immaterial, unborn and undying force. It is called Brahman.

2) There are individual souls which are unbreakable and eternal parts of the universal soul. They are named Atman. Brahman and Atman are one and indivisible, yet the Atman living in the world of senses as nature, seems to exist apart from Brahman. This apparent separateness is Maya or illusion.

3) Nature is the manifestation of the supreme energy . . .

Brahman, and is in continuous evolution according to its immutable law.

4) So long as we live in illusion we place our faith in ever-changing things of nature. The effect of the fickle nature incites our pains and pleasures as experiences in our life. Only through the realisation or reabsorption of oneself into Brahman can one become free from worldly sensations of pains and pleasure.

5) Activities are the incidence of life. Every person acts according to his soul, mind and the senses and produces his destiny as misfortunes or fortunes. For there cannot be a result without action in the past. Thus each soul receives many experiences birth . . . After birth and gradually shakes off illusions of separateness and proceeds through self purification towards oneness.[8]

Central to Hinduism is the law of karma, the idea that one's deeds in this lifetime are determined by the quality of other lifetimes. The Sanskrit word, *karma*, represents the accumulated actions, positive and negative, of former lifetimes that help to create one's present *dharma*, one's 'assigned' duties in this lifetime.

The karma of the individual is the factor which determines the progress of the soul through its various incarnations. Karma appears in three aspects: Sanchita, the sum or result of acts committed in the previous incarnation, Prarabda, acts of the present incarnation which are subject both to the influence of the previous life and to the exercise of free will in the present one, and Agami, future, unrealised acts. Thus the progress of the soul from one incarnation to another is conditioned by a mixture of free will, karma and fate.[9]

Ever since Eastern religions and spirituality have been introduced into mainstream Western culture, much of the Sanskrit terminology has been misunderstood here. Many Westerners loosely use the word 'karma' to describe anything that happens which seems fated. If, for instance, we receive a gift from someone soon after we bought a gift for someone else, we call it 'karma'. We have, of course, lifted its meaning from the traditional definition which does, in fact, refer to the act of getting back what we have given. What Hindus are referring to, however, are

important acts which will have their consequences
throughout the course of many lifetimes.

Dr B. V. Raman, one of India's foremost modern Hindu
astrologers, describes the laws of karma as follows:

> According to ancient texts when one dies, his soul which is
> enveloped in a subtle body and invested with the sum-total
> of good and bad Karma passes after some time into another
> body leaving off his gross body, as a man casts off worn-
> out clothes and puts on new ones. His reincarnation takes
> place in a physical body corresponding with the deeds done
> by him in his previous life. The processes of death and
> birth go on until the person concerned attains
> emancipation. The cardinal doctrine of Karma therefore is
> the law of cause and effect in accordance with the maxim
> 'as a man soweth so shall he reap'.[10]

As an illustration of life in India, the Vedas describe a
society consisting of priests, warriors, merchants, artisans
and slaves, whose classifications form the descending class
order which eventually became the rigid Hindu caste
system. Those five categories are equivalent to the
contemporary caste system of Brahmins (priests and the
well-educated), Kshatrias (rulers and warriors), Vaishya
(merchants), Shudra (farm labourers), and the lowest class,
Harijans or Untouchables (outcasts), who do not work or
own property and often support themselves by begging on
the streets. Whereas the Brahmin caste once consisted only
of priests, contemporary Brahmins — still the highest rung
on the ladder — now include the well-educated and
wealthy.

Although the caste system is not an aspect of Hinduism
per se, and is almost universally considered politically
unjust, it is still an accepted socio-economic division of the
Hindu population. The Hindu accepts that the caste he has
been born into, the family he was born into and the
profession he was chosen for (many times his father's or
father-in-law's) all exist because of the soul's journey
through previous lifetimes. If he committed sins, crimes or
was dishonourable in his last life then he will pay for his
indiscretions by being born into a lowly caste in this
incarnation. If he was honourable, then he will be
rewarded this time around: moreover, obligations

performed within one's caste will determine who and what one will be in the next life.

> Hence a Brahmin in this life may be born as a Harijan in the next life; a rich man in this life may be born as a poor man in the next life and vice versa. Thus the station of life or the degree of wealth, etc., that one has attained in this life is mostly due to the Karma at his credit in the previous life.[11]

Though there are no definite astronomical rules set down in the Vedas, the numerous references to the Sun, the Moon, certain stars, the months and the seasons indicate that the authors were familiar with Mesopotamian astronomy and astrology.[12] These references are to be found in the Rig-Vedas, the earliest of the four Vedic books. Though it was the Babylonians who first used a lunar-based calendar and a thorough astrological system, we know from records of this period that the Indians, too, had developed a soli-lunar calendar and the year was already being divided into 12 months. There are no names for these 12 months as such but there is mention in the Vedas of a wheel of time divided into 12 parts.

1300 BC–AD 300

The period extending from 1300 BC until AD 300 was dominated by the *Vedanga Jyotish,* a separate body of work and an adjunct to the written laws of Vedic worship. In addition to containing the calendric and astronomical principles that were formulated and set down during the previous Vedic Age, the *Vedanga Jyotish* also describes life in India at that time. (A secondary function of most ancient religious texts has always been to illustrate daily life in a particular culture; the Bible is a good example of this.)

The *Vedanga Jyotish* is referred to as one of the six limbs of the Vedas, with 'Vedanga' indicating anything relating to the Vedas and 'Jyotish' meaning astronomy. Today, Jyotish, as it is taught in the universities in India, has come to include both the study of astronomical and astrological principles. In this time-period, however, it consisted solely of the precise mathematical rules affecting planetary movements, much of which was influenced by the discoveries of the Babylonians and the Greeks.

Due to foreign conquests and invasions from the Near and Middle East there were, in this period of Indian history, a plethora of philosophies which not only modified the arts and sciences but drastically changed life in general. After annexing Babylonia and Egypt, Alexander the Great extended his empire into India's northwest province of Punjab in around 323 BC. The Greek empire, now incorporating Mesopotamian and Egyptian culture, became so powerful as it spread from Asia Minor to Northwest India that Greek remained the language throughout the entire East for quite some time.

Though they made remarkable contributions in the areas of religion, art, literature and sciences, the Indians who lived between 300 BC and AD 400 rejected Greek astronomical and astrological findings due to the hostility of their political and religious leaders towards any form of fortune-telling. This hostility was especially prevalent in the third century BC when a great portion of the population rallied together under the leadership of the Buddhist emperor Asoka, whose religion disavowed the belief in predestination and, ultimately, astrology.

Very simply stated, Buddhism, the dominant religion of this period, teaches that the path of moderation will lead towards liberation in this lifetime, whereas the Hindu belief is that we must work hard in order to obtain a better place in the next one. The Buddha was adamant in his opposition to astrology, which then consisted of lunar conjunctions with other planets and omens based on the appearance of comets and eclipses. He ridiculed these types of omens and held astrology in great contempt. Even those Hindu political leaders who were anti-Buddhist were also anti-astrology as they felt it discouraged people from showing any personal initiative. The Indians accepted these condemnations and continued to reject astrology as a belief system.[13]

Just like the Babylonian priests, the monks in India were in a perfect position to carry out astronomical studies due to their solitude and the access they had to materials and instruments. But because astronomical knowledge became confused with astrological omens, the cultivation of scientific astronomy was also forbidden in the monasteries throughout India. This thwarted the germination of astrological thought until Buddhism declined and astronomical calculations were again resumed. It was around 100 BC that the study of astrology, condemned by the Buddha, slowly began to find its way back into the mainstream of religious thought. The city of Ujjain became the centre where ideas were disseminated and practitioners of astrology could combine Western ideas with Eastern methodology. Ujjain was, in fact, later adopted as the Indian 'Greenwich' from which point east and west longitudes were recorded.

Between the appearance of the writings of the Greek astronomer, Hipparchus, in 100 BC and the publication of Ptolemy's astronomical treatise, *Tetrabiblios*, in AD 150, there was an enormous rise in horoscopic astrology throughout the West. The concept of the individual horoscope rapidly spread to the rest of the world and was reintroduced into India between 100 BC and AD 200, during the regime of the Saka and Kusana Rulers. With the Greek influence on Hindu astrology and mythology (Table 1.3), the Indian gods and goddesses took on some of the characteristics of the Greek deities and the days of the week in India were soon named after the planets. The qualities and names of the zodiacal signs were also retranslated from the Greek into Sanskrit. But it was not until around AD 400, the beginning of the Siddhantic period, that these Greek techniques were fully utilized and assimilated into Indian culture.

AD 400-1200

This period was marked by the use of the Siddhantic calendar, which was based on the Siddhantas, five scientific astronomical treatises written around AD 400. One of the texts, the Surya Siddhanta, was said to have been described by the Sun God to Asura Maya, the architect of the gods, who then revealed it to the Indian rishis, the same stars who revealed the Vedas to the Brahmin priests. The Surya Siddhanta, still referred to today, describes the Hindu version of the creation of the world, including the creation of the Sun, the Moon and the planets. The universe is taken to be geocentric and the

Table 1.3

Different Names of Zodiacal Signs

Beginning and ending of the signs	Names of the signs and symbol	English equivalent	Greek names	Varaha Mihira	Indian names	Babylonian names
0° – 30°	♈ Aries	Ram	Krios	Kriya	Mesha	Ku or Iku (Ram)
30 – 60	♉ Taurus	Bull	Tauros	Tāburi	Vrishaba	Te-te (Bull)
60 – 90	♊ Gemini	Twins	Didumoi	Jituma	Mithuna	Masmasu (Twins)
90 – 120	♋ Cancer	Crab	Karxinos	Kulīra	Kataka	Nangaru (Crab)
120 – 150	♌ Leo	Lion	Leon	Leya	Simha	Aru (Lion)
150 – 180	♍ Virgo	Virgin	Parthenos	Pathona	Kanyā	Ki (Virgin)
180 – 210	♎ Libra	Balance	Zugos	Jūka	Thula	Nuru (Scales)
210 – 240	♏ Scorpio	Scorpion	Scorpios	Kaurpa	Vrischika	Akrabu (Scorpion)
240 – 270	♐ Sagittarius	Archer	Tozeutes	Tauksika	Dhanus	Pa (Archer)
270 – 300	♑ Capricorn	Goat	Ligoxeros	Ākokera	Makara	Sahu (Goat)
300 – 330	♒ Aquarius	Water Bearer	Gdroxoos	Hrdroga	Kumbha	Gu (Water carrier)
330 – 360	♓ Pisces	Fish	Ichthues	Antyabha	Meena	Zib (Fish)

A comparison of the various astrological names: the Greek names, themselves of Babylonian origin, were translated into Indian names:

Table 1.3. It can be easily inferred from the table that the names are of Babylonian origin, but their exact significance is not always known. It has been assumed that the symbols used to denote the signs have been devised from a representation of the figure of the animal or object after which the sign has been named, for example, the mouth and horns of the Ram, the same of the Bull, and so on. It is seen that Vaharamihira's alternative names given in column 5 are simply Greek names corrupted in course of transmission and as adopted for Sanskrit . . . the purely Sanskrit names given in column 6 are all translations of Greek names with the exceptions of: twins, which becomes Mithuna or 'amorous couple', the archer, which becomes the 'bow', the Goat, which becomes the crocodile, water bearer, which becomes the water pot. Some of them appear to have been translations of Babylonian names. The Babylonian names are given in the seventh column, with their meanings . . . it is thus seen that the names of the zodiacal signs are originally of Babylonian origin. They were taken over almost without change by the Greeks and subsequently by the Romans and the Hindus from Greco-Chaldean astrology.[14]

planets are listed in descending order according to their proximity to the earth. Beginning with the farthest and ending with the closest planet, they are recorded as follows: Saturn, Jupiter, Mars, Sun, Venus, Mercury, Moon.[15]

The Siddhantic calendar was a soli-lunar calendar which incorporated the lunar calculations of the Babylonians, the zodiacal signs of the Greeks, plus the uniquely Indian lunar measurements, the tithi and the nakshatra.* The Indian lunar day, called a tithi, is measured by the length of time it takes for the Moon to travel 12°, one-thirtieth of a lunar month or 360°. Beginning with the New Moon — the conjunction of the Moon and the Sun — one tithi is completed when the waxing Moon moves ahead of the Sun by 12°. The tithis are numbered from 1 to 15 with the end of the fifteenth tithi, or 180°, being the Full Moon.

---

* Nakshatras will be discussed in more detail in Chapter 8.

Moving from Full Moon and back again to New Moon, the tithis of the waning Moon are also numbered from 1 to 15, with the end of the fifteenth tithi or 360° equalling the New Moon. This gives us 30 tithis in a lunar month. By counting 30 lunar days from the New Moon or conjunction, the Moon has travelled 360° from New Moon to Full Moon and back again to New Moon completing its monthly phases. The *average* lunar day or the time it takes the tithi to travel 12° is ±23.62 hours, a little less than the solar day of 23 hours 56 minutes measured from sunrise to sunrise. Because of the irregularity in the Moon's motion, the length of the individual tithi can be anything from 20 to 26 hours.[16] Since Siddhantic times, the Hindu lunar calendar has been marked off by these tithis rather than by our solar days. Even today holidays and important dates are always listed on the Hindu lunar calendar according to the tithi or lunar day.

The individual days were also marked off according to which lunar mansion — or nakshatra — the Moon occupied during the evening. The nakshatras, another unique feature of the Hindu calendar, are more commonly called 'moon mansions'. Of the thousands of cuneiform tablets dating from between 1500 BC and the first century AD which have been translated into English, there are none which have extensive references to moon mansions. Due to the present accuracy in calculating the tithi and the nakshatra, the actual measurements have changed greatly over the centuries. What remains the same is that they are as significant in Hindu timekeeping today as they were when first recorded in the Siddhantas.

The authors of the *Surya Siddhanta* supported the concept of the Tropical Zodiac which uses the spring equinox, or equinoctial point, to designate the symbolic first degree of Aries and the beginning of the astrological year. This was due to a phenomenon called the Precession of the Equinoxes, the retrograde movement of the equinoctial point through the constellations of the zodiac.* This concept of the Precession was brought to India by the Greeks and was included in the writings of the *Surya*

---

* This will be further detailed in Chapter 2.

Siddhanta. By observing the shifting of the equinoctial and solstitial points due to the Precession of the Equinoxes, Hindu astronomers determined their own rate for this motion instead of utilizing the rate already determined by the Greek astronomer Hipparchus.

Although these points were supported by the originators of the Surya Siddhanta, the writers of subsequent Hindu calendars rejected their use. Instead of using the equinoctial point to indicate the start of the astrological year, later Hindu calendar-makers decided to use the first degree of the *actual* constellation Aries to indicate its commencement. This 'fixed degree of Aries' formed the basis of the Sidereal — or Nirayana — Zodiac, the one still used by Hindus today and the major difference between their system and ours.

It was during this Siddhantic period that the first Hindu astrologers began to emerge. Influenced by Greek horoscopy and Siddhantic mathematical rules, the astronomers in India discovered that, by drawing a map of the sky at the exact moment of birth, a picture of the person's character and life could be determined. For the Hindu astrologer, the horoscope represented the stage a man's soul had reached and why his particular caste suited him. Different planetary configurations were indicative of character traits, accumulated past karma and present dharma.

> Astrology reveals the result of our past karma, expressed probably in terms of what we crudely call planetary influences. Astrology reveals the consequence of our actions which we do not remember in this life and are untraceable in this birth . . . planets, therefore, indicate the results of previous karma and hence there is nothing like fate or destiny in its absolute sense controlling us.[17]
> . . . The future is a reflection of the past. The horoscope simply indicates the future.[18]

By applying concepts of karma and reincarnation, the horoscope illustrates the way to fulfil our mission in this life based on the deeds we have performed in previous lives. Though astrology was never mentioned in the Vedas per se, all Indian astrologers were Hindus and thus adherents of Vedic thought. What the Vedas and every other religious schema ultimately have in common with astrology is the belief in the harmony of the universe. Astrologers expound on this by simply regarding the stars as an extension of ourselves.

By basing their craft on Vedic principles, many astrologers attributed their knowledge to divine sources. After AD 500, however, Indian astronomers ceased claiming *divine* authorship of their treatises and began to acknowledge their own writings. The earliest known Indian astrologers were Aryabhata (AD 476-523) and Parasara (5th century AD) whose *Hora Sastra* was the first major astrological treatise to appear. But the most revered astrologer of all was Vaharamihira (AD 505-587), a student of Parasara and transmitter of the knowledge that Parasara was unable to convey to the public. Vaharamihira practised astrology at the court of King Vikramaditya, and he did what Ptolemy did for Greek astronomy in his supreme work, *Tetrabiblios*. Vaharamihira summarized all the astronomical and astrological knowledge available in India in a series of definitive books. Among his many astronomical works, which include *Daivajna-Vallabha* and *Brihat Samhita*, it is his masterwork *Brihat Jataka* which is still considered to be India's foremost astrological text. The *Brihat Jataka* describes the planets, Moon's nodes, zodiacal signs and houses in the light of Vedantic thought by showing how their placements in the horoscope resulted from past deeds and influence present purpose.* He further elaborates on a variety of categorizations and techniques (to which I will refer throughout this book) used to delineate character and forecast events. Vaharamihira's methodical approach gave Hindu Astrology its scientific status and influenced generations of practitioners in this field. Other astrological works influenced by the teachings of Vaharamihira and still used by modern astrologers are Kalyana Varma's treatise, *Saravali*, also written in the sixth century AD, and Mantreswar's *Phaladeepika* written during the sixteenth century AD. These books are similar in form and content to the *Brihat Jataka* with certain variations due to the

---

* In this book I do not include Vedic interpretations since they have no significance for our lives, but they are extremely meaningful for Hindus, who go to astrologers to find out about their lives.

different authorships. Included in the *Phaladeepika* were new astrological and astronomical discoveries not available in Vaharamihira's era and more sophisticated forecasting techniques. (I will be using these works as points of reference throughout this book.)

Although a fatalistic approach to astrology is anathema to our concept of free will, the horoscope's validation of present deeds based on past actions, the mainstay of Hinduism, is certainly one reason why astrology has remained a vital part of Hindu life. Even those Indians who do not visit astrologers respect its legitimacy as an art and a science and recognize the astrologer as an influential figure within the Hindu community.

1200-1757

The Siddhantic calendar, minus the implementation of the Precession of the Equinoxes, continued to be used as India's official calendar until AD 1200, when India fell under Islamic domination. Throughout Muslim rule from 1200 to 1757, their Hejira calendar — completely lunar — was introduced and used for civil and administrative affairs. Hindu communities dispersed throughout India managed to maintain their independence and retained their Hindu calendars for religious purposes. These calendars were, however, mathematically incorrect since so many Indian observatories had either been destroyed by Turkish armies or simply abandoned by their astronomers. This left the task of calendar-making solely in the hands of regional astrologers who had little knowledge of actual astronomy and depended on direct observations and unscientific ancient treatises for their calculations.[19] Due to the complete lack of uniformity and disagreement over (a) which starting year to use for the calendar, and (b) the precise positioning of the first degree of Aries, almost every region in India developed its own soli-lunar calendar — with its own unique cultural and historical tradition. Holidays and religious festivities were celebrated on different days throughout India because of the variable date and time of the first degree of Aries, the first day of their New Year. As a result, all regional calendars conflicted in epoch, New Year's Day and naming of the months.[20]

1757–Present

With the advent of British rule in 1757, the Christian Gregorian calendar* replaced the Muslim calendar as the official calendar of India. The Gregorian calendar uses the Egyptian solar year of 365¼ days, the length of time it takes for the earth to revolve around the Sun. The four cardinal points determine the seasons and the length of the year; the extra quarter day is made up with the inclusion of a leap year every fourth year. The Gregorian calendar was used for official timekeeping, civil and administrative matters and anything else linking India to the rest of the world. Throughout each governmental regime, however, every religious community always retained its own regional calendar. This applied not only to the Hindu communities, but also to the Muslim communities who continued to use their medieval Hejira calendar and the Buddhists, Jains and Christians who had their individual calendars and time-keeping methods.

By the time India emerged as an independent nation in 1947 under the rulership of Pandit Jawaharlal Nehru, there were still two types of calendars in use — the official Gregorian solar calendar and the regional religious lunar calendars. While weeding out remnants of the bureaucracy left behind by the British, the Government found this practice of varying calendars much too disconcerting. In 1952, five years after the last British troops left India, the Government of India appointed the Calendar Reform Committee to rectify 'the Hindu calendar problem'.

The actual purpose of the Calendar Reform Committee was to investigate:

1. whether the Christian Gregorian calendar, the international calendar, should be upheld as the official calendar of India since it had been imposed by the British from whom they were now independent.

2. whether there should be one unified religious calendar which would serve all the practising Hindu communities throughout the country and meet the Committee's requirements for holidays to be uniformly celebrated

---

* The Gregorian calendar is used for official functions by all Christian countries and most non-Christian countries.

throughout the country rather than on different days of the year.

In 1955 their recommendations were published in the *Report of the Calendar Reform Committee*. In answer to the first question, the Calendar Reform Committee recommended the retention of the Gregorian calendar as the only official calendar in India. Because it had been successfully utilized for so many years, the Committee felt the Gregorian calendar was vital to ensure that timekeeping in India would keep pace with the rest of the world.

In response to the second more complicated question, the Calendar Reform Committee felt that there should only be one religious calendar used throughout the country. Because each region disagrees about the precise calculation of the first degree of the *actual* constellation Aries, holidays tend to fall on different days throughout the country. In addition, due to the Precession of the Equinoxes, that first degree of Aries (the first day of the New Year) is consistently moving farther away from 21 March, the first day of spring. Ultimately, certain holidays will fall in different seasons than were originally intended. It is not unusual — according to the Chinese or Hebrew lunar calendar — for religious holidays to fall on different days each year due to their coincidence with the New Moon and the Full Moon. It *is* uncommon, however, for those events to be celebrated progressively later each year.

Though the Hindu population seemed quite comfortable with their calendars just as they had been under British rule, these inconsistencies nonetheless presented the Committee with a dilemma. In response, the Calendar Reform Committee recommended setting up a yearly 'official Indian ephemeris and nautical almanac' published by the Government of India which would show the positions of the Sun, the Moon, the planets and other heavenly bodies.[21] The almanac would include listings of the tithi and the nakshatra and, most importantly, one unified Hindu calendar, called the National Calendar, which would be both civil and religious to be used by Hindus throughout India. The Indian New Year would commence on the vernal equinox, the Tropical Zodiac's first degree of Aries, as it was originally set down in the

Siddhantas. Since this publication would be in the hands of the Government, the listings of tithis and nakshatras would be astronomically correct and celebrations could be held on the 'correct' day throughout India. The Calendar Reform Committee further recommended that the calendar would be implemented on 21 March 1956. The Ayanamsa would be Lahiri's Ayanamsa of 23°15' and there would be six seasons divided by climatic changes: summer (grisma), rains (varsa), autumn (sarat), late autumn (hemanta), winter (susna), and spring (vasanta).

The Government of India soon realized that requiring the Hindu community to accept the recommendations of the Calendar Reform Committee would be as impossible a task as getting all Indians to speak one language. This became especially evident during the 1963 Durga Puja Festival in honour of the goddess Durga. The government declared that all of India should celebrate this festival on a certain date but, since India is a country comprised of diverse languages, traditions and even different patron gods and goddesses, the Hindus used their regional dates and completely ignored the date and time designated by the government.[22]

The government decided that if no attention was being paid to their recommendations, they could at least supply correct astronomical data. An official almanac was to be published each year containing 'an ephemeris showing the true planetary positions and other relevant information leaving the preparation of the religious calendar to the persons most qualified for the work.'[23] The planets are listed in the Indian ephemeris according to their positions at sunrise (an arbitrary hour) as opposed to our ephemeris which lists the planets at either noon or midnight (fixed times). The city of Ujjain provides the central time zone from which the listings in the ephemeris emanate, equivalent to the way Greenwich, England is used to convey 0° longitude. The day is not divided into hours and minutes but into ghatis and vighatis. There are 2$\frac{1}{2}$ ghatis in an hour and 60 ghatis in a day. Each ghati is further divided into 60 vighatis. By supplying data, the government ensured the availability of mathematically accurate calculations. The rest was left up to each Hindu community.

Since the development of the calendar went hand in hand with the development of religious and astrological thought in India, some of the recommendations of the Calendar Reform Committee affected astrological timekeeping as well. The official ephemeris was a reference book astrologers could use for calculating the positions of the planets according to the Sidereal Zodiac. Like the calendar, the astrology of India has always remained both solar and lunar, combining the influence of the Greco-Chaldean school with their own unique calculations and philosophy of life. Many modern Indian astrologers still use techniques dating from Siddhantic times synthesized with more modern methods used in the West. The bulk of their teachings, however, can still be traced back to the writings of the earliest astronomers and astrologers and, most importantly, to the Hindu Vedic tradition. What this indicates is how steadfast Hindu astrology has actually remained.

2
SIDEREAL ASTROLOGY VS. TROPICAL ASTROLOGY

One of the unique features of Hindu astrology is its use of the Sidereal Zodiac (Nirayana) instead of our own Tropical Zodiac (Sayana). Although this distinction was briefly mentioned in the previous chapter, it is important to review the technical differences between the two zodiacs in more detail.

By the time Babylonia was annexed by Alexander the Great in approximately 330 BC, the Greeks had inherited an astrological legacy that included the discovery of the zodiacal belt, the movement of the four cardinal points through the constellations known as the Precession of the Equinoxes and the creation of the earliest individual horoscopes. Though most astronomers were already dividing the sky into 12 star groupings, it was the Greeks who apparently first named these groups according to their various shapes and sizes. These groupings became the 12 signs of the zodiac, and the zodiacal belt is so-called because of the imaginary belt the signs seem to form around the constellations. This circular belt measures 360° and each zodiacal sign consists equally of 30°.

According to the Greeks and most other Western cultures, the commencement of the astrological year — the first degree of Aries — always falls on 21 or 22 March, the date of the vernal (spring) equinox. The vernal equinox is defined as the point at which the celestial equator intersects with the ecliptic, the apparent path of the Sun travelling through the constellations as it is viewed from the earth. Because it is the *earth* that is actually revolving around the *Sun*, the Sun only *appears*

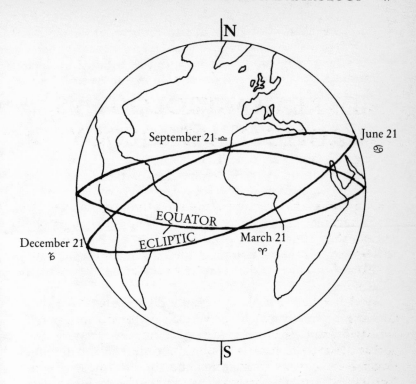

Fig 2.1. The above diagram depicts the equinoxes: the points at which the equator intersects with the ecliptic, the apparent path the Sun takes travelling through the zodiac. According to the Tropical Zodiac, 0° Aries is always the sign of the vernal equinox.

to be moving through the signs of the zodiac, or zodiacal belt. (Fig 2.1)

Around the time of the birth of Christ, the equinoctial point fell on the first degree of the group of stars known as Aries, the first sign of the zodiac. Since the earth's orbit is elliptical rather than circular in motion, the equinoctial point never returns to its exact starting place when the year is over. Instead, the equinox moves retrogradely and increases at a rate of approximately 50.23 seconds per year. This slow and steady movement of the vernal equinox through the zodiacal belt is called the Precession of the Equinoxes. Although the equinox always occurs on the same date each year, on 21 March, it no longer falls in the actual constellation of Aries due to the retrograde motion of the Precession.*

It is this retrograding Precession of the Equinoxes which determines the Planetary Ages of Man — the Age of Aries, Age of Pisces, Age of Aquarius, etc. At an annual precessional rate of 50.23 seconds, it takes approximately 71.67 years for the equinoctial point to advance only one degree or 60' (71.67 × 50.23 sec = 3600 sec or 1°). If we take 71.67 years (the time it takes for the equinox to move 1°) and multiply it by 30° (one sign of the zodiac), the product is approximately 2,150 years. According to these calculations, 2,150 years after the equinoctial point of intersection embarked on its journey through the constellation Pisces (thus defining the current Piscean Age), that point will begin its retrograde movement through the sign of Aquarius to welcome the long-awaited Aquarian epoch.

Because there has always been a disagreement as to (a) the exact year in which the very first vernal equinox fell in Aries, and (b) the precise yearly increment of the Precession, there has always been a difference of opinion among astrologers as to when the Age of Aquarius will actually begin. The assignment for the beginning of the Aquarian Age may range anywhere from 1787 to 2150.

The Hindus have their own system of epochs which has absolutely nothing to do with the Precession of the Equinoxes and the Planetary Ages of Man. These epochs are known as yugas. The four yugas are four planetary eras which, when added together, make up the Maha Yuga, literally meaning 'great year'. The Maha Yuga consists of 4,320,000 years and is divided up as follows:

Krtiayuga (Golden Age)	1,728,000 years
Tretayuga (Silver Age)	1,296,000 years
Dvaparayuga (Copper Age)	864,000 years
Kaliyuga (Earthen Age)	432,000 years
	4,320,000 years[1]

* Traditional Hindu astrologers and calendar-makers do not use the Precession of the Equinoxes at all in their calculations. Although the Precession was mentioned in the Siddhantas, it was never really accepted in India. Most modern Hindu astrologers, however, do refer to both zodiacs.

Fig 2.2. The shrine of Mata Kali in Kathmandu, Nepal. Photo
courtesy of Roy Doremus.

Maha Yuga represents a period of spiritual and material decline starting from the Golden Age of Krtiayuga and continues throughout the other yugas. We are presently in Kali Yuga which began in 3102 BC when there was a grand conjunction in the sign of Virgo. The number of years comprising Kali Yuga — 432,000 years — is equivalent to the number of years in the Great Babylonian Year, making it plausible that this information was brought over to India from the Near East.[2] Kali Yuga, the period of ultimate evil and destruction, is symbolized by the Goddess of Destruction, Mata (Mother) Kali (Fig 2.2), who is always pictured surrounded by serpents and standing over her dead husband, Shiva, the God of Creation and Destruction. According to the Hindus, when Kali Yuga is completed, the world as we know it will come to an end.

The difference between the two zodiacs — our Tropical (Sayana) Zodiac and the Hindu Sidereal (Nirayana) Zodiac — lies in the placement of that first degree of Aries, the beginning of the astrological year. The Tropical Zodiac is known as a symbolic or movable zodiac because 21 March, the vernal equinox and beginning of spring, represents 0° Aries though it has not actually coincided with the equinox for centuries. The Sidereal Zodiac, on the other hand, is a fixed zodiac because the beginning of the Hindu astrological year is always the first degree of the actual constellation of Aries though its exact date and time has gradually shifted each year. (Fig 2.3)

The difference between the *actual* 0° of Aries and the equinoctial point, the Tropical Zodiac's *symbolic* 0° Aries, is called the Ayanamsa and is one of the most important factors in Hindu Astrology. The Ayanamsa used in the course of this book is the one based on the calculations of the late astrologer, K. S. Krishnamurti, whose books and teachings were introduced to me by my first Jyotish teacher and whose ephemeris I have always used with great satisfaction.

Table 2.1 is the Ayanamsa table found in the Krishnamurti ephemeris. Krishnamurti's Ayanamsa is based on the annual precessional rate of 50.23 seconds with the original year of the two coinciding zodiacs given as AD 291. This rate of precessional movement was the very first Ayanamsa and the yearly rate by which the initial Equinox

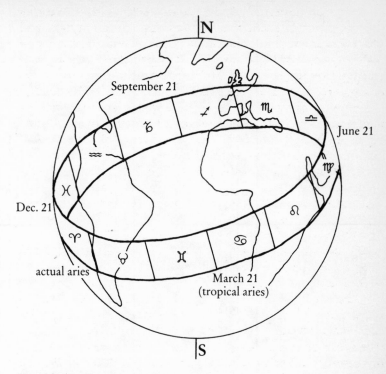

Fig 2.3. The above diagram depicts the actual position of Aries and the one used by followers of the Sidereal Zodiac. According to the Tropical Zodiac, however, 0° Aries is always the position of the vernal equinox.

moved away from its position of 0° Aries. If the difference between a particular year and AD 291 were multiplied by 50.23 seconds, the products would be the Ayanamsas listed in Table 2.1. Referring to Table 2.1, we see, for instance, that Krishnamurti's Ayanamsa will be 23°37' in 1990. This means that in that year the actual degree corresponding to the Tropical Zodiac's 0° Aries will be 6°25' of Pisces, 0° Aries minus 1990's Ayanamsa of 23°37'.

The other Ayanamsa most often used is the one found in the official Indian ephemeris compiled by Lahiri, the official astrologer of the Indian Government and Secretary of the Calendar Reform Committee. Lahiri calculated the rate of precession to be 50.27 seconds and the year of the two coinciding zodiacs as AD 285. Because Lahiri's figures

Year	Ayanamsa		Year	Ayanamsa		Year	Ayanamsa	
	deg.	mt.		deg.	mt.		deg.	mt.
1840	21	31	1894	22	17	1948	23	02
1841	21	32	1895	22	18	1949	23	03
1842	21	33	1896	22	18	1950	23	04
1843	21	34	1897	22	19	1951	23	04
1844	21	35	1898	22	20	1952	23	05
1845	21	36	1899	22	21	1953	23	06
1846	21	37	1900	22	22	1954	23	07
1847	21	37	1901	22	23	1955	23	08
1848	21	38	1902	22	23	1956	23	09
1849	21	39	1903	22	24	1957	23	10
1850	21	40	1904	22	25	1958	23	10
1851	21	41	1905	22	26	1959	23	11
1852	21	42	1906	22	27	1960	23	12
1853	21	42	1907	22	28	1961	23	13
1854	21	43	1908	22	29	1962	23	14
1855	21	44	1909	22	30	1963	23	15
1856	21	45	1910	22	31	1964	23	15
1857	21	46	1911	22	32	1965	23	16
1858	21	47	1912	22	33	1966	23	17
1859	21	47	1913	22	33	1967	23	18
1860	21	48	1914	22	34	1968	23	19
1861	21	49	1915	22	35	1969	23	20
1862	21	50	1916	22	36	1970	23	20
1863	21	51	1917	22	37	1971	23	21
1864	21	52	1918	22	38	1972	23	22
1865	21	52	1919	22	38	1973	23	23
1866	21	53	1920	22	39	1974	23	24
1867	21	54	1921	22	39	1975	23	25
1868	21	55	1922	22	40	1976	23	25
1869	21	56	1923	22	41	1977	23	26
1870	21	57	1924	22	42	1978	23	27
1871	21	57	1925	22	43	1979	23	28
1872	21	58	1926	22	44	1980	23	29
1873	21	59	1927	22	44	1981	23	30
1874	22	00	1928	22	45	1982	23	30
1875	22	01	1929	22	46	1983	23	31
1876	22	02	1930	22	47	1984	23	32
1877	22	02	1931	22	48	1985	23	33
1878	22	03	1932	22	49	1986	23	34
1879	22	04	1933	22	49	1987	23	35
1880	22	05	1934	22	50	1988	23	35
1881	22	06	1935	22	51	1989	23	36
1882	22	07	1936	22	52	1990	23	37
1883	22	08	1937	22	53	1991	23	38
1884	22	08	1938	22	54	1992	23	39
1885	22	09	1940	22	54	1993	23	40
1886	22	10	1941	22	55	1994	23	41

Year	Ayanamsa		Year	Ayanamsa		Year	Ayanamsa	
	deg.	mt.		deg.	mt.		deg.	mt.
1887	22	11	1941	22	56	1995	23	41
1888	22	12	1942	22	57	1996	23	42
1889	22	13	1943	22	58	1997	23	43
1890	22	13	1944	22	59	1998	23	44
1891	22	14	1945	22	59	1999	23	45
1892	22	15	1946	23	00	2000	23	46
1893	22	16	1947	23	01	2001	23	47

Table 2.1   The list of Ayanamsas between the years 1840 and 2001 according to Krishnamurti.[3]

are so close to those of Krishnamurti, the difference between their Ayanamsas is negligible.[4] This is very important since Lahiri is the official astrologer of India and the official almanac is published according to his calculations.

The variety of Ayanamsas, like the varying dates of the beginning of the Aquarian Age, are attributed to the fact that astrologers disagree about the exact annual rate of Precession and the year in which the first degree of Aries actually coincided with the vernal equinox. The Greek astronomer Hipparchus placed that year at AD 280, and it is this discrepancy which has led to the variety of starting dates in calendars throughout India. Other popular Ayanamsas include those calculated by Dr B.V. Raman, the world-famous Indian astrologer and writer,* and by Cyril Fagan, who championed the use of the Sidereal Zodiac in the West and determined that the starting year was AD 213.

Throughout this book we will be constructing charts according to the Sidereal Zodiac. Since the Indian ephemeris is set up much differently than ours, and would be almost impossible to decipher, we will not use it to calculate planetary positions. Instead, we'll subtract the Ayanamsa of the year of birth from the Sayana (or Tropical) position of each planet to arrive at its Nirayana (or Sidereal) position. The Sanskrit word 'Nir-ayana' simply means without 'ayan'or Ayanamsa.

* Dr. B. V. Raman's *The Astrological Magazine*, English language books and astrology school in Bangalore, have all aided in the dissemination of Indian astrology throughout the Western World.

Using the charts of Annemarie and Barbara,* the following steps illustrate how to calculate the Nirayana planetary positions using the appropriate Ayanamsa. Let's begin with Annemarie who was born on 26 December 1952 at 5:50 Greenwich Mean Time. The first step is to look at Table 2.1 and find the year of Annemarie's birth with its corresponding Ayanamsa. Because this date is so close to 1953 and because the Ayanamsa is only listed in degrees and minutes and not seconds, it is more accurate to use the 1953 Ayanamsa of 23°6' rather than the Ayanamsa from 1952.

The next step is to subtract the Ayanamsa of 23°6' from the corresponding Sayana placements of the planets, the Moon's nodes, and the Ascendant at the exact moment of Annemarie's birth. Table 2.2 lists the corresponding Tropical and Sidereal positions in Annemarie's chart.

Table 2.2 Annemarie's Planets

Planets	Tropical or Sayana Position	Sidereal or Nirayana Position
Sun	4 Capricorn 26	11 Sagittarius 20
Moon	5 Taurus 5	11 Aries 59
Mercury	14 Sagittarius 7	21 Scorpio 1
Venus	18 Aquarius 14	25 Capricorn 8
Mars	26 Aquarius 25	3 Aquarius 19
Jupiter	11 Taurus 8	18 Aries 2
Saturn	25 Libra 52	2 Libra 46
North Node	14 Aquarius 23	21 Capricorn 17
South Node	14 Leo 23	21 Cancer 17
Ascendant	21 Scorpio 40	28 Libra 34

Let's take one more example, Barbara. Her birth date is 30 January 1960, and the time of her birth is 16:59 Greenwich Mean Time. The Ayanamsa table indicates that in 1960 this figure was 23°12'. Table 2.3 shows the results of subtracting this number from the positions of each planet.

---

* Throughout this book, the charts of Annemarie and Barbara, two clients, will be used to illustrate the calculation and interpretation of the Hindu chart known as the Rasi Chakra.

Table 2.3 Barbara's Planets

Planets	Tropical or Sayana Position	Sidereal or Nirayana Position
Sun	9 Aquarius 49	16 Capricorn 37
Moon	12 Pisces 13	19 Aquarius 1
Mercury	12 Aquarius 42	19 Capricorn 30
Venus	4 Capricorn 16	11 Sagittarius 4
Mars	12 Capricorn 16	19 Sagittarius 4
Jupiter	24 Sagittarius 52	1 Sagittarius 40
Saturn	12 Capricorn 52	19 Sagittarius 40
North Node	25 Virgo 26	2 Virgo 14
South Node	25 Pisces 26	2 Pisces 14
Ascendant	0 Gemini 28	7 Taurus 16

According to the Tropical Zodiac, Barbara has three planets in Capricorn and one planet in Sagittarius. Using the Sidereal Zodiac, however, she has four planets in Sagittarius and two planets in Capricorn. This will present no real contradiction since Sidereal astrology is interpreted very differently from our own astrology.

The trans-Saturnian planets — Uranus, Neptune and Pluto — are not used in Hindu astrology since they were discovered with the aid of a telescope in 1781, 1846, and 1930, respectively, and therefore were not included in ancient scriptures. Although modern Hindu astrologers, Raman and Krishnamurti, incorporate Uranus, Neptune and Pluto into their horoscope interpretation as do Western 'Siderealists' (Western astrologers who use the Sidereal Zodiac), most Hindu astrologers still only use that which has been handed down to them by the astrological sages.

There will *always* be arguments between the two schools of astrology — Tropical and Sidereal — who each insist that its own form of horoscopy is the most reliable. Critics of astrology like to refer to the existence of two zodiacs as valid proof of astrology's inconsistency and unreliability. Most astrologers, however, do not necessarily see this as an indication of astrological chaos and readily acknowledge the coexistence of two systems. Interpretation of the horoscope according to the Sidereal Zodiac, based on the actual planetary placements, concentrates on the external factors of our lives. Since Indians are event-oriented and mostly interested in fulfilling the dharma to which they were assigned, they are concerned with external matters of education, marriage, children, finances, profession and health. Astrologers utilizing the Tropical Zodiac interpret the planetary symbols as being representative of the aforementioned issues *plus* the personal psychology and attitudes which lie behind them, including internal factors such as longings, needs, fears, hopes and dreams. Most importantly, however, the Tropical Zodiac emphasizes the fact that with a thorough understanding of ourselves, we can alter many external factors and take control of our lives so that we may better attain our goals.

The two astrological systems, much like two different schools of psychological thought, reach separate but equally significant conclusions as well as some of the same conclusions even though the steps employed to reach those conclusions may be very different indeed.

3

CONSTRUCTING THE HOROSCOPE

There are five areas of Hindu astrology:

1. *Jataka* (Natal): horoscopic study of an individual for the entire span of life (this type of horoscope is generally drawn up for a child at birth)

2. *Varshaphala* (Predictive): one year's prediction for an individual

3. *Prashna* (Horary): chart of the moment

4. *Muhurtas* (Electional): auspicious times during the day for a desired act

5. *Samhita* (Mundane): astrology of a country or study of weather conditions, epidemics, wars, calamities, etc.

For the purposes of this book, we will only concentrate on Jataka, the study of the individual horoscope.

Table 3.1 and Table 3.2 represent both the planets and the zodiacal signs used in Hindu astrology. Table 3.1 consists of four columns and lists their anglicized names in Column A, their corresponding Sanskrit names in Column B, a transliteral pronunciation in Column C, and their symbols (glyphs) in Column D. Table 3.2 is structured in the same manner with the addition of the planetary rulers of the zodiacal signs listed in Column E.

Table 3:1 Planets

A	B	C	D
Planets	Grahas	Pronunciation*	Glyphs
The Sun	Ravi	RA-vi	☉
	Surya	SUR-ya	
The Moon	Chandra	CHAN-dra	☽
Mars	Kuja	Ku-JA	♂
Mercury	Budha	Bud-HA	☿
Jupiter	Guru	Gu-RU	♃
Venus	Sukra	SU-kra	♀
Saturn	Sani	SA-ni	♄
North Node	Rahu	RA-hu	☊
South Node	Kethu	Ké-TU	☋

* Accented syllable is in CAPS

Table 3:2 Signs of the Zodiac

A	B	C	D	E
Zodiacal signs	Rasis	Pronunciation*	Glyphs	Planetary Ruler
1) Aries	Mesha	Me-SA	♈	Mars
2) Taurus	Vrishaba	VRISH-aba	♉	Venus
3) Gemini	Mithuna	Mithu-NA	♊	Mercury
4) Cancer	Kataka	Kata-KA	♋	Moon
5) Leo	Simha	SIM-ha	♌	Sun
6) Virgo	Kanya	Kan-YA	♍	Mercury
7) Libra	Thula	Too-LA	♎	Venus
8) Scorpio	Vrischika	VRISCH-ika	♏	Mars
9) Sagittarius	Dhanus	DHA-nu	♐	Jupiter
10) Capricorn	Makara	MA-kara	♑	Saturn
11) Aquarius	Kumbha	Kum-BHA	♒	Saturn
12) Pisces	Meena	MEE-na	♓	Jupiter

* Accented syllable is in CAPS

The Sanskrit word, 'graha', literally meaning 'rotating body,' can be applied to each of the above nine heavenly bodies used in Hindu Astrology — the Sun, the Moon, the five planets and the Moon's Nodes. The Sun and the Moon, called the two 'lights' in ancient cultures, are classified as planets in most astrological systems. The order of the Sun, the Moon and the planets in Hindu Astrology always corresponds with the order of the days of the week which they rule — Sunday (Sun) through Saturday (Saturn). In Sanskrit, English and in most European languages, the names of the days of the week are derived from the names of the planets.

Unlike the planets, Rahu and Kethu (Sanskrit for Dragon's Head and Dragon's Tail) are not physical bodies with shape or mass but are the two intersecting points formed where the orbit of the Sun cuts the orbit of the Moon (Fig 3.1). They are always 180° apart, in opposition

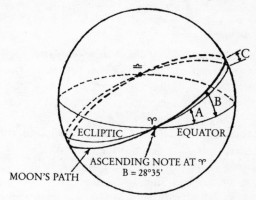

A = OBLIQUITY OF ECLIPTIC (23°27')
B = MOON'S MAXIMUM DECLINATION
C = MOON'S LATITUDE (5°08')

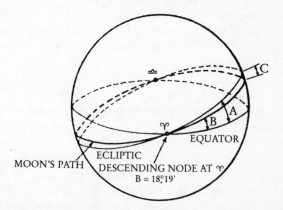

Fig 3.1 Diagram of how the Moon's Nodes are formed (reproduced from *The Astrologer's Astronomical Handbook* by Jeff Mayo).

to each other. The point formed after the Moon has travelled from south to north is called the Ascending or North Node, more commonly known as the Dragon's Head. The Dragon's Tail is the Descending or South Node and is the point formed after the Moon has moved in its course from North to South.[1]

Symbolically, Rahu and Kethu serve the same function as the planets in both the birth chart and in the planetary periods called dasas. The Nodes are not, however, always assigned the same categories as planets. They do not correspond to days of the week nor can they ever rule a zodiacal sign or house.

With some understanding of the Sidereal Zodiac behind us, let's now move on to the actual construction of the Hindu horoscope, the Rasi Chakra. Our word 'horoscope' means 'picture of the hour' and is derived from two Greek words — 'hora' meaning hour and 'scope' meaning 'picture' or 'vision'. The Sanskrit 'Rasi Chakra' consists of 'Rasi' meaning 'constellation' or 'zodiacal sign' and 'Chakra' denoting 'wheel'. Literally, then, the Rasi Chakra is defined as a 'zodiacal wheel'.* Because of the Hindu belief in reincarnation, the description of a person's life as one spoke on the continuing wheel of many lifetimes perfectly epitomizes their concept of astrology. The chakra, or wheel, does not, however, apply to the *drawing* of the birth chart which is constructed in the shape of a rectangle. Though the layout of the rectangular chart varies from region to region, the calculations and basic interpretation of the chart remain the same throughout India. (Figs 3.2 and 3.3)

The 12 signs of the zodiac are always divided into twelve equilateral areas of the horoscope called bhavas, Sanskrit for houses of the chart. The Lagna, Sanskrit for Ascendant or first house, forms one of the most important concepts in Hindu astrology and consists of the entire zodiacal sign in which the ascending degree is placed. Even if the Ascendant falls on 29° of Libra, for example, the first house will still cover the entire sign of Libra. Because the

---

* The Chakras are the seven energy centres of the body, and are described in Leadbetter's book, *The Chakras*, as 'wheels of energy'.

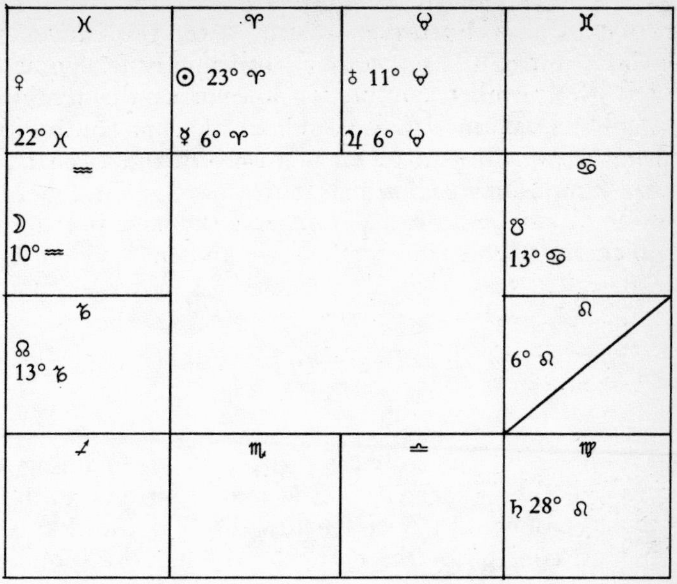

South Indian Chart

♓ ♀ 22° ♓	♈ ☉ 23° ♈ ☿ 6° ♈	♉ ♂ 11° ♉ ♃ 6° ♉	♊
♒ ☽ 10° ♒			♋ ☋ 13° ♋
♑ ☊ 13° ♑			♌ 6° ♌
♐	♏	♎	♍ ♄ 28° ♌

Fig 3.2 South Indian Chart

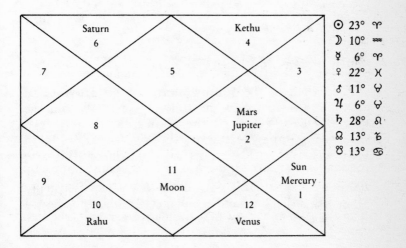

Saturn 6		Kethu 4	☉ 23° ♈
7	5	3	☽ 10° ♒
	8	Mars Jupiter 2	☿ 6° ♈
9	11 Moon	Sun Mercury 1	♀ 22° ♓
10 Rahu		12 Venus	♂ 11° ♉

☉ 23° ♈
☽ 10° ♒
☿ 6° ♈
♀ 22° ♓
♂ 11° ♉
♃ 6° ♉
♄ 28° ♌
☊ 13° ♑
☋ 13° ♋

Fig 3.3 North Indian Chart

sign of the Ascendant may be seen on the horizon at the moment of birth, it is sometimes called the rising sign. That is why the Ascendant of a person born around sunrise will inevitably be the same zodiacal sign as the Sun sign. Instead of using an astrological glyph to represent the sign of the Lagna, Hindus instead use its corresponding number as follows:

Aries	= 1	Libra	= 7
Taurus	= 2	Scorpio	= 8
Gemini	= 3	Sagittarius	= 9
Cancer	= 4	Capricorn	= 10
Leo	= 5	Aquarius	= 11
Virgo	= 6	Pisces	= 12

The numbers of the zodiacal signs of the remaining 11 houses are then inserted in sequential order counter-clockwise around the Rasi Chakra. Each house, like the Ascendant, consists of the entire 30° of its corresponding sign. The planetary ruler or lord of each house, vital to horoscope interpretation, is defined as the ruler of the zodiacal sign found within that house.

Figs 3.2 and 3.3 illustrate two basic versions of the horoscope, the North Indian and South Indian. Though there are many other variations, these are the two most commonly used.

A. South Indian Model (See Fig 3.2)

Originally used in the southwestern coastal province of Kerala, it is drawn up in the following way. Within the rectangle, the first sign of the zodiac, Aries, is placed second from upper left with the signs following in clockwise fashion. The signs are stationary and are, therefore, always placed in the same boxes. The house occupied by the zodiacal sign of the Ascendant is usually filled in with a diagonal and the planets are then positioned in their respective signs and houses.

B. North Indian Model (See Fig 3.3)

Since I studied astrology in Benares (Varanasi), a city in the north central province of Uttar Pradesh, the North Indian chart is the model I will employ throughout this book. In the North Indian chart, the signs are not stationary but the *Ascendant* and the *houses* remain in fixed positions around the chart. The Ascendant, always marked by the number of its corresponding sign, is placed in the upper central position. The subsequent signs are then placed in their sequential order counter-clockwise around the chart. The Ascendant never changes *its* placement just as in the chart from South India the signs never change *their* placements.

Using the North Indian chart as our model, let's construct the charts of Annemarie and Barbara. The first step is to take the Nirayana positions of the planets and Ascendant of Annemarie's chart. Once again, below is a listing of her planets (Grahas) and the Ascendant (Lagna).

Annemarie's Planets

Ravi	(Sun)	11 Dhanus 20	(Sagittarius)
Chandra	(Moon)	11 Mesha 59	(Aries)
Kuja	(Mars)	3 Kumbha 19	(Aquarius)
Budha	(Mercury)	21 Vrischika 1	(Scorpio)
Guru	(Jupiter)	18 Mesha 2	(Aries)
Sukra	(Venus)	25 Makara 8	(Capricorn)
Sani	(Saturn)	2 Thula 46	(Libra)
Rahu	(North Node)	21 Makara 17	(Capricorn)
Kethu	(South Node)	21 Kataka 17	(Cancer)
Lagna	(Ascendant)	28 Thula 34	(Libra)

The following diagrams illustrate the steps taken in order to draw Annemarie's Rasi Chakra to completion.

Steps to Construct a Rasi Chakra

Step 1. Fig 3.4 is a blank rectangle around which the planets will be placed. The rectangle is first filled in with an 'X' drawn from corner to corner (Fig 3.5) and then with a diamond (Fig 3.6) dividing the rectangle into 12 sections which will become the 12 houses of the Rasi Chakra.

Step 2. The most important position, top centre, will be the Ascendant with the subsequent houses sequentially marked around the horoscope (Fig 3.7). Insert Number 7 — the number of Annemarie's Libra Ascendant — in the top central position to indicate that the entire 30° of Libra

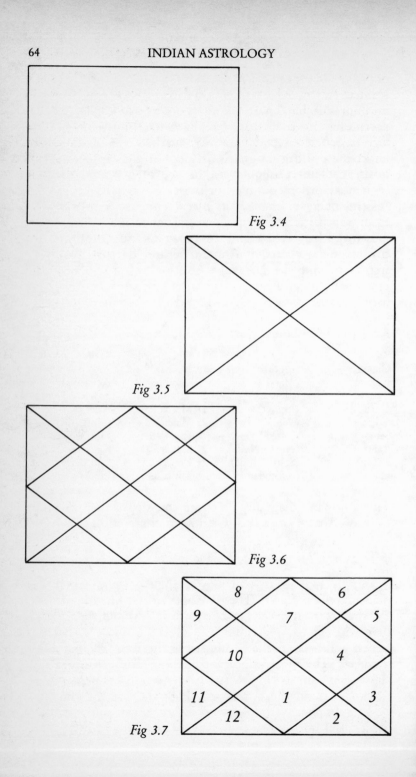

Fig 3.4

Fig 3.5

Fig 3.6

Fig 3.7

occupies the first house. The Ascendant lord, therefore, is Venus, the ruler of Libra. Moving counter-clockwise around the chart, insert the succeeding numbers in their ascending order. The second house comprises the entire sign of Scorpio with Mars as its ruler, the third house is the entire sign of Sagittarius with Jupiter as its ruler, etc. Each house, therefore, simply consists of the entire zodiacal sign.

Step 3. Fig 3.8 is the definitive version of Annemarie's chart accomplished by placing the planets in their proper signs/houses around the horoscope. The names of the planets are written out in longhand rather than using the glyphs to represent them. Their exact degrees and minutes are listed alongside the Rasi Chakra.

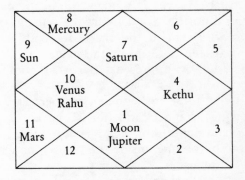

Fig 3.8 Annemarie's Rasi Chakra

Let's now do the same with Barbara's chart. Barbara's planets and Ascendant are listed as follows.

Barbara's Planets

Ravi	(Sun)	16 Makara 27	(Capricorn)
Chandra	(Moon)	19 Kumbha 1	(Cancer)
Kuja	(Mars)	19 Dhanus 4	(Sagittarius)
Budha	(Mercury)	19 Makara 30	(Capricorn)
Guru	(Jupiter)	1 Dhanus 40	(Sagittarius)
Sukra	(Venus)	11 Dhanus 4	(Sagittarius)
Sani	(Saturn)	19 Dhanus 40	(Sagittarius)
Rahu	(North Node)	2 Kanya 14	(Virgo)
Kethu	(South Node)	2 Meena 14	(Pisces)
Lagna	(Ascendant)	7 Vrishaba 16	(Taurus)

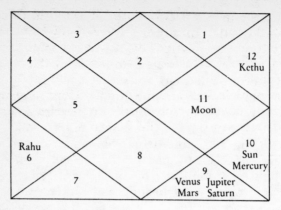

Fig 3.9 Barbara's Rasi Chakra

Using a Vrishaba-Taurus Ascendant, fill in the number 2 in the top central positions and insert the remaining numbers counterclockwise around the chart. As with Annemarie's chart, the next step is to insert the planets in their proper signs/houses. Fig 3.9 represents Barbara's completed Rasi Chakra.

The charts of these two women are perfect illustrations of the drawing of the Hindu horoscope or Rasi Chakra. The degrees and minutes of each planet may be listed either alongside the horoscope, inside the bhavas, or written on a separate piece of paper according to the way an astrologer finds it most practical and/or aesthetically pleasing. (I have always recorded them alongside the chart as in Fig 3.3.) In the South Indian chart, the planets and their positions are listed within the drawing itself as in Fig 3.2.

The Rasi Chakra is visually simpler than its Western counterpart. A Western horoscope is drawn with many aspect lines connecting the planets. They are often multi-coloured, making it simpler to depict the various aspects. These lines only make the Western horoscope *appear* more intricate than its Hindu counterpart. In reality, the interpretation of the Hindu chart is no less complicated than that of the Western horoscope.

The Moon Chart

There are other types of Hindu charts that are constructed

in the same manner as the Rasi Chakra though used for different interpretive purposes. The Moon Chart (Fig 3.10), constructed by placing the Moon in the Ascendant position, is only used in conjunction with the horoscopes of women.*

The Moon Chart is a supplementary chart used to obtain information not always obvious from the birth chart alone. Interpreted similarly, the Moon Chart may verify

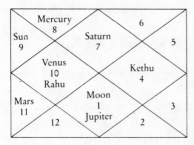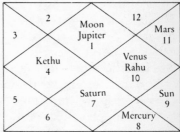

Rasi Chakra   Annemarie   Moon Chart

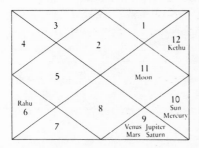

Rasi Chakra   Barbara   Moon Chart

Fig. 3.10 These are Annemarie's and Barbara's Rasi Chakra charts juxtaposed with their Moon Charts. In Annemarie's Moon Chart, the seventh house, occupied by the Moon, is placed as the Ascendant and in Barbara's Moon Chart, the tenth house is placed as her Ascendant.

* In charts where the Moon already occupies the first house, the Rasi Chakra and the Moon Chart are identical.

conclusions already reached by analysing the Rasi Chakra. When certain themes — positive or negative — appear in both charts, those tendencies are especially dominant throughout life. It is also considered by some astrologers to be superior to the Rasi Chakra when describing the woman's character.

Navamsa Chart

In Hindu astrology, there are 16 Varga (short for Shodasavarga) charts — formed by using a particular number to divide the Rasi. Used alongside the Rasi Chakra and the Moon Chart in horoscope analysis, the Navamsa chart is the most significant Varga chart and an extremely important interpretive device. It is formed by dividing each Rasi — 30° — into nine equal sections of three and one third degrees called Navamsas. Table 3.3 illustrates this principle of division. Beginning with the first degree of Aries, the zodiacal signs and degrees are placed in Column A, their planetary rulers in Column B and their corresponding Navamsa Signs and Planetary Lords in Column C. As seen from the table, nine sub-zodiacs — from Aries to Pisces — of 40° each (360 divided by 9) are then formed.

Table 3.3

COLUMN A	COLUMN B	COLUMN C	
Degrees and Sign	Planetary Lord	Navamsa and its Lord	
0.00–3.20 Aries	Mars	Aries	Mars
3.20–6.40 "	"	Taurus	Venus
6.40–10.00 "	"	Gemini	Mercury
10.00–13.20 "	"	Cancer	Moon
13.20–16.40 "	"	Leo	Sun
16.40–20.00 "	"	Virgo	Mercury
20.00–23.20 "	"	Libra	Venus
23.20–26.40 "	"	Scorpio	Mars
26.40–30.00 "	"	Sagittarius	Jupiter
0.00–3.20 Taurus	Venus	Capricorn	Saturn
3.20–6.40 "	"	Aquarius	Saturn

Degrees and Sign	Planetary Lord	Navamsa and its Lord	
6.40-10.00 "	"	Pisces	Jupiter
10.00-13.20 "	"	Aries	Mars
13.20-16.40 "	"	Taurus	Venus
16.40-20.00 "	"	Gemini	Mercury
20.00-23.20 "	"	Cancer	Moon
23.20-26.40 "	"	Leo	Sun
26.40-30.00 "	"	Virgo	Mercury
0.00-3.20 Gemini	Mercury	Libra	Venus
3.20-6.40 "	"	Scorpio	Mars
6.40-10.00 "	"	Sagittarius	Jupiter
10.00-13.20 "	"	Capricorn	Saturn
13.20-16.40 "	"	Aquarius	Saturn
16.40-20.00 "	"	Pisces	Jupiter
20.00-23.20 "	"	Aries	Mars
23.20-26.40 "	"	Taurus	Venus
26.40-30.00 "	"	Gemini	Mercury
0.00-3.20 Cancer	Moon	Cancer	Moon
3.20-6.40 "	"	Leo	Sun
6.40-10.00 "	"	Virgo	Mercury
10.00-13.20 "	"	Libra	Venus
13.20-16.40 "	"	Scorpio	Mars
16.40-20.00 "	"	Sagittarius	Jupiter
20.00-23.20 "	"	Capricorn	Saturn
23.20-26.40 "	"	Aquarius	Saturn
26.40-30.00 "	"	Pisces	Jupiter
0.00-3.20 Leo	Sun	Aries	Mars
3.20-6.40 "	"	Taurus	Venus
6.40-10.00 "	"	Gemini	Mercury
10.00-13.20 "	"	Cancer	Moon
13.20-16.40 "	"	Leo	Sun
16.40-20.00 "	"	Virgo	Mercury
20.00-23.20 "	"	Libra	Venus
23.20-26.40 "	"	Scorpio	Mars
26.40-30.00 "	"	Sagittarius	Jupiter
0.00-3.20 Virgo	Mercury	Capricorn	Saturn
3.20-6.40 "	"	Aquarius	Saturn
6.40-10.00 "	"	Pisces	Jupiter
10.00-13.20 "	"	Aries	Mars
13.20-16.40 "	"	Taurus	Venus
16.40-20.00 "	"	Gemini	Mercury
20.00-23.20 "	"	Cancer	Moon

Degrees and Sign	Planetary Lord	Navamsa and its Lord	
23.20-26.40 "	"	Leo	Sun
26.40-30.00 "	"	Virgo	Mercury
0.00-3.20 Libra	Venus	Libra	Venus
3.20-6.40 "	"	Scorpio	Mars
6.40-10.00 "	"	Sagittarius	Jupiter
10.00-13.20 "	"	Capricorn	Saturn
13.20-16.40 "	"	Aquarius	Saturn
16.40-20.00 "	"	Pisces	Jupiter
20.00-23.20 "	"	Aries	Mars
23.20-26.40 "	"	Taurus	Venus
26.40-30.00 "	"	Gemini	Mercury
0.00-3.20 Scorpio	Mars	Cancer	Moon
3.20-6.40 "	"	Leo	Sun
6.40-10.00 "	"	Virgo	Mercury
10.00-13.20 "	"	Libra	Venus
13.20-16.40 "	"	Scorpio	Mars
16.40-20.00 "	"	Sagittarius	Jupiter
20.00-23.20 "	"	Capricorn	Saturn
23.20-26.40 "	"	Aquarius	Saturn
26.40-30.00 "	"	Pisces	Jupiter
0.00-3.20 Sagittarius	Jupiter	Aries	Mars
3.20-6.40 "	"	Taurus	Venus
6.40 10.00 "	"	Gemini	Mercury
10.00-13.20 "	"	Cancer	Moon
13.20-16.40 "	"	Leo	Sun
16.40-20.00 "	"	Virgo	Mercury
20.00-23.20 "	"	Libra	Venus
23.20-26.40 "	"	Scorpio	Mars
26.40-30.00 "	"	Sagittarius	Jupiter
0.00-3.20 Capricorn	Saturn	Capricorn	Saturn
3.20-6.40 "	"	Aquarius	Saturn
6.40-10.00 "	"	Pisces	Jupiter
10.00-13.20 "	"	Aries	Mars
13.20-16.40 "	"	Taurus	Venus
16.40-20.00 "	"	Gemini	Mercury
20.00-23.20 "	"	Cancer	Moon
23.20-26.40 "	"	Leo	Sun
26.40-30.00 "	"	Virgo	Mercury

Degrees and Sign	Planetary Lord	Navamsa and its Lord	
0.00-3.20 Aquarius	Saturn	Libra	Venus
3.20-6.40 "	"	Scorpio	Mars
6.40-10.00 "	"	Sagittarius	Jupiter
10.00-13.20 "	"	Capricorn	Saturn
13.20-16.40 "	"	Aquarius	Saturn
16.40-20.00 "	"	Pisces	Jupiter
20.00-23.20 "	"	Aries	Mars
23.20-26.40 "	"	Taurus	Venus
26.40-30.00 "	"	Gemini	Mercury
0.00-3.20 Pisces	Jupiter	Cancer	Moon
3.20-6.40 "	"	Leo	Sun
6.40-10.00 "	"	Virgo	Mercury
10.00-13.20 "	"	Libra	Venus
13.20-16.40 "	"	Scorpio	Mars
16.40-20.00 "	"	Sagittarius	Jupiter
20.00-23.20 "	"	Capricorn	Saturn
23.20-26.40 "	"	Aquarius	Saturn
26.40-30.00 "	"	Pisces	Jupiter

In order to actually construct the Navamsa Chart, the natal planets must first be converted to their corresponding Navamsa signs. Referring to Table 3.3, Annemarie's planets and their Navamsa signs are listed as follows:

Annemarie's Planets		*Navamsa*
Sun	11 Sagittarius 20	Cancer
Moon	11 Aries 59	Cancer
Mars	21 Scorpio 1	Capricorn
Mercury	25 Capricorn 8	Leo
Jupiter	3 Aquarius 19	Libra
Venus	18 Aries 2	Virgo
Saturn	2 Libra 46	Libra
North Node	21 Capricorn 17	Cancer
South Node	21 Cancer 17	Capricorn
Ascendant	28 Libra 34	Gemini

The Navamsa chart is drawn according to the same principle as the Moon Chart: the Navamsa sign of the natal Ascendant is placed in the first house position. In Annemarie's example, the corresponding Navamsa sign of her Ascendant — 28 Libra 34 — is Gemini. Fig 3.11 is

Annemarie's Navamsa Chart drawn to completion when the planets are placed around the chart in their corresponding Navamsa positions.

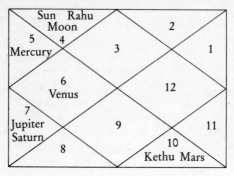

Fig 3.11 Annemarie's Navamsa Chart

Barbara's planets and their corresponding Navamsa signs are listed as follows and Fig 3.12 represents Barbara's Navamsa Chart when drawn to completion.

Barbara's Planets		*Navamsa*
Sun	16 Capricorn 37	Aquarius
Moon	19 Aquarius 1	Pisces
Mars	19 Sagittarius 4	Virgo
Mercury	19 Capricorn 30	Gemini
Jupiter	1 Sagittarius 40	Aries
Venus	11 Sagittarius 4	Cancer
Saturn	19 Sagittarius 40	Virgo
North Node	2 Virgo 14	Capricorn
South Node	2 Pisces 26	Cancer
Ascendant	7 Taurus 16	Pisces

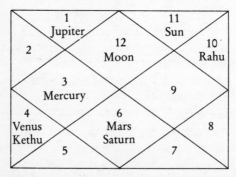

Fig 3.12 Barbara's Navamsa Chart

Interpreting the Navamsa Chart in conjunction with the Rasi Chakra and the Moon Chart provides the Hindu astrologer with a more in-depth look at the nature of the individual. The Navamsa Chart is examined in the same manner as the birth chart and any major themes of the Navamsa Chart will be incorporated into the interpretation of the Rasi Chakra. For example, Annemarie's Navamsa Chart has an emphasized second house. The quest for money and possessions (second house themes) will be a strong aspect of her life even though it may not be obvious from the Rasi Chakra alone. In addition, a theme which recurs in both the Rasi Chakra and the Navamsa Chart also becomes a dominant factor. In any event a final judgment of the Rasi Chakra is reserved until the astrologer consults both the Moon Chart and the Navamsa Chart.

The Navamsa Chart is primarily used by astrologers to determine whether two marriage partners are compatible. Comparing the Navamsa Charts of the prospective bride and groom to see whether the two charts are complementary is a method considered by astrologers to be infinitely more reliable than comparing the two Rasi Chakras. This method of chart comparison is analogous to synastry, the technique in Western astrology by which cross-aspects are drawn up between two horoscopes in order to see which characteristics of each partner will both help and hinder the other.

Vargas

Including the Rasi Chakra and the Navamsa Chart, there are altogether 16 vargas (degree divisional charts) which the Hindus can use to judge a nativity. The Rasi Chakra itself is considered to be a varga because the Rasi is divisible by one unit while the Navamsa Chart is formed by dividing the Rasi into nine units. Based on the same principles as the Navamsa Chart, the Vargas most commonly used in India are constructed as follows:

Hora
Dividing the Rasi by two, each hora is comprised of 15° forming two sub-zodiacs from Aries to Pisces.

Degrees and Sign	Hora
1–15 Aries	Aries
16–30 Aries	Taurus
1–15 Taurus	Gemini
16–30 Taurus	Cancer
1–15 Gemini	Leo
16–30 Gemini	Virgo
1–15 Cancer	Libra
16–30 Cancer	Scorpio
1–15 Leo	Sagittarius
16–30 Leo	Capricorn
1–15 Virgo	Aquarius
16–30 Virgo	Pisces

1–15 Libra	Aries
16–30 Libra	Taurus
1–15 Scorpio	Gemini
16–30 Scorpio	Cancer
1–15 Sagittarius	Leo
16–30 Sagittarius	Virgo
1–15 Capricorn	Libra
16–30 Capricorn	Scorpio
1–15 Aquarius	Sagittarius
16–30 Aquarius	Capricorn
1–15 Pisces	Aquarius
16–30 Pisces	Pisces

Dreccan

Each sign is divided by three into dreccans of 10° each. In Western astrology, these divisions are known as decanates. The Dreccan Charts are slightly different from the other Varga charts in that the three corresponding zodiacal signs are listed in order of their element. The dreccans are as follows:

Degrees and Sign	Dreccan	Element
0–10 Aries	Aries	
11–20 Aries	Leo	Fire
21–30 Aries	Sagittarius	
0–10 Taurus	Taurus	
11–20 Taurus	Virgo	Earth
21–30 Taurus	Capricorn	
0–10 Gemini	Gemini	
11–20 Gemini	Libra	Air
21–30 Gemini	Aquarius	
0–10 Cancer	Cancer	

Degrees and Sign	Dreccan	Element
11–20 Cancer	Scorpio	Water
21–30 Cancer	Pisces	
0–10 Leo	Leo	
11–20 Leo	Sagittarius	Fire
21–30 Leo	Aries	
0–10 Virgo	Virgo	
11–20 Virgo	Capricorn	Earth
21–30 Virgo	Taurus	
1–10 Libra	Libra	
11–20 Libra	Aquarius	Air
21–30 Libra	Gemini	
0–10 Scorpio	Scorpio	
11–20 Scorpio	Pisces	Water
21–30 Scorpio	Cancer	
0–10 Sagittarius	Sagittarius	
11–20 Sagittarius	Aries	Fire
21–30 Sagittarius	Leo	
0–10 Capricorn	Capricorn	
11–20 Capricorn	Taurus	Earth
21–30 Capricorn	Virgo	
0–10 Aquarius	Aquarius	
11–20 Aquarius	Gemini	Air
21–30 Aquarius	Libra	
0–10 Pisces	Pisces	
11–20 Pisces	Cancer	Water
21–30 Pisces	Scorpio	

Panchamsa

Each sign is divided by five into panchamsas of 6°. There will also be five sub-zodiacs from Aries to Pisces as follows:

Degrees and Sign		Panchamsa
0–6	Aries	Aries
7–12	"	Taurus
13–18	"	Gemini
19–24	"	Cancer
25–30	"	Leo
0–6	Taurus	Virgo
7–12	"	Libra
13–18	"	Scorpio
19–24	"	Sagittarius
25–30	"	Capricorn
0–6	Gemini	Aquarius
7–12	"	Pisces

Degrees and Sign		Panchamsa
13–18	"	Aries
19–24	"	Taurus
25–30	"	Gemini
0–6	Cancer	Cancer
7–12	"	Leo
13–18	"	Virgo
19–24	"	Libra
25–30	"	Scorpio
0–6	Leo	Sagittarius
7–12	"	Capricorn
13–18	"	Aquarius
19–24	"	Pisces
25–30	"	Aries
0–6	Virgo	Taurus
7–12	"	Gemini
13–18	"	Cancer
19–24	"	Leo
25–30	"	Virgo
0–6	Libra	Libra
7–12	"	Scorpio
13–18	"	Sagittarius
19–24	"	Capricorn
25–30	"	Aquarius
0–6	Scorpio	Pisces
7–12	"	Aries
13–18	"	Taurus
19–24	"	Gemini
25–30	"	Cancer
0–6	Sagittarius	Leo
7–12	"	Virgo
13–18	"	Libra
19–24	"	Scorpio
25–30	"	Sagittarius
0–6	Capricorn	Capricorn
7–12	"	Aquarius
13–18	"	Pisces
19–24	"	Aries
25–30	"	Taurus
0–6	Aquarius	Gemini
7–12	"	Cancer

Degrees and Sign		Panchamsa
13–18	"	Leo
19–24	"	Virgo
25–30	"	Libra
0–6	Pisces	Scorpio
7–12	"	Sagittarius
13–18	"	Capricorn
19–24	"	Aquarius
25–30	"	Pisces

Septamsa

Each sign is divided by seven into septamsas of 4° 17' resulting in seven sub-zodiacs from Aries to Pisces.

Degrees and Sign		Septamsa
0– 4.17	Aries	Aries
4.17– 8.34	"	Taurus
8.34–12.51	"	Gemini
12.51–17.08	"	Cancer
17.08–21.25	"	Leo
21.25–25.42	"	Virgo
25.42–30.00	"	Libra
0– 4.17	Taurus	Scorpio
4.17– 8.34	"	Sagittarius
8.34–12.51	"	Capricorn
12.51–17.08	"	Aquarius
17.08–21.25	"	Pisces
21.25–25.42	"	Aries
25.42–30.00	"	Taurus
0– 4.17	Gemini	Gemini
4.17– 8.34	"	Cancer
8.34–12.51	"	Leo
12.51–17.08	"	Virgo
17.08–21.25	"	Libra
21.25–25.42	"	Scorpio
25.42–30.00	"	Sagittarius
0– 4.17	Cancer	Capricorn
4.17– 8.34	"	Aquarius
8.34–12.51	"	Pisces
12.51–17.08	"	Aries
17.08–21.25	"	Taurus

Degrees and Sign		Septamsa
21.25–25.42	"	Gemini
25.42–30.00	"	Cancer
0 – 4.17	Leo	Leo
4.17– 8.34	"	Virgo
8.34–12.51	"	Libra
12.51–17.08	"	Scorpio
17.08–21.25	"	Sagittarius
21.25–25.42	"	Capricorn
25.42–30.00	"	Aquarius
0– 4.17	Virgo	Pisces

4.17– 8.34	"	Aries
8.34–12.51	"	Taurus
12.51–17.08	"	Gemini
17.08–21.25	"	Cancer
21.25–25.42	"	Leo
25.42–30.00	"	Virgo
0– 4.17	Libra	Libra
4.17–8.34	"	Scorpio
8.34–12.51	"	Sagittarius
12.51–17.08	"	Capricorn
17.08–21.25	"	Aquarius
21.25–25.42	"	Pisces

25.42–30.00	Aries	
0– 4.17	Scorpio	Taurus
4.17– 8.34	"	Gemini
8.34–12.51	"	Cancer
12.51–17.08	"	Leo
17.08–21.25	"	Virgo
21.25–25.42	"	Libra
25.42–30.00	"	Scorpio
0–4.17	Sagittarius	Sagittarius
4.17–8.34	"	Capricorn
8.34–12.51	"	Aquarius
12.51–17.08	"	Pisces

17.08–21.25	"	Aries
21.25–25.42	"	Taurus
25.42–30.00	"	Gemini
0– 4.17	Capricorn	Cancer
4.17– 8.34	"	Leo

Degrees and Sign		Septamsa
8.34–12.51	"	Virgo
12.51–17.08	"	Libra
17.08–21.25	"	Scorpio
21.25–25.42	"	Sagittarius
25.42–30.00	"	Capricorn
0– 4.17	Aquarius	Aquarius
4.17– 8.34	"	Pisces
8.34–12.51	"	Aries
12.51–17.08	"	Taurus
17.08–21.25	"	Gemini
21.25–25.42	"	Cancer
25.42–30.00	"	Leo
0– 4.17	Pisces	Virgo
4.17– 8.34	"	Libra
8.34–12.51	"	Scorpio
12.51–17.08	"	Sagittarius
17.08–21.25	"	Capricorn
21.25–25.42	"	Aquarius
25.42–30.00	"	Pisces

The balance of the vargas — too numerous to mention here — are not used as regularly as the aforementioned charts. Each of the remaining varga charts represents a different phase of life and is used to gain added insight into the Rasi Chakra. It is up to the discretion of the individual astrologer which of the the varga charts he will utilize since they are not mandatory for chart interpretation. The Navamsa Chart is, however, employed by all astrologers to: (a) learn more about the individual and (b) to arrange a marriage, one of the most important steps a Hindu takes in life.

Harmonics

Though an entire chapter could easily be devoted to both the philosophical and mathematical correlations between varga charts and harmonics charts, it is a subject that will unfortunately be briefly covered.

In the same way that varga charts are formed by using different numerals to divide the Rasi (30°), harmonic charts — their Western equivalent — are formed by using those same numerals to divide the zodiac (360°). The late John Addey perfected the system of harmonics by basing it on the same principles as Hindu Astrology:

> . . . this old tradition in Hindu astrology of creating sub-cycle charts is really a practical application of the idea of harmonics. Each division of the circle into a subordinate number of cycles or circles has its own significance, derived from the symbolism of the number by which the division is made. By dividing up the original circle of the Zodiac into a number of lesser circles one is, in effect, considering the distribution of the natal positions within the sub-circle of a particular horoscope. It is true perhaps that the Indian astrologer may think of this technique as one in which each sign is divided by a particular number — in this case nine — but in point of fact, what he has done first and foremost is to divide the whole circle by nine, and then divide each of those nine divisions into a little Zodiac of twelve signs.[2]

Like the vargas, harmonic charts are sub-zodiacs used to identify character traits and subtle parts of the personality that could not be noticed using the horoscope alone. By advocating the usage of harmonics charts based on multiples ranging from 2 to 12, Addey, the father of Harmonics, revolutionized astrology by discovering more in-depth ways of looking at the chart in addition to using newer aspect combinations. He found the most significant harmonics charts, however, to be the fifth harmonic, the seventh harmonic and the ninth harmonic — based on divisions of five, seven and nine and comparable to the most commonly used vargas — the Panchamsa, Septamsa and Navamsa Charts.

To explain this in more detail: the navamsa chart, for instance, is formed by dividing the Rasi by nine into Navamsas of $3^1/3°$ The first 40° of the zodiac completes one sub-zodiac from Aries to Pisces. (See Table 3.3) Altogether there will be nine sub-zodiacs and for this reason, the ninth Harmonic Chart correlates with the Navamsa chart. To take this one step further any planets that are in conjunction (0°) or in opposition (180°) in the Ninth Harmonic Chart will form a novile aspect (40°) in the Rasi Chakra. In the Fifth Harmonic Chart the conjunctions and oppositions form quintiles and bi-quintiles (72° and 144°) while the first 72° of the Panchamsa Chart comprises the first of the five sub-zodiacs. Finally, in the Seventh Harmonic Chart the conjunctions and oppositions form septiles (51$^{1}/_{2}$°) while the first 51$^{1}/_{2}$°of the Septamsa chart comprises the first of the seven sub-zodiacs. Through Addey's work and persistence, aspects based on these divisions are used today in Western astrology alongside the more traditional square, opposition, sextile and trine (based on multiples of two and three and are seen by the second and third Harmonics Charts).

But more importantly, John Addey hoped that the study of harmonics might lead to a new commitment towards a unification of Eastern and Western principles based in part on the universality of numbers and the rhythms of the universe. In his own words:

> The picture that has so emerged is one of the harmonics, that is the rhythms and sub-rhythms, of cosmic periods, which can be demonstrated to provide the basis of all astrological doctrine both ancient and modern.[3]. . .This is only one of the many ways in which the new approach to astrology in terms of harmonics promises a reunion of the Eastern and Western traditions in astrology and, indeed, seems likely to illuminate Indian astrology for Indians as much as Western astrology for Westerners.[4]

PART II
INTERPRETATION

4
DEFINING THE PLANETS, SIGNS AND HOUSES

In India, the Rasi Chakra has traditionally been used to determine the nature of one's past lives as well as the direction of one's present life. Before the Rasi Chakra can be interpreted, however, it is necessary to first define the planets, signs and houses, the basic elements of the Hindu chart. Each planet in the birth chart represents a different quality — the capacity for love, intelligence, work, emotions — and adopts the identity of the house it rules. The expression of the planets is further modified by: (a) the zodiacal sign in which the planet is placed at the precise moment of birth and (b) the house the planet occupies. Interpretation of the horoscope, however, is ultimately dependent on the way an astrologer synthesizes these elements and judges their influences.

The following descriptions of the elements have been divided into two categories: (1) authentic delineations taken from translations of ancient writings and (2) their modern interpretations. The books in which these writings are found include *Brihat Jataka* by Vaharamihira, *Saravali* by Kalyana Varma and *Phaladeepika* by Mantreswar. Some of these depictions cannot be applied to our lives but have been included for the purposes of historical documentation. Other descriptions have been reworked in order for these elements to be applicable in a contemporary horoscope.

The Planets (Grahas)
The following descriptions include both positive and negative qualities of the planetary symbols. Whether they manifest as beneficial or difficult influences depends upon

Table 4.1. Planets*

Planet	Ruling Sign	Body part	Day	Gem	Colour	Sense	God(dess)
Sun	Leo	Heart Spine	Sunday	Ruby	Copper	Soul	God Shiva
Moon	Cancer	Breasts	Monday	Pearl	White	Mind	Goddess Parvati
Mars	Aries Scorpio	Head	Tuesday	Coral	Red	Sight	God Kamara
Mercury	Gemini Virgo	Lungs	Wednesday	Emerald	Green	Smell	God Vishnu
Jupiter	Sagittarius Pisces	Thighs	Thursday	Topaz	Yellow	Hearing	God Brahma
Venus	Taurus Libra	Kidneys Eyes	Friday	Diamond	Multi-Colour	Taste	Goddess Lakshmi (Vishnu's Wife)
Saturn	Capricorn Aquarius	Bones Teeth	Saturday	Sapphire	Black	Touch	God Yama

* The components of this chart are compiled from different sources. For instance, the colours are taken from the *Brihat Jataka* while the gemstones, Gods and Goddesses are taken from *Phaladeepika*.

their association with the other elements in the chart. (It is interesting to note that the writers of the ancient scriptures endowed the planets with human characteristics.)

The Sun (Ravi)

Ravi rules Leo (Simha), the body parts are the heart and spine, the day of the week is Sunday, the God is Shiva, the gemstone is ruby, and the colour is copper. Other parts of the body include man's right eye, woman's left eye, mouth, spleen, throat and brain. The associated profession may involve business inherited from the father, dealings in copper and gold, and government service. The Sun indicates administrators, kings, dictators, and heads of state. Acquisition of wealth comes from fruit trees, medicine, wool, metals. The Sun is the soul.[1]

> The Sun has somewhat yellow eyes, is of the height of the length of the two arms stretched out, of bilious nature and with very little hair on his head.[2] The Sun is of bilious temperament, lord of bones, limited quantity of hair, dark red form, reddish brown eyes, red, square built body, valiant, wrathful broad shoulders. He is a Shiva worshipper, doctor, minister, king, performer of sacrifice. It has to do with matters concerning the self, copper, gold, father, auspiciousness, happiness, dignity, power, glory, influence, health, vigor, fortune and the God Shiva.[3]

The Sun represents Prana, Sanskrit for the 'breath of life'. Hindus pray to the Sun in order to regain vitality. It symbolizes the deity Brahma, the Creator, and Hindus perform religious rites throughout the year on holidays celebrating the Sun and its power. The Sun is considered to be the self, the father, and the career. The Sun gives activity, authority, steadiness, self-acquisition, strong will and good fortune. The person with a powerful Sun in the horoscope will be an over-achiever and (at times) bossy, aggressive and outspoken. There can also be too much preoccupation with status and recognition.

If the planet is well-placed there will be ambition, brilliance, command, dignity, energy, fame, generosity, health, individuality, optimism, royalty, success, vitality, and warmth, and the native will have a cheerful outlook on life. If the planet is ill-placed there will be arrogance, dominance and egoism, jealousy, lavishness, over-ambition, irritability and anger. Illnesses associated with the Sun include heart disease, skin disease and fever of undetermined sources.

The Moon (Chandra)

Chandra rules Cancer (Kataka), the body part is the breasts, the day of the week is Monday, the Goddess is Parvati, the gemstone is pearl, and the colour is white. Other parts of the body include the left eye of the male, right eye of female, stomach, oesophagus, uterus, ovaries, lymphatic system and bladder. Profession involves anything associated with shipping, water products, pearls, corals, agriculture, cattle, clothes, service under a woman. The Moon* represents both the mind and the body. [4]

> The Moon has a thin and round body, is of an exceedingly windy and phlegmatic nature, is learned and has a soft voice and beautiful eyes . . . [5] The Moon has a huge body, is young and old, lean and white, has fine lovely eyes, black and thin hair, governs blood, is soft in speech, wears white, is yellowish in color, has wind and phlegm in his composition and is mild in temperament. It has to do with matters concerning mother, mental tranquility, fruits, tenderness, flowers, fame, pearls, milk, sweet substances, women, bodily health, beauty, heart, understanding and affluence. The Moon is female and is concerned with the sea. [6]

The Moon represents the personality which reflects the light of the Sun — one's identity and essence — to the outside world. As a watery planet, its emphasis in the birth chart promotes frequent changing of feelings, residences and careers. It is receptive rather than initiating and symbolizes the mother, the mind and the body. The Moon is associated with family life, the home and clandestine affairs. Its placement in the horoscope reveals the conditions surrounding the person's infancy and, in a woman's chart, the ability to conceive. An afflicted Moon may cause upset stomachs and frequent vomiting.

If the planet is well-placed there will be love of home and maternal concerns. If the planet is ill-placed there will be changeability, vacillating nature, stomach and other nervous

---

* Mercury rules over speech and represents the way ideas are communicated to others whereas the Moon as mind reflects our personalities.

ailments, inconsistencies and indulgence with food and sex. Diseases are eye diseases, lunacy, hysteria, and paralysis.

Mars (Kuja)

Kuja rules both Aries (Mesha) and Scorpio (Vrischika), the part of the body is the head, the day of the week is Tuesday, the God is Kamara, the gemstone is coral and the colour is red. Other body parts include external sex organs, left ear, muscular system, uterus, pelvis, and prostate. Professions are hunters, the military, dentists, surgeons, butchers and barbers. Wealth is acquired through metals, battles, gold, cooking, acquisition of land, acts of oppression and spying. Mars represents strength and the sense that it rules is sight.[7]

> Mars has sharp and cruel eyes and a young body, is generous, of bilious nature, of unsteady mind, and has a narrow middle.[8] Mars has slender waist, curled and shining hair, fierce eyes, is bilious and cruel in nature, red, wrathful but generous. It rules matters pertaining to strength, products from the earth, brothers, war, courage, fire, enemies, attachment to females, mental dignity. It has to do with courage, disease, younger brothers, lands, foes, blood, paternal relations. He is a cook, and an arms bearer, a goldsmith and a thief.[9]

According to the Hindus, Mars is commander-in-chief of the celestial forces. It is a fiery and dry planet noted for both its constructive and destructive energy. It represents ambition, desires and the animal instinct in man. Mars-dominated people approach life with the utmost enthusiasm and physical energy. There is a tendency to act before thinking and, if afflicted in the birth chart, its influence may contribute to drinking, violence and aggression.

If the planet is well-placed there will be self-confidence, endurance, impulse for ventures and heroic deeds, strength, courage, combativeness, sharp wit, and a go-ahead spirit. There will also be mental activity and muscular strength, good organizing ability, an independent spirit, character, strong determination, ambition and leadership qualities. If the planet is ill-placed there will be rashness, loss of temper, foolhardiness, a quarrelsome nature and alcohol indulgence. Diseases are smallpox, measles, mumps, bleeding, infections and a tendency towards high fever.

Mercury (Budha)

Budha rules Gemini (Mithuna) and Virgo (Kanya), the body part is lungs, the day of the week is Wednesday, the God is Vishnu, the gemstone is emerald, the colour is green. Other parts of the body include the solar plexus and the nervous system. Professions are salesmen, agents, orators, and linguists. Wealth is acquired through poetry, scriptures, clerical work, astrology, vedas and mantras. Mercury is speech and the sense it rules is smell.[10]

> Mercury has an impediment in his speech, is fond of joke, and is of a bilious, windy and phlegmatic nature . . .[11] Mercury is green, full of nerves, pleasant in speech, red and broad eyes, and is fond of fun. It has to do with matters pertaining to learning, eloquence, skill in fine arts, dexterity in speech, maternal uncle, aptness for acquiring knowledge, cleverness and the mechanical arts. It has to do with relatives, discrimination, friends, speech and action. He is a cowherd, learned man, artisan, accountant.[12]

Mercury is the planet of communication and it indicates one's level of intelligence. It rules the solar plexus and central nervous system. There is moodiness and forgetfulness, along with logic, sharpness of wit, and an ability to learn quickly. If this planet is prominent in the chart, there will be frequent short trips since the Mercury-dominated person is quite adaptable to new situations. There is a fondness for the occult sciences, versatility, mathematical and engineering skills.

If the planet is well-placed, the subject has an inquiring and analytical mind and the ability to grasp ideas quickly. If the planet is ill-placed, there will be lack of concentration, vacillation, and restlessness that must be tempered. There will be cunning, mischievousness, conceit, talkativeness, eccentricities, and general instability. Illnesses may include nervous ailments, eye disease, sore throat, anaemia, and itchiness.

Jupiter (Guru)

Guru rules Sagittarius (Dhanus) and Pisces (Meena), the body part is the thigh, the day of the week is Thursday, the God is Brahma, the gemstone is topaz, the colour is yellow. Other parts of the body and its functions include the liver, circulation of the blood in arteries and fat content in the body. There may also be a tendency towards growths and cysts. Profession relates to educational interests, law, religion, philosophy and banking. Wealth is acquired with the help of Brahmins, through morality, religion or banking. Jupiter is knowledge and health.[13]

> Jupiter has a big body, yellow hairs and eyes, high intellectual powers, and a phlegmatic nature . . .[14] Jupiter has body of yellowish hue and eyes and hair are brown, fat and elevated chest, big body, phlegmatic, intelligent and is after wealth. It has to do with knowledge, good qualities, teaching, prosperity, reverence to Gods, wisdom, and conquering of the senses. He is an astrologer, preceptor, minister, important personage and Brahmin. It is genius, wealth, physical development, sons and knowledge. The sense it rules is hearing.[15]

As the largest planet, Jupiter represents the areas of our lives through which we learn and grow. Jupiter brings both material and spiritual expansion to whichever house of the horoscope it occupies and typifies the principles of learning, teaching, travelling, religion, the law and sharing ideas with others. It typifies the social aspect of the individual as well as the moral, ethical and religious issues affecting his/her life. There is mobility and a love of honesty and integrity. An emphasized Jupiter endows one with athletic ability and a love of outdoor sports, adventure and risk-taking.

If the planet is well-placed there will be judiciousness, steady habits, concentration and meditation. There is benevolence, fruitfulness and optimism. The disposition will be generous and candid. There is high reasoning ability and proper judgment along with geniality, generosity, joviality, prosperity and good health. If the planet is ill-placed there will be extremism, liberalism, extravagance, lavishness, over-optimism, carelessness, debts, disputes, speculative failure, religious fanaticism, misjudgment and miscalculation. Diseases are liver ailments, hip injuries, jaundice, hernia and dermatological problems.

Although Jupiter (Guru) represents the principles of learning and teaching in the birth chart, the literal and more complex definition of the Sanskrit word 'guru' is:

venerable, respectable, person (father, mother, or any relative older than one's self) . . . spiritual parent or preceptor (from whom a youth receives the initiatory Mantra or prayer). [16]

Very simply stated a guru is 'one who transmits knowledge'.

In recent years, many people have gone to India to study certain yogic and/or meditative techniques from skilled practitioners and religious adepts. Many of these yogis and swamis have grown long beards, are draped in either flowing robes or thin loincloths and have renounced the material world. Though this attire and attitude towards possessions is quite typical for a man of religion in India, it creates an ominous and distrustful feeling for Westerners. Furthermore, because of the notoriety that a handful of swamis have received, we associate 'gurus' with these few who cannot possibly convey the sanctity that a religious teacher represents in Indian society.

Though most often a guru is defined as a *religious* master, he may also be a teacher of music, astrology or any sacred art or science. What does distinguish him, however, from an institutional teacher is the intense relationship that he cultivates with his disciple and the way in which his field of expertise complements his spiritual practice. The guru usually meets his student daily for an actual lesson. Instead of monetary payment for the tutelage, it is not unusual for a disciple to serve his guru by performing duties ranging from administrative work to preparing tea. Some pupils live with the guru's family and help with the day-to-day running of the household. In addition to receiving traditional instruction, the pupil spends as much time as he can in the presence of his teacher in order to observe him and, ultimately, absorb the guru's knowledge. In essence, the student is devoted to his teacher and is available to serve him at all times. Their arrangement is comparable to the master/apprentice relationship of feudal times and is the most intensive and efficient way to become proficient in a chosen field.

Most religious teachers, Indian musicians and astrologers learn their craft from individual gurus. Both Indian classical music compositions and many astrological techniques not included in ancient texts have been orally transmitted through generations and remain a testament to the importance of the guru/student relationship. Even Westerners who study in India regard their teachers as gurus because they too have been instructed in this unique and intense manner. I, too, was taught by a guru whom I saw every day over a six-month period and I addressed him the way an Indian student addresses a teacher — as 'Guru-ji' — literally meaning 'my teacher'.

Venus (Sukra)

Sukra rules Taurus (Vrishaba) and Libra (Thula), the day of the week is Friday, the Goddess is Lakshmi, the gemstone is diamond, the colour is 'multi-coloured'. Parts of the body include eyes, generative system, throat, chin, cheeks and kidneys. Professions may include musician, filmmaker, actor, transport worker, jeweller, and tailor. Wealth is acquired through women's merchandise, animals, music and dance, silver, silk and poetry. Venus represents desire and the sense that it rules is taste.[17]

> Venus leads a comfortable life, has a beautiful body, fair eyes, a windy and phlegmatic nature, and black curling hairs . . .[18] Venus wears multi-colors, black curled hair, limbs and body are huge, wind and phlegm, green and lovely and broad eyes, and he treasures his virility. It has to do with matters pertaining to clothes, song and dance and music, wife, happiness, flowers, poetry, charming speech and marriage. Venus is a musician, wealthy man, sensualist, merchant, dancer, weaver, peacock. It has to do with wives, vehicles, ornaments, love affairs, pleasure.[19]

Venus is the brightest and most visible star and, because it could clearly be seen rising and setting with the Sun, was commonly called the Morning and Evening Star. This planet, like the goddess of the same name, exemplifies the concepts of love, passion and emotional expression. In Hindu mythology, the goddess of love is called Kama, and one's capacity for giving and receiving love depends on the position of Venus in the birth chart. The *Kama Sutra*, the ancient Hindu book illustrating love-making techniques, literally means 'Song of Venus' as 'Sutra' means 'verse' or 'song' and 'Kama' is another name for Venus.

If the planet is well-placed, there will be kindness,

sociability, pleasant nature, good looks, attentiveness, good marriage, generosity, cheerfulness, artistic nature, general success and popularity with others. If the planet is ill-placed, there will be sloth, amorousness, extravagance, excessive behaviour, eating or overspending and a general inability to control one's emotions. Diseases are eye infections, ovarian problems, difficulties with the skin, swellings and anaemia.

Saturn (Sani)

Sani rules Capricorn (Makara) and Aquarius (Kumbha), the day of the week is Saturday, the God is Yama, the gemstone is sapphire, and the colour is black. Parts of the body include bones, hair, ears and teeth. Profession may involve working with metal, iron, wool, or leather products. Wealth is acquired through roots and fruits, servants, sculpture, woods. Saturn represents sorrow and it is associated with the sense of touch.[20]

> Saturn is lazy, has eyes of gold color, a thin and tall body, large teeth, stiff hair, and is of a windy nature . . .[21] Saturn is dark, lame, windy in composition, deep eyes with lean, tall body full of arteries and veins, idle and calumniating, governs muscle, cruel and has no pity, dull headed, large nails, teeth, stiff hair and limbs, dirty and of a slow disposition, fierce and black. It has to do with longevity, death, fear, misery, sickness, misfortune, servitude, captivity and poverty. It defines the period of a person's life, livelihood, cause of death, adversity and servants. Saturn is an oil monger, servant, vile person, blacksmith.[22]

If the planet is well-placed there will be prudence, frugality, self-control, loyalty and steadfastness. Through any obstacles, the influence is one of perseverance, industrious-ness, and remarkable patience. If the planet is ill-placed there will be laziness, lethargy, delays, consolidation, and depression. Illnesses are related to weak knees, bones and teeth, arthritis, and gallstones.

North Node (Rahu)

> The Dragon's head is black, tall, has skin disease, is a heretic, speaks falsehoods, is cunning, and is devoid of intellect. Gemstone is agate. Rahu indicates paternal grandfather.[23]

South Node (Kethu)

> The Dragon's Tail is red, fierce in look, inhales smoke, has bruised limbs, is lean and malicious. Gemstone is turquoise. Kethu indicates maternal grandfather.[24]

Rahu and Kethu are considered to be difficult points, and create problems in the areas of life represented by the houses they occupy. Rahu indicates excesses of all types and Kethu represents hardships and isolation. Both Nodes also represent dissatisfaction, aimless travels and dishonesty. If they are well-placed and well-aspected, however, they can enhance the houses in which they are placed. Rahu will give power and material success, while Kethu may bring a spiritual and meditative influence to the chart.

Rasis, or Signs of the Zodiac

The zodiacal sign, or Rasi, that each planet occupies further modifies planetary definitions by illustrating the way in which the energy of that planet may be expressed. Most importantly, the meaning of each house of the Rasi Chakra is determined by the zodiacal sign occupying that house in combination with its planetary ruler. The following are general descriptions of the 12 zodiacal signs and may be applied to people whose Ascendant* matches that particular sign of the zodiac.

Aries (Mesha)

Aries (Mesha) is symbolized by a ram which is by nature rash, combative, lascivious, springy and hardy. With Mars ruling this sign, people born under the sign of Aries are active, ambitious, bold, confident, courageous and impulsive. They are always interested in challenges and, once they have achieved what they have sought, they move on to the next project. They possess a childlike naivety and Aries natives must learn to cultivate patience and to think before they act. They have an abundant amount of physical energy which should always be

---

* It is customary in the West to identify ourselves by our Sun sign whereas in India one is identified by the Lagna, or Ascendant, of the chart.

Table 4.2. Signs of the Zodiac

Sign	Ruler	Body Part[25]	Colour[26]	Direction	Element	Gender	Positive/negative	Fruitful/barren
Aries	Mars	Head	Red	East	Fire	Masculine	+	Barren
Taurus	Venus	Face	White	South	Earth	Feminine	-	Semi-fruitful
Gemini	Mercury	Arms	Green	West	Air	Masculine	+	Barren
Cancer	Moon	Heart	Pink	North	Water	Feminine	-	Fruitful
Leo	Sun	Stomach	Brown	East	Fire	Masculine	+	Barren
Virgo	Mercury	Hips	Grey	South	Earth	Feminine	-	Barren
Libra	Venus	Abdomen	(Multi-)	West	Air	Masculine	+	Semi-fruitful
Scorpio	Mars	Genitals	Black	North	Water	Feminine	-	Fruitful
Sagittarius	Jupiter	Thighs	Gold	East	Fire	Masculine	+	Semi-fruitful
Capricorn	Saturn	Knees	Yellow	South	Earth	Feminine	-	Barren
Aquarius	Saturn	Ankles	Brown	West	Air	Masculine	+	
Pisces	Jupiter	Feet	White	North	Water	Feminine	-	Fruitful

expressed. If it is not released, this energy is likely to emerge as aggression, anger and hostility.

Taurus (Vrishaba)
As a sign depicted by the fierce and fiery bull, Taureans are productive, persevering, stubborn and are always trying to convince others that their views are correct. Venus, the ruler of Taurus, endows these people with kindness, patience, charm and a fondness and talent for the arts and luxuries. They are sensual, extremely passionate, possessive and jealous. They are straightforward and direct and, as opposed to the previous sign of Aries, ponder for a long time before making a decision. Once they have a goal in mind, however, they are almost obsessive about attaining it. They are even-tempered and while it takes some time before anger is ignited, their temper can be vile and difficult to control. The accumulation of wealth is a major preoccupation and Taureans are either extremely well-off or notoriously wasteful. With difficult aspects they may be inflexible, slow, lazy and overly indulgent by overeating or spending too much money.

Gemini (Mithuna)
Signified by the symbol of the twins, the dual nature of Gemini appears in their versatility, restlessness and need to be involved simultaneously in more than one project at any given time. Boredom is their worst enemy and they always seem to be searching for intellectual stimulation and other people to engage in conversation. As a Mercury-ruled air sign, Gemini rules communications and mental energy. They often play the devil's advocate for the sole purpose of stirring up a discourse and a debate. Gemini natives are adaptable, extremely intelligent, mechanical and quick witted. One of their difficulties is an inability to concentrate and a constant need for instant gratification which causes them to give up rather easily. With difficult aspects, they can be too scattered, restless and insensitive.

Cancer (Kataka)
This sign is symbolized by a crab and the ruling planet, the Moon, provides Cancerians with a fertile imagination, an emotional disposition and a tendency towards moodiness

and introversion. Their inclination is towards an artistic medium and their minds are extremely retentive. Due to extreme sensitivity, there may be nervous irritability and, at times, meaningless chatter which compensates for their general insecurity and shyness. They are sentimental but their personalities are extremely changeable, ranging from extreme warmth to secrecy which is often mistaken for coldness. Cancerians feel safe and secure surrounded by family and the comforts of home though they sometimes go through their entire lives searching for it. With difficult aspects, they can be quick-tempered, irritable and dishonest.

Leo (Simha)
Represented by the lion, king of the jungle, Leos must be in control of their lives at all times. They do not like working for others and everything they do must have their personal stamp. But Leo can also represent one of the most generous and magnanimous signs of the zodiac, capable of being wonderful hosts and hostesses. In addition to being constructive and inventive, Leos are good organizers, directors and 'ideas men' who leave the detailed and technical work to others. They enjoy being admired and praised for their accomplishments and desperately need the approval of others. Difficult aspects make them too demanding, too authoritative and too egotistic to concern themselves with the needs and opinions of others.

Virgo (Kanya)
As the sign of the virgin, Virgos search for purity through cleanliness, good health, proper diet and exercise. They are sensitive, reserved, self-conscious, critical and fastidious. As they are ruled by inconstant Mercury, Virgos are prone to change whether it be through multiple residences, jobs or points of view. They are conscientious and methodical workers capable of functioning under any adversity and also make excellent secretaries, organizers and editors. Virgos can be very insecure and reserved, qualities which may be interpreted as lack of warmth and good will. Because they are perfectionists, they are often dissatisfied and too critical of themselves as well as others. With difficult aspects, Virgos tend to have a pessimistic outlook

on life spending too much time analysing and worrying which may adversely affect their health.

Libra (Thula)
Libra is symbolized by a pair of justice scales indicating their love of balance and harmony. With Venus ruling this sign, they are adverse to arguments and are always gentle, soft-spoken, modest and courteous. They like beautiful objects and, like Venus-ruled Taureans, enjoy luxuries, having a good time and patronizing the arts. Librans are not particularly self-motivated, do not like being alone and can be much too preoccupied with finding a marriage partner. In fact, relationships usually direct the course of their lives. They have a difficult time making decisions and can be lazy, excessive with drugs and alcohol, and especially indulgent where affairs of the heart are concerned. With difficult aspects, there is too much concern with appearances and they too often adjust their personalities to suit their present partners.

Scorpio (Vrischika)
Scorpions are tireless workers as well as incredible extremists. They work very hard — sometimes too hard — trying to control their emotions. They know that admitting their true feelings means that, in addition to expressing love, they must also confront the accompanying jealousy, pain and anger. Scorpions are amazing workaholics, and the more challenges they accept the more outlets they will have for all their energy. They are extremely determined, business-oriented, and possess a fertile imagination and sharp intelligence. Their need to communicate and form relationships is expressed not only through business dealings but through their sometimes insatiable sexuality. They have deep intuition, powerful emotions and extremely high standards which they set for themselves and others. With difficult aspects, they can be ruthless and relentless in achieving their goals. To this end, there is a self-destructive tendency which can result in alcohol and drug abuse.

Sagittarius (Dhanus)
Sagittarius is symbolized by the centaur — half horse and

half-man — who is always pictured pointing his bow and arrow towards the sky. Eternally optimistic and hopeful about the future, Sagittarians try to persuade others to develop this same attitude. They are always searching for the key to knowledge and happiness without working too hard to attain it, have very high principles and are sometimes frank to the point of being painfully brutal. They have a joy and enthusiasm for life and a love of sports, travelling to foreign countries, learning and teaching. These people enjoy meeting foreigners and very often live abroad or marry foreigners. There is interest in pursuing higher degrees in religion, philosophy or the law. With difficult aspects they can be arrogant, bossy and terribly indulgent with food and alcohol, especially when attending social functions (which they rarely miss).

Capricorn (Makara)
In accordance with their symbol of the mountain goat, Capricorns have immense organizational skills and an overwhelming desire and ability to achieve their goals at any cost. Whatever Capricorns set out to do will be followed through to the end despite any obstacles encountered along the way. They are economical, frugal, cautious and very rarely proceed without planning in advance. They are good and loyal friends, honest, upright, and persevering to a fault without ever complaining. These people are faithful and extremely good providers but need secure homes to which they can always return and reflect upon their busy lives. They are born leaders and possess great executive abilities. Capricorns can be extremely disciplined and calculating to the point of ruthlessness. They are very reserved and usually speak only when they have something important to say. Some people mistake the Capricornian reserve for coldness and insensitivity. For Capricorns, however, it is a way to pursue their goals without allowing extraneous emotions to stand in the way. Difficult aspects make them pessimistic, depressive, shy, uncommunicative and ruthless.

Aquarius (Kumbha)
Aquarius, an air sign, is often mistaken for a water sign since it is symbolized by someone carrying the waters of

humanity and pouring it over the earth. The element, air, represents the desire to communicate brotherhood and freedom to the rest of the world. Aquarians have inventive minds and are always seeking innovative projects in which they may become involved. They are very socially conscious and are identified with groups fighting social and political injustices. Interests range from technology to astrology and social work. They love meeting new people with whom they can exchange ideas, and always enjoy surrounding themselves with others dedicated to the same causes. They have difficulties being intimate with one person because of their involvement with groups and causes. Their difficulties include a highly strung nature, day-to-day impatience and an inflexibility to change habits and patterns which would put their lives on a more even keel.

Pisces (Meena)

There is honesty, love of the arts and an incredible empathy and compassion towards people. They lean towards cultivating a spiritual life or live abroad. They have vivid imaginations and relate to the world through their feelings and instincts. Pisceans are sometimes incapable of making a decision due to a lack of faith in their own judgment. They do not always express themselves clearly but are willing to help other people at a moment's notice. At times Pisceans live in a world of their own creation and have difficulty facing reality. Because of this they are sometimes withdrawn and moody. Their lack of clarity makes them difficult to understand but they are, none the less, extremely sensitive and incapable of hurting others. If they have hurt someone's feelings they tend to feel guilt and remorse. With difficult aspects, there is lack of confidence, dishonesty and self-destructive tendencies leading to either overeating or drug and alcohol abuse.

Houses or Bhavas

One of the most important elements of the horoscope is the zodiacal house or 'bhava'. In Sanskrit, the word 'bhava' literally means 'state of being'. In addition to representing 12 different areas of one's life, the houses are also categorized according to their auspicious or inauspicious natures. The most beneficial houses in the zodiac are the fifth and ninth houses, Trikona houses. Any planet placed in the fifth or ninth house, or ruling either of these houses, generally becomes a beneficial influence in the chart. Also auspicious are the angular first, fourth, seventh and tenth houses known as Kendra houses. The sixth, eighth and twelfth houses, Dusthana houses, are what Hindus call evil houses but which I will call 'difficult'. The Upachaya houses, the third, sixth, tenth and eleventh houses, are classified as 'bothersome'. Later in the book we will see the importance of each planet as it is identified with the house it rules. We will also see how the aforementioned house categories may be altered by the quality of occupying planets. The following descriptions attributed to the houses combine both Eastern and Western definitions.

First House (Ascendant or Lagna)
(body, fame, limbs, general appearance, head [27])
The sign occupying the first house is also the sign of the Lagna (or Ascendant) and defines the mood of the entire horoscope. It determines character, appearance, the manner in which a person approaches life in general and how he/she is viewed. It is the manner in which others view this person. The first house is an indicator of childhood and the influence of one's formative years in determining the personality and general outlook on life. Health is evaluated through the corresponding body parts and organs of both the ascending sign and the sign of the sixth house.

Second House (family, wealth, right eye, speech,
truthfulness, learning, face [28])
The second house deals with assets, basic talents and capacities for being successful. It also indicates activities within one's personal control, power and quality of speech, imagination, eyes, neck and throat. It represents our approach to finances and how we earn and spend money. An analysis of the second house illustrates the effects of our primary education and the way in which we learn.

Third House (brothers, bravery, meals, right ear,
courage, breast[29])
The third house tells of travels, changes of residence,

neighbours, communications, siblings, hands, arms, ears and shoulders. This house indicates the nature of the relationship with brothers and sisters and defines the nature of the siblings themselves. By being defined as the house of courage, it determines whether one may or may not embark on adventurous journeys in the course of one's life.

Fourth House (relations, education, mother, house, land, comfort, sister's son, maternal uncle, heart[30])

It is the house of the mother, the domestic environment, the conditions of the latter part of one's life, stomach and breasts. In addition to information concerning the home and the mother, this house indicates the level of one's education.

Fifth House (offspring, intelligence, previous karma, Vedic knowledge, entertainment, education, belly[31])

It is a house concerned with one's intelligence, one's children, creative and pleasurable pursuits, and the expression of passion. The fifth house has always been associated with love affairs as opposed to the seventh house which concerns itself with marriage and committed relationships. It indicates the way in which we use our spare time to develop hobbies and creative interest.

Sixth House (enemies, kinsmen, diseases, humiliation, debt, anxiety, servants, hip[32])

The condition of the sixth house will affect the person's work habits, health and the propensity for serving and helping others. The general constitution is indicated by the first house whereas physical vulnerability is defined by the corresponding body part or organ of the planet ruling the sixth house.

Seventh House (wife or husband, generosity, respect, desire, passion, groin[33])

The seventh house describes the marriage partner and how the individual relates to that partner. It also describes litigation, legal partnerships and business partnerships.

Eighth House (duration of life, death, mental pain, sorrow, obstacles, sexual organs[34])

It is the house of the marriage partner's financial capacity, the money one receives through marriage, partnerships, or lawsuits. It also affects chronic illnesses, business projects, chronic diseases, obstacles, and one's sexuality.

Ninth House (deeds of virtue, father, medicine, anything auspicious, luck, worship, duty, fortune, thighs[35])

The ninth house indicates the nature of the father, higher education and the way personal philosophy and/or religion affects our approach to life. It also indicates foreign travel, languages, hips, thighs and defines the nature of the relationship to the father.

Tenth House (vocation, knowledge, clothes, honour, occupation, commerce, knees[36])

The tenth house points out career choices, describes the way we would like others to view us, the position of our father in society, and our own status in the world.*

Eleventh House (income, fulfilment, eldest brother, good news, earnings, left ear, calves, result of capabilities, legs and ankles[37])

The eleventh house shows us the way in which we relate to groups of people, our friendships, community participation, and the things that we gain in life. It also represents our hopes, goals and the ability to fulfil our ambitions.

Twelfth House (loss, bad deeds, travels, misery, left eye, feet[38])

The twelfth house is indicative of that which is beyond our personal control. It is a house traditionally related to isolation, imprisonment, limitations and the inability to

* Since a Hindu woman does not usually pursue a career, the tenth house traditionally indicates her father and his profession. Since modern Western women do not have these restrictions, the tenth house of a woman's chart will be interpreted as both her profession *and* her father's.

communicate with others. This house also relates to anything one must do in solitude like doing research, practising meditative techniques, praying, reading or simply having the ability to be alone with oneself. It is also the house of expenditures showing how we spend that which we either earn or borrow.

After interpreting the horoscope, the Hindu astrologer may offer certain suggestions by utilizing the categories of the signs and planets listed in Table 4.1 and Table 4.2. For instance, in India, medical astrology is a very specialized field used by astrologers, physicians, and healers. Medically speaking, each planet and sign of the zodiac is analogous to a body part or organ. To learn about a person's health we generally look to the zodiacal signs found on the Ascendant and the sixth house with their corresponding planetary rulers. The part or organ associated with that sign or planet is a vulnerable area of the body and may flare up during times of possible health crises.

If the sign or planet is well-placed in the chart, then this will usually not present a serious problem. If that sign or planet, however, is exceptionally weak in the context of the birth chart, the astrologer may prescribe wearing certain amulet(s) of the matching 'healing' gemstone(s) to be worn around the neck or placed on an altar. A stone or stones may remedy the general ailment, improve the state of the afflicted planet or simply provide general protection for the person before a crisis arises. The astrologer or healer may also recommend praying to the afflicted planet's corresponding god or goddess on a certain day of the week. The planet's colour is taken into account when choosing the flower to be placed on the altar when chanting certain prayers or mantras (the Sanskrit word for 'sacred song'). The remedies corresponding with the strongest planets in the chart are sometimes also used as added protection against illness.

At first glance these healing rituals may seem somewhat strange, but it is quite typical in any culture or religion to pray to a god at a time of crisis. Because Hinduism is a polytheistic culture, the prayers are simply directed toward a particular deity determined partially by the region one lives in and partially by the contents of the horoscope. As for gemstones, there are many people all over the world who attest to the fact that stones contain physical properties which restore vitality, alleviate migraines, and even calm the nervous system. Wearing an amulet may simply give the person the *feeling* of being helped thus restoring confidence and vitality. For this reason alone, the astrologer may recommend wearing one.

Table 4.1 and Table 4.2 illustrate the way in which the ancient Hindus liked to categorize and co-relate planets, zodiacal signs, days of the week, colour, etc. Some of the categories of the zodiacal signs — such as planetary rulership, element and modality — are used in Hindu astrology in the same way as in Western astrology, that is, to provide more information about the quality of the sign. The direction associated with the sign of the Moon or the sign on the Ascendant at the moment a journey begins is, for instance, important for the astrologer when ascertaining whether a journey to a certain place will be beneficial. For example, if the Moon is in the sign of Aries at the moment a journey commences, the trip will be forecast as successful because Aries is an auspicious sign for beginnings.[39] Direction is also an important consideration for an astrologer when advising about marriage: the sign which is prominent in the client's chart signifies the direction (from the client's birthplace) to which the astrologer looks for a prospective marriage partner.

According to the *Phaladeepika*, a woman's ability to conceive is determined by whether the signs occupying the fifth and seventh houses of the Rasi Chakra and the Moon Chart are fruitful, semi-fruitful or barren (see Table 4.1). With fruitful and semi-fruitful signs occupying these houses, pregnancy is almost guaranteed. If however, there are barren signs ruling these houses, the astrologer may predict difficulty in conceiving, or, in extreme cases, child-lessness. Because of the availability — especially in the West — of birth control as well as unique fertilization methods, it is very difficult to apply these ancient formulas to determine conception in modern horoscopes. A woman whose chart may have originally indicated that she would have a certain number of children may have fewer children or even none at all. (More detailed information about conception and childbirth is included in Chapter 9.)

Using the aforementioned definitions of the planets, signs and houses, the following chapters illustrate the actual steps involved in interpreting the Rasi Chakra according to the rules of Hindu astrology. The principles I will demonstrate are a cross-section of methods I have tested over the years, and which I feel the Western astrologer may comfortably utilize. In the end, however, judgement is always up to the discretion of the individual Astrologer and the application of his analytical skills and intuitive ability.

5
Ascendant Combinations

Now that we have defined the elements of the birth chart, the first step in interpreting the Rasi Chakra is to describe each of the 12 signs as it appears on the Ascendant. Since Hindu astrology employs an equal house system, each of the 12 Ascendants only produces one combination of zodiacal signs/planets ruling each sequential house. What follows, therefore, are 144 basic delineations — 12 zodiacal sign combinations for 12 Ascendants (12 × 12 = 144) — of the 12 zodiacal signs and rulers which respectively occupy and rule the houses of the 12 different Ascendants. This chapter should deepen the astrologer's understanding of what the planets, signs and houses actually represent.

The descriptions for the Taurus and Libra Ascendants should be read with reference to the charts of Barbara and Annemarie, respectively. It is also important to remember that the classifications of people as 'Arians', 'Taureans', etc. refer to their Ascendant and not to their Sun sign.

Mesha (Aries) Lagna

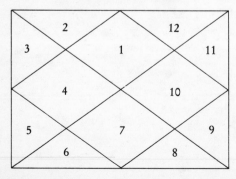

Round eyes, weak knees, passionate, afraid of the water, eats sparingly, longs for women, uses his legs, fickle, speaks falsehoods . . .[1]

People born under this sign are of middle stature. They possess a lean and muscular body and are neither stout nor thick. Their complexion will be ruddy and they will have a fairly long neck and face. Their head will be broad at the temples and narrow at the chin. They have bushy eyebrows, eyes gray to grayish brown with sharp sight. Their hair will be wiry, color varying from dark to sandy.[2]

Health is indicated by the first and sixth houses. The influence of Mars — the fighter — provides Arians with overall good health and resistance to infections. They are, however, prone to colds and fevers and (due to their over-exertion and intense activities) migraine headaches. Since their enthusiasm is boundless, the result could be either limitless energy or total exhaustion.

Their approach to life is usually impulsive with a tendency to act first and think later. Arians are sports-oriented, love the outdoors, and become restless and bored easily. To this end, they must learn to finish projects that they begin before they lose interest. Though they often view everything from the perspective of their own experiences, their egocentricity stems from childlike innocence rather than from any type of vindictiveness. None the less, Arians are considered by their friends to be good-natured and generous.

Taurus on the Second House Cusp. With Taurus on the second house cusp, Arians are obsessed with finances and the attainment of financial security. They are usually economically well-established and enjoy accumulating works of art and other collectibles. Though they may be considered extravagant by some, their plans for the future almost always include wise investments and savings accounts.

Gemini on the Third House Cusp. As the third sign of the zodiac, Gemini is in its natural place in the third house. Arians are usually excellent speakers and story-tellers of great inventiveness. Their need to chatter incessantly shortens their attention span and they have difficulty listening to others. Since they love to travel, their residences and jobs may change frequently.

Cancer on the Fourth House Cusp. Attitude towards home is reflected by the fourth house and, in this case, Cancer, a sign associated with the mother and with emotional and domestic stability. Although an Arian's mother may have been traditional and loving, she may also have been overbearing and domineering. Consequently, these close-knit family ties are responsible for making Arians good but often controlling parents — similar to their own mothers. As the centre of their recreational activities, their homes are a source of pride in which furnishings represent achievements. Arians prefer to work at home or in close proximity to it. In fact, their search for domestic tranquillity and a compatible partner are the most important goals in their lives.

Leo on the Fifth House Cusp. Leo is in its natural place in the fifth house. Both Leo and Aries are barren signs; because of their self-involvement and artistic temperaments, Arian parents may have difficulty in giving enough time to their children during the formative years. As their children mature, however, Arians may ironically find it hard to refrain from attempting to control their destinies. With the right balance of discipline and encouragement, their children will be creative, academically productive and a continual source of pride. Arians are also extremely passionate and sensual, and enjoy recreational activities such as the theatre, concerts, movies, sports and other physical activities.

Virgo on the Sixth House Cusp. Since Mercury rules the sixth house, Arians often have high-strung temperaments and have unstable job histories. They are usually happier being self-employed since working for others often creates inevitable conflicts and problems with authority figures. Unless their anger is given a proper outlet, their inability to handle stress and pressure may predispose them to ulcers. In addition to stomach problems, the influence of Virgo on the sixth house gives Arians sensitive digestive systems and intestinal tracts. To maintain their health and to increase resistance to illness, they require a great deal of physical activity, fresh air and a diet consisting largely of fruit, vegetables, and water to cleanse their system.

Libra on the Seventh House Cusp. As the ruler of the seventh house, Venus represents the type of partner an

Arian desires: beautiful, charming, sophisticated and, above all, devoted. However, Arians are also extremely jealous since their partners are also attractive to others. Their spouses are, for the most part, passionate and share their need for loyalty and domestic tranquillity.

Scorpio on the Eighth House Cusp. Since Mars is the ruler of the eighth house, impulsiveness and hasty decision-making cause Arians to spend and invest money rather foolishly. This placement may be detrimental to the partner's finances and to business ventures generally. Arians are short-term thinkers rather than long-term planners. When emotionally aroused, they can also be argumentative and hot-tempered.

Sagittarius on the Ninth House Cusp. As ruler of the ninth house of Sagittarius, Jupiter describes the father as being well-educated, religious, magnanimous and fair-minded. Arians themselves are ethical, religious, enjoy travelling and are interested in learning languages. They love a good debate and very often play the devil's advocate in order to argue the opposite point of view. They are prone to exaggeration and, because they are also eloquent, they make very good actors and public speakers.

Capricorn on the Tenth House Cusp. Their organizational skills and their drive to succeed are among Arians' most positive qualities. Despite obstacles, they can work hard and remain fixed on their objectives, thus attaining their goals. Professions represented by Capricorn on the tenth house are managers, directors, administrators and most other positions which require practical and leadership skills as well as the potential for growth. Professional sports and the performing arts may also prove to be satisfying outlets for their Martian temperaments.

Aquarius on the Eleventh House Cusp. Though they are extremely social and open-minded, Arians are quite selective when choosing friends and colleagues. With Saturn ruling this house, there will be a large circle of acquaintances but only a handful of true friends. These friends, however, will be extremely important to them — almost as important as their immediate families — and will usually consist of people sharing the same social and political interests.

Pisces on the Twelfth House Cusp. There will be a

tendency for Arians to spend periods of time alone in order to explore their more religious and silent side. Even though they may spend extravagantly (including contributions to worthwhile causes) they are conscientious and, with Taurus occupying the second house, their funds will always be replenished.

Vrishaba (Taurus) Lagna

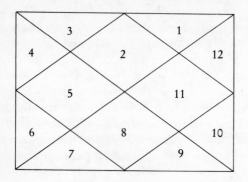

Broad thighs, big face, agriculture, happy in middle and end of life, fond of women, forgiving disposition, hardships, cattle, marks or moles on back, face and sides . . . [3]

The stature will be middle, body is plump, forehead is broad, neck is thick and stout. Eyes are bright, hair dark and complexion is clear. They are solidly built and are stocky with big shoulders and well developed muscles. [4]

Since Venus rules the two houses associated with health matters — the ascendant and the sixth house — Taureans may feel the effects of self-indulgence, especially of overeating and overspending. They may also find that they have difficulties with their thyroids, and are prone to sore throats, stiff necks, swollen glands, poor eyesight and bad skin. When they are ill, they prefer to suffer in silence rather than depend on others.

Taureans are very good listeners who do not speak much unless they have something important to say. They are patient, persevering and extremely loyal to their families, friends, and colleagues. They are sensual, passionate and faithful as well as jealous and possessive. Although Taureans are basically even-tempered, once their temper *is* ignited, they transform into bulls (after whom they are named) and see 'red'. Taureans are amazingly productive and are relentless to the point of obsession. They are, however, inflexible and need to be in control at all times. When things do not go according to plan, they find it difficult to readjust.

Gemini on the Second House Cusp. Since the restless planet Mercury rules the second house, the state of a Taurean's finances is perpetually fluctuating. Some of the 'down' periods may stem from unwise investments, frivolous spending and unexpected job changes. Their frugality and sensible attitude towards money, however, usually steers them back on the right track, thereby counteracting the effects of Gemini in the second house.

Cancer on the Third House Cusp. The third house of communications is represented by Cancer and its planetary ruler, the Moon. The collective and associative quality of the sign of Cancer contributes to the Taureans' extremely retentive memory. They perceive the world in terms of images and colours and are, therefore, often accomplished musicians and painters. They are not, however, lucid speakers and prefer to listen and reflect rather than direct the conversation.

Leo on the Fourth House Cusp. Because Taureans spent so much time alone when they were children, they were able to develop artistic hobbies and talents. As parents, they are usually stern and their attitudes towards their children reflect the way they were treated as youngsters. Taureans take great pride in their homes, and their furnishings reflect the Leonine penchant for luxury, ornateness and extravagance. They act as though they are lords and ladies of the manor. Their children are taught to respect their surroundings, and regard their homes in the same way.

Virgo on the Fifth House Cusp. Mercury, the ruler of the fifth house, causes changeability in relationships, often leading to insecurity and a cynical attitude towards love and partnerships. Since Virgo is considered to be a 'barren' sign, many Taureans, in fact, consciously choose *not* to have children. There may be difficulties conceiving children or there may be children later in life. Impulsive spending, hasty investments and gambling should be avoided, since restless Mercury rules both this house and the second house of finances.

Libra on the Sixth House Cusp. Since Venus rules the sixth house, Taureans need absolute harmony in their work environment, and they try to ensure camaraderie between themselves and their co-workers. Taureans enjoy any type of work that deals with the public such as advertising, sales, distribution, representation or the service professions. As far as their health is concerned, their tendency toward overindulgence may cause problems with their eyes and their kidneys (ruled by Venus) or with their abdomens (ruled by Libra).

Scorpio on the Seventh House Cusp. In describing the partner, Mars/Scorpio typifies people who are not only passionate, sensual and emotional but argumentative and jealous as well. Taureans will probably marry more than once and their unions will be challenging and marked by many major arguments and periods of crisis. They can learn from these difficult times, however, in order to cultivate more successful channels of communication with their spouses.

Sagittarius on the Eighth House Cusp. Jupiter rules the eighth house, which pertains to legacies and the finances of others, especially those of the spouse. Because Jupiter is the 'greater benefic', it is very likely that Taureans will inherit money at some time in their lives. Hindu astrological scriptures attribute this likelihood to the fact that 'they command the good will and sincere affection of their relatives'.

Capricorn on the Ninth House Cusp. Taureans have a conservative philosophy of life which is reflected in behaviour often considered by their friends to be too structured, inflexible and rigid. The father may have either been a strict disciplinarian or deeply religious, someone who instilled the meaning of hard work and responsibility in his children. Because they are patient and wish to communicate ethical values, Taureans make good teachers and counsellors.

Aquarius on the Tenth House Cusp. Saturn is a very beneficial planet in this chart since it rules both the ninth and tenth auspicious houses. The profession, as seen from the tenth house, has its best expression through careers involving contact with other people and can range from social work and community organizing to advertising. Their professions will reflect the Taurean need for financial stability accompanied by the Aquarian need for freedom of expression and service to others.

Pisces on the Eleventh House Cusp. Jupiter, the ruler of the eleventh house, provides Taureans with constantly expanding circles of friends and acquaintances linked by their artistic, religious or social interests. Due to the humanitarian nature of Pisces, Taureans may be involved with volunteer work and will most likely meet their friends through community meetings or social organizing.

Aries on the Twelfth House Cusp. Since the Martian-ruled twelfth house governs expenditures and because Taureans enjoy owning expensive things, they tend to spend rather extravagantly. Their overwhelming desire for economic stability, however, eventually wins out to temper these indulgent habits.

Mithuna (Gemini) Lagna

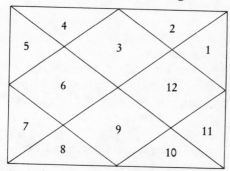

Black eyes, curled hairs, sporting with women, can interpret other people's thoughts, elevated nose, music and dance, home-keeping . . .[5]

Gemini gives a tall, upright, straight body and the hands will be long. The legs will be thin and the veins will be visible. The eyes will be hazel and the look quick, sharp and active. Nose will be long. Complexion will vary according to the ascendant.[6]

Geminis ruin their health through worry and anxiety which may weaken their already delicate nervous systems. Good health and physical well-being is easily maintained with sufficient rest, fresh air, correct eating habits and plenty of exercise. Gemini rules the lungs, making these people prone to colds, bronchitis, pneumonia and, at worst, emphysema. They should avoid smoking, and try to pace their lives to allow time for relaxation.

Geminis may satisfy their need for constant mental stimulation through meaningful conversations and diversions such as lectures, museums, films, concerts and the theatre. They are intelligent, witty, wonderful conversationalists, but very poor listeners. Their greatest challenge is to finish what they begin and to devote their energy to one project at a time. Because they are usually involved with two projects at once, they never seem to be totally successful with either.

Cancer on the Second House Cusp. Since Cancer, as ruler of the second house, symbolizes the means by which these people earn money, Geminis may find themselves in the restaurant or music business. They may also be art collectors, architects or historians. Like the phases of the Moon (the ruler of Cancer), their finances tend to fluctuate. Their early education may have been marked by restlessness and an inability to concentrate.

Leo on the Third House Cusp. Geminis are talkative, outgoing and — like the Sun which rules the third house of communications — self-assured. Though they are intelligent, mentally disciplined and highly creative, they often feel inferior to their siblings whom they perceive to be more successful.

Virgo on the Fourth House Cusp. As ruler of the fourth house, Mercury endows Geminis with restlessness and the need to change residences frequently. This need for change often stems from their own unstable upbringings: their parents may have been separated, or one parent may have been estranged from his/her children. In any event, their childhoods were usually marked by the early loss of one or both parents or constant moving from place to place.

Libra on the Fifth House Cusp. Geminis adore flattery, appreciate admiration and demand respect. They are passionate, charming, sensual, artistic and feel most productive only when they are involved in a relationship or working in a creative partnership. Their children will be both physically attractive and artistically gifted.

Scorpio on the Sixth House Cusp. Scorpio-ruled illnesses affecting Geminis include complaints from constipation, haemorrhoids, and infections of the bladder, colon or reproductive system. As ruler of the sixth house, Mars may cause problems with co-workers and a tendency towards 'workaholism'. Geminis must learn to work co-operatively with others, continue to remain self-employed or hire others to work for them. In the latter situation, they must also learn to be less rigid with their employees.

Sagittarius on the Seventh House Cusp. Sagittarius describes the marriage partner who will probably be a lawyer, teacher, theosophist, journalist, linguist or in another profession ruled by Jupiter. They enjoy travelling for both work and pleasure, and are apt to meet their spouses while vacationing. The partner may either be foreign or well-travelled. With this placement, Geminis usually have attentive and loving partners who are also successful, good-natured, and considerate. It is a good placement for a successful marital partnership.

Capricorn on the Eighth House Cusp. Since the eighth house is the second house from the house of partnership, it describes the assets of the partner. To this end, the spouse's achievements are represented by the financially successful sign of Capricorn, and they may satisfy the Gemini's need for material security. Since Saturn rules this house, investment decisions should be made only after ample research and with great foresight.

Aquarius on the Ninth House Cusp. Independent thinking and, at times, unusual social or religious philosophy govern the way Geminis live their lives. Even their friends often consider them to be eccentric and radical. Their work usually involves righting social injustices or working for an idealistic goal. When Geminis were children, the father might have been difficult to reach, though intellectually stimulating.

Pisces on the Tenth House Cusp. Geminis strive to be recognized for their sensitivity, generosity and artistic talents. They are very often confused about which profession to choose and may vacillate between several before finally deciding on one career. Due to their varied interests, they often have more than one line of work or many hobbies. The way in which Jupiter, ruler of the tenth house, is aspected will indicate whether opportunities will be seized or overlooked.

Aries on the Eleventh House Cusp. Because Mars colours this house, Gemini women may have complicated pregnancies and/or deliveries. (This may also indicate giving birth by Caesarean section.) Geminis have difficulty working in groups since they are extremely opinionated and often blurt out statements without realizing they are offensive to others. Because of this lack of self-control, there will almost certainly be irreparable conflicts with friends and/or colleagues throughout their lives.

Taurus on the Twelfth House Cusp. This placement concurs with other indications in the horoscope that Geminis have the ability to be quite economical, even frugal. Despite this trait, they enjoy spending money on aesthetically-pleasing objects, antiques and other collectibles.

Kataka (Cancer) Lagna

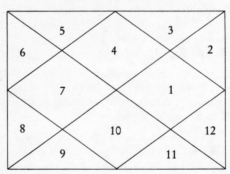

Henpecked, fleshy neck, surrounded by friends, possesses houses, elevated buttocks, rich, short, fast in walking, intelligent, fond of water, possesses few sons . . .[7]

Physical features are clumsy body and slender limbs. Cancerians generally have a large upper body. As age advances, they acquire, by overeating, a prominent abdomen. Face is wide between the ears and the mouth will be large with nice teeth of chalky colour. The hair will be brown and the complexion pale. As the limbs are extremely slender when compared to the large upper body, the whole body appears top heavy and one will walk with a rolling gait.[8]

Like the phases of the Moon (which rules Cancer), the health of these people fluctuates in conjunction with their emotional states. Controlling their indulgent natures by adapting to a reasonable diet and partaking in physical exercise will allow them to lead healthy lives. Their most vulnerable areas are the digestive and pulmonary systems, and they have a tendency towards gastric and asthmatic disturbances.

Cancerians are very sensitive, moody, introverted and mysterious. They are motivated by their desire to nurture and to be of service to others. In extreme situations, they may beome 'co-dependents' — people who need to control others and develop relationships with weak and addictive personalities. They find it easy to give their time to others but find it difficult to ask for assistance in times of crisis. Although they are emotional, Cancerians are not very communicative about their deepest feelings. Instead they release their emotions through art, poetry or music.

Leo on the Second House Cusp. Since Leo rules the second house of finances, the Cancerians' self-image is inextricably tied to their acquisition of money and the accumulation of material possessions. In accordance with the security Cancerians so desperately need, this placement ensures sufficient earnings which should guarantee independence and financial security throughout their lives.

Virgo on the Third House Cusp. Cancerians have extremely good memories and are analytical, mentally alert and retentive. Since Virgo occupies the third house, Cancerians have an aptitude for mathematics, engineering and computer programming, especially if Mercury — ruler of the third house — is aspected by Saturn. (Saturn's influence allows the mind to be disciplined and concentrated.) They may also be prone to pessimism and self-doubt and are equally critical of themselves as they are of others.

Libra on the Fourth House Cusp. As described by Libra, the mother most likely enjoyed her traditional role within the family. Cancerian adults strive for the same strong family values as those instilled in childhood. They also need partners who share their vision of a harmonious family life and an aesthetically pleasing home furnished with beautiful and valuable art objects.

Scorpio on the Fifth House Cusp. Due to the impulsive character of Mars-ruled Scorpio, this placement reflects a tendency toward gambling or spending money foolishly. Because they can be secretive and do not articulate their feelings or thoughts, Cancerians may experience conflicts with spouses and/or with their children. On the positive side, there is a love of sports, adventure, theatre, music and films. Their boundless energy enables them to enjoy thoroughly whatever they are doing, and to be happy with whoever they find themselves.

Sagittarius on the Sixth House Cusp. If Cancerians are overindulgent, this placement may be accompanied by ailments involving the liver or pancreas which is ruled by Jupiter, lord of Sagittarius. Their work may involve the use of oratorical, theatrical, legal, or teaching skills. Due to the nature of their work, there may be a need to travel a great deal. Although they enjoy frequenting exotic places, they soon get tired and homesick.

Capricorn on the Seventh House Cusp. With Saturn-ruled Capricorn in the seventh house, there is usually an age gap between a Cancerian and their spouse. Partners may be selected for an ability to fulfil a parental role and to supply Cancerians with the domesticity they desire. Marriage may also occur later in life. Due to the Cancerian's taciturnity and their need for solitude and secrecy, they seek partners with whom they can communicate non-verbally.

Aquarius on the Eighth House Cusp. Cancerians must be extremely cautious in choosing their business ventures. There is no room for speculation and financial risk-taking with Saturn ruling the business-oriented eighth house. If they invest wisely, however, they will reap long-term profits. It is advantageous for Cancerians to follow their intuition rather than depend on the advice of others where finances are concerned.

Pisces on the Ninth House Cusp. As a description of the father, Pisces points to a religious-minded or artistic figure whose honesty, fairness and spirituality have influenced the way Cancerians approach life. Cancerians love travelling and have a unique ability for learning languages and mimicking accents and speech patterns.

Aries on the Tenth House Cusp. Their careers are coloured by the influence of Mars-ruled Aries which gives them the propensity to become professional athletes, military men, pilots or to do work involving physical activity. They have a great drive to reach the top in their chosen field. This is a perfect placement for doctors and surgeons who combine the caring qualities of the Cancer Ascendant with the ambition and passion inherent in the sign of Aries.

Taurus on the Eleventh House Cusp. With Venus-ruled Taurus on the eleventh house cusp, a Cancerian's circle of friends and acquaintances are mostly women. Since they are loners by nature and strong individualists, Cancerians do not have many intimate friends. Instead, they have one or two confidantes with whom they are especially close and friendships will last a lifetime.

Gemini on the Twelfth House Cusp. There may be financial fluctuation due to the erratic manner in which Cancerians spend their money. Depending on their moods, they either hoard it or spend it extravagantly. With Mercury ruling the twelfth house, Cancerians have the ability to spend long hours doing research or work that involves detailed planning. Computer technology is a common metier among Cancerians, and may be reaffirmed by the other placements around the horoscope.

Simha (Leo) Lagna

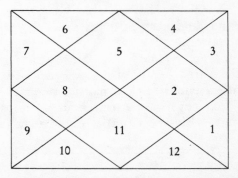

Reddish eyes, large cheeks, broad face, arrogant and powerful, angry at trifles, obedient to his mother . . .[9]

One will have well developed bones and broad shoulders and forehead. He will be tall, well built and muscular. Never will he be plump or ugly. His stature will be full and his appearance majestic, imposing, commanding and dignified, as Leo is fixed and fiery. Complexion will vary according to the exact position of the ascendant, and planets occupying or aspecting the ascendant.[10]

People with Leo Ascendants have strong constitutions. Due to self-induced stress and rigidity, however, they often develop chronic back trouble, and are prone to high blood pressure which may result in heart attacks. Colds and flu are due to a tendency to overwork. If they do become ill, which is not frequent, they recover rapidly. Leo represents the heart, the spinal column, spinal marrow, nerves and nerve fibres.

Leos are very concerned with their appearance and pride themselves on their independence and self-sufficiency. While they may exude extreme self-confidence, there is a need for constant reassurance that they are loved and needed. They are generous, creative, expressive, brutally honest and thrive on admiration and flattery. Though they sometimes give the impression of being self-involved, they are generally magnanimous and loyal to the people they love and who love them.

Virgo on the Second House Cusp. As children, Leos have inquisitive minds and for that reason actually love going to school and enjoy learning. Their financial situations are not as auspicious, however, and as ruler of the second house, Mercury's influence is one of economic fluctuation throughout their lives. They are able, however, to use their analytical minds and keen business sense to help increase their earning power.

Libra on the Third House Cusp. Since Venus-ruled Libra occupies the third house, Leos are usually eloquent speakers with a talent for journalism, poetry, acting and public speaking. They have harmonious relationships with their siblings who are usually equally talented and intelligent.

Scorpio on the Fourth House Cusp. The mother,

personified by Mars-ruled Scorpio, may have a problematic relationship with her Leo children who very often leave home when relatively young. When they become responsible adults, Leos usually mend their differences with their mothers and close, meaningful relationships may develop. These people often move frequently due to changes in their domestic situations and difficulties with their landlords.

Sagittarius on the Fifth House Cusp. Beneficent, expansive Jupiter ruling this house may compel Leos towards fulfilment through creative self-expression. They may also be content to work with children in addition to parenting. One of their biggest challenges is to balance both of these activities in order to feel completely fulfilled. They are optimistic people with an ability to remain hopeful and move forward even in the wake of adversity. Leos are hopeless romantics and often exercise poor judgment by exaggerating the importance of certain relationships.

Capricorn on the Sixth House Cusp. The sixth house is ruled by Capricorn which is associated with weak knees and bones, and sensitive skin, teeth and gums. As far as their work is concerned, Leos are ambitious, talented and can master practically any skill they wish. They are also very proficient at detailed work and/or organizational duties. Things do not always come easily, however, and Leos must work hard for the positions they attain and the money they earn.

Aquarius on the Seventh House Cusp. Since Saturn rules the seventh house of marriage, Leos' pragmatism is reflected in their desire for a partnership based on companionship rather than romantic love. They crave intellectually stimulating partners from whom they can learn about interesting and unusual subjects. This often results in relationships with older, well-educated and more sophisticated men/women. Ideally they would both belong to the same political groups and/or social organizations, though this in itself should not be a criterion for a relationship.

Pisces on the Eighth House Cusp. Since the eighth house represents the finances of the partner, Jupiter-ruled Pisces indicates that their partners have the ability to earn vast amounts of money and then spend it just as quickly. Leos do not use very good judgement with regard to their own finances and should, therefore, be cautious before entrusting money to people who profess to know more than they do. They are more fortunate, however, with inheritances and gifts which are bestowed on them because they are likeable and they usually remain amicable with families and friends.

Aries on the Ninth House Cusp. Due to the influence of Mars-ruled Aries on the ninth house governing ideas and philosophies, Leos tend to be argumentative and insistent that their opinions about politics, religion and ethics are the right ones. They enjoy travelling and have a vital need to exercise their independence at all times.

Taurus on the Tenth House Cusp. Because Taurus — a practical earth sign — occupies this house, Leos usually choose a career which will enable them to earn enough money to support their extravagances and love of travel. Professions may be related to banking, entrepreneurial activities or the stock market. Since the artistic planet Venus also rules the tenth house, the career may also be related to dancing, sculpture, jewellery making, designing or music (especially singing since Taurus rules the throat). They also make good builders and farmers as they enjoy the countryside.

Gemini on the Eleventh House Cusp. Leos enjoy cultivating friendships with interesting people who are well-educated, literary and creative. They are proud of their diversified acquaintances as typified by Mercury-ruled Gemini. They enjoy belonging to groups who share their open-mindedness and general inquisitiveness, and with whom they can discuss a myriad of subjects. Because they love to learn they often enrol in courses and will study virtually any subject they find interesting.

Cancer on the Twelfth House Cusp. Leos have a tendency to be withdrawn and spend long periods of time in self-imposed confinement either reflecting, writing or retreating from the pressures of the world. They also tend to spend money indulgently and — more often than not — irrationally.

Kanni (Virgo) Lagna

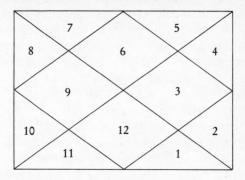

Shoulders and arms droop, enjoys wealth of others, truthful and speaks kindly, fond of enjoyment, limited children . . .[11]

Virgo is tall with a slender body, and he or she will have dark hair and eyes. Eyebrows will be curved with much of hair growth. Voice will be thin and even shrill. They will walk quickly and never have a pot belly. Due to their activity, they often appear younger than their actual age. Nose is straight, indicating that they are very clever and necessarily cunning. The forehead near the eyebrows will be pronounced. Expression of their eyes will be honest and frank. Among Westerners, most of the Virgoans will have beautiful blue eyes. That is because Venus-ruled Libra, representing beauty, is on the cusp of the second house which has to do with the eyes.[12]

Virgos are temperate people whose chances for good health and general well-being are increased because they strive toward moderation. Ailments include digestive and intestinal troubles, dysentery and ulcers. Vulnerable parts of the body are the stomach and nervous system. However, with the inclusion of vitamin B supplements, a balanced diet and regular exercise, these ailments can be avoided.

They are self-conscious and insecure when meeting new people. Virgos tend to analyse everything and are very detail-oriented. At times, they are so finicky about minor details that nothing seems to get accomplished. They are good-natured, shy, and gentle but their reserved manner can be mistaken for coldness.

Libra on the Second House Cusp. Since Venus rules the

second house, Virgos are more successful doing business in conjunction with a partner than on their own. Under the influence of Libra, the sign personifying marriage, they may form business relationships with their spouses which can range from owning a boutique to collecting art or antique furniture.

Scorpio on the Third House Cusp. Due to the competitive nature of Mars-ruled Scorpio, these people may experience conflicts or difficult relationships with siblings. Virgos are assertive speakers who, unfortunately, do not exhibit the same intensity and concentration when it comes to listening. They enjoy participating in a debate and very often play the role of devil's advocate simply to stir up an argument. Above all, however, they are extremely intelligent, analytical, insightful and possess probing and penetrating minds.

Sagittarius on the Fourth House Cusp. Virgos very often reside in countries other than the ones in which they were born. This may be due to marriage to a foreigner or simply a desire to live in an exotic place. In any event, they will speak at least one other language fluently and will become involved with international affairs. Their parents were very warm-hearted people who may have been foreign, religious or academically inclined. Virgos are usually fortunate in finding suitable homes in the neighbourhoods in which they wish to live and may even dabble in real estate successfully.

Capricorn on the Fifth House Cusp. Virgos are perfectionists with a somewhat authoritarian and rigid approach to raising a family. As a result, they may choose to remain childless or not to have children until they are well into their thirties. Since they are extremely critical, they may date many people before finally deciding on a partner.

Aquarius on the Sixth House Cusp. The combination of Virgo on the Ascendant and Aquarius on the sixth house works to create a highly strung and nervous temperament. As a result, Virgos are prone to heart disease and related circulatory problems. Relaxation, proper diet and exercise, however, reduces the possibility of developing hypertension. As ruler of the sixth house, Saturn's influence may also lead to rheumatism and arthritis later in life.

Pisces on the Seventh House Cusp. Virgos thrive on being needed and, accordingly, choose partners who need their assistance and sympathy. Partners are often creative and artistic and may be teachers, dancers, writers or artists. Because Virgos are usually attracted to exotic places, there is a very strong possibility their spouses may be foreign (especially since this influence has already appeared on the chart with a Virgo Ascendant, that is, Sagittarius on the fourth house).

Aries on the Eighth House Cusp. Since Mars rules the eighth house of business investments, there may be hasty decisions and faulty judgment resulting in unnecessary monetary losses. Many of those decisions will be made by the partner who is not very economical. There also may be lawsuits which will not be settled in the Virgo's favour. Due to their insecurity, Virgos may be possessive and jealous of their loved ones. They have great physical strength and, in line with this, are very good athletes.

Taurus on the Ninth House Cusp. Virgos must work hard for their qualifications in higher education but, with determination, they usually achieve their goals. Because the ninth house — the house of travel — is ruled by Venus, there is an indication that the partner may be foreign or that they may be involved with international business activities (this theme has already been seen in the interpretation of the fourth and seventh houses).

Gemini on the Tenth House Cusp. Since Mercury-ruled Gemini occupies the tenth house of profession, Virgos will have careers involving journalism, writing, advertising or any medium through which ideas and opinions must be communicated. They also make good business people, sales people and lawyers. Other possible work includes agents, distributors, bookkeepers, editors and translators.

Cancer on the Eleventh House Cusp. As ruler of the eleventh house, the Moon indicates that many of the friendships Virgos acquire will be with women. Virgos are devoted people and their friendships last for many years. Insecurity and self-doubt, however, sometimes cause them to question the loyalty of others.

Leo on the Twelfth House Cusp. These people tend to squander money since the Sun is not well-placed as ruler of the twelfth house and their altruism often defeats their own best interests. On the positive side, however, Virgos are able to be alone for long periods of time and are excellent researchers who can master spiritual and physical disciplines.

Thula (Libra) Lagna

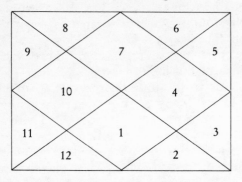

Lean and frail body, wandering, God-worshipping, tall, clever, brave . . .[13]

The person born with Libra as ascendant is tall with a well-proportioned body. His limbs are slender but strong. His appearance is graceful with a sweet smile and his countenance attractive. Eyebrows add to beauty.[14]

Librans can be excessive when it comes to drinking and eating and are very often extremely lazy. For these reasons, they are prone to illnesses which directly relate to their indulgent natures such as kidney ailments, bladder infections, bad skin and digestive problems. These difficulties are, however, easily avoidable through temperate habits and less time devoted to social activities which tend to encourage alcohol and drug abuse. Because Librans are very concerned with acceptance by their peers, these difficulties can be averted by choosing friends wisely.

Since Venus is the ruler of the ascendant, Librans are always impeccably dressed and are often obsessed with their appearances. They enjoy 'dressing up' and using an abundance of make-up and jewellery for others to admire. They are overly concerned with pleasing others, and very often their decisions mirror the opinions of others, thus revealing an inability to make a decision. Librans are intent listeners and, because they relate well on a one-to-one basis, they make good therapists, counsellors and teachers. Their desire to be of service to others extends to the point that they reserve too little time for themselves.

Scorpio on the Second House Cusp. As children, their schooling was probably marred by rebelliousness and an inability to concentrate. Because Mars rules the second house, Librans are comfortable working outdoors and make good physical education teachers and professional athletes. They may find it difficult to concentrate on one profession and are always seeking a way to earn 'easy money' — often leading to ruthless or dishonest business dealings.

Sagittarius on the Third House Cusp. Librans interact very well with their siblings and are popular with friends, neighbours and colleagues. They enjoy travelling and are very concerned with religious, ethical and philosophical issues. Since Jupiter-ruled Sagittarius occupies the third house of communications, there is a tendency to exaggerate and sometimes be brutally honest. As a result, they may appear insensitive to others, though 'mental cruelty' is never the intention.

Capricorn on the Fourth House Cusp. The fourth house of Saturn-ruled Capricorn is usually interpreted by traditional astrologers as having 'an unhappy mother and rigid childhood'. There may have been an early separation or loss of one parent, but this influence can also mean that the parents were strict disciplinarians. They enjoy working at home and living in an organized and beautiful environment.

Aquarius on the Fifth House Cusp. Since Librans are very active socially and politically — as indicated by the influence of Aquarius — they may decide to have children later in life or not at all. They are honest about the fact that they do not have enough time to devote to their spouses or to their children. They are not particularly fond of large families and usually have only one or two children, with whom they form intense relationships. Their offspring will be highly intelligent, independent and creative.

Pisces on the Sixth House Cusp. Illness, as represented by Pisces, may relate to water retention, and swelling of the lymph nodes — the first signal of infection. They may also have weak feet, poor posture and back trouble. As far as work is concerned, they find it very difficult to follow orders and are, therefore, more comfortable in a partnership or being self-employed. Librans are usually involved in professions where they can express and explore their creativity.

Aries on the Seventh House Cusp. Although Librans spend their entire lives searching for the 'perfect' relationship, none the less they often choose the 'wrong' partner. They are jealous and possessive and their partners are usually independent, short-tempered and impulsive — qualities of the sign of Aries. It is not unusual for Librans to marry more than once and their partnerships are always challenging and difficult though in the end rewarding and worth the effort. Because they dislike being alone, they work very hard to make their unions successful ones.

Taurus on the Eighth House Cusp. They usually marry people who not only have good earning potential but who also have the ability to invest wisely. Librans and their partners enjoy collecting books, jewellery, antiques, etc. and they both take great pride in their possessions. Because Librans enjoy communicating with other people, many opportunities will present themselves through these connections and meetings.

Gemini on the Ninth House Cusp. Librans have a talent for advertising, writing, journalism and teaching. These skills may take them abroad where they may reside for several years to satisfy their restlessness. The father was probably extremely intelligent and an excellent role model for his children. Librans love to debate and become well-versed in current affairs by reading voraciously and by associating with many different types of people.

Cancer on the Tenth House Cusp. Since Cancer occupies the tenth house, professions suited to Librans relate to caring for others and may include therapy, nursing, or social work. They are excellent helpers since they pay attention to the problems of others, a quality they incorporate into their work. Librans enjoy working with people, being involved in real estate and interior decorating. Other professions and interests may include owning a restaurant or shop, cooking, dealing in antiques, studying history or architecture.

Leo on the Eleventh House Cusp. As a barren sign occupying the eleventh house governing childbirth, Leo may limit the number of children Librans usually have. They are very generous with friends and are active in community groups and social causes both professionally and voluntarily. Because of their leadership abilities and need for recognition, they are often the organizers of these groups.

Virgo on the Twelfth House Cusp. The Mercury-ruled sign of Virgo on the twelfth house cusp provides these people with the ability to spend hours in solitude doing research, exploring their creativity, or simply meditating and reflecting. This placement provides Librans with a talent for working independently, but there is also a tendency to become depressed and overly analytical about themselves and the world at large.

Vrischika (Scorpio) Lagna

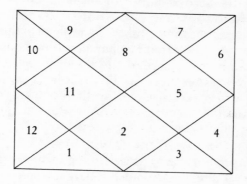

Broad eyes, broad chest, round loins and knees, diseases at an early age, will separate from parents, cruel acts, honored by sovereign . . .[15]

The body will be well-proportioned. Hands are generally long. The stature is above average. They will have a broad face, commanding appearance, short, curly hair and muscular body. Good personality.[16]

Scorpions are prone to bladder infections and problems related to their reproductive systems. Due to their highly strung nature and the stressful circumstances they themselves create, Scorpions may be prone to back and heart problems. They should be more aware that their eating and drinking habits may cause their digestive systems to malfunction. When they become depressed, there may be a tendency towards extreme behaviour such as alcohol and drug abuse.

Their immense ambition and single-minded determination enables them to carry almost anything through to its logical conclusion. In achieving goals, their relentless drive may turn into ruthlessness which can ultimately destroy everything they've created. They do not always know how to handle their successes. Scorpions are often authoritarian, inflexible, and find it difficult to make major changes when things do not go their way.

Sagittarius on the Second House Cusp. Innovative Scorpions always seem to have financial opportunities lying at their doorsteps. Due to Jupiter-ruled Sagittarius occupying the second house of material assets, however, money often slips away as soon it is earned. Their optimism and uncanny ability to replenish their supply sees them through seemingly hopeless situations. Because Jupiter rules both the second and the fifth houses, they are interested in speculation. If Jupiter is well-placed, Scorpions will make wise and profitable investments. If it is ill-placed, they tend to be foolhardy and incur heavy losses.

Capricorn on the Third House Cusp. Scorpions have difficulty communicating their feelings which affects their rapport with siblings, friends, colleagues and neighbours. They have the ability to concentrate intensely, and are almost obsessive about the things that truly interest them. They are very serious, extremely depressive, and sometimes even reclusive.

Aquarius on the Fourth House Cusp. Saturn-ruled Aquarius occupying the fourth house represents the difficult relationship they often have with the mother. The childhood homes of many Scorpions were probably modestly furnished but always filled with their parents' friends, colleagues and acquaintances. These people were most probably intellectually stimulating and shared the same political and social beliefs as their parents.

Pisces on the Fifth House Cusp. Children form a major part of Scorpions' lives and Jupiter, the ruler of the fruitful sign of Pisces, represents learning through their children and their parenting experiences. These people are attracted to the arts and will either participate in or patronize sporting events, concerts, theatre and dance performances.

Aries on the Sixth House Cusp. The effect of Mars-ruled Aries occupying the sixth house predisposes these people to chills, colds, fevers and headaches. Due to the impulsive nature of both Aries in the sixth house and the Scorpio Ascendant, there may be an uncommon number of cuts, bruises and burns due to minor accidents incurred during childhood.

Taurus on the Seventh House Cusp. Since the conservative sign of Taurus inhabits the seventh house, Scorpions generally bring old-fashioned values to their marriages. Because of their ultimate commitment to this sacred institution, they are cautious when choosing a partner. Once they are in love and finally decide to marry, they are passionate, jealous and demand both loyalty and fidelity. Because the seventh house is ruled by Venus, Scorpions need partners who are comforting, loving and patient. In return they will be reliable, generous and faithful.

Gemini on the Eighth House Cusp. With Gemini occupying the eighth house, these people have an instinct for financial dealings. This quality enables Scorpions to begin innovative projects, to raise financial backing and to be quite successful managing their own businesses and those of others. They tend, however, to manipulate others and their dealings are not always above-board.

Cancer on the Ninth House Cusp. Many people with Scorpio Ascendants live abroad since Cancer, symbol of home and family, is on the cusp of the ninth house of foreign travel. They have an uncanny ability for languages and their interest in subjects such as anthropology, history or architecture could lead to academic careers. Their fathers were probably home-loving individuals who found it difficult to express their deepest feelings. These men may have been artistic or musically inclined.

Leo on the Tenth House Cusp. The tenth house of Leo makes these people enterprising and ambitious with the need to control their destinies. They prefer to work independently of others or to be in charge of all situations of a professional nature. Career options associated with Leo are actors, directors, entrepreneurs and executives. Their ideal preference, however, is ultimately self-employment.

Virgo on the Eleventh House Cusp. Mercury-ruled Virgo on the eleventh house cusp indicates a preference for friends and acquaintances who are intelligent and who share the same intellectual and artistic pursuits. Due to the Scorpions' extreme sensitivity, their need to be appreciated, and their difficulty trusting people, it takes a long time for them to acquire true friends. Their circle of friends changes because they are overly critical and are often intolerant of the weaknesses of others. If they were more compassionate towards others, they would ultimately be easier on themselves as well.

Libra on the Twelfth House Cusp. Venus-ruled Libra on the twelfth house indicates that these people incur many debts due to indulgences and extravagances. Their self-image is based on the value of possessions but they often find it difficult to live up to the image they are attempting to project.

Dhanus (Sagittarius) Lagna

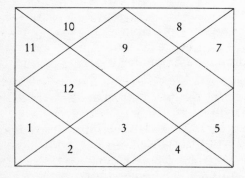

Long face and neck, ears and nose are big, intent on business, short, favourite of king, eloquent, liberal in gifts, destroying his enemies . . .[17]

Sagittarians are well-proportioned with a well-developed body. They will have a tall large forehead, high and bushy eyebrows, long nose, bright eyes, charming appearance, graceful look and fair complexion.[18]

Because these fun-loving people are constantly attending social functions, the opportunity to indulge in food, drugs and alcohol is heightened. Their health is affected by a tendency towards excessive behaviour and they must work hard at practising self-control and discipline. Problem areas include the hips, pancreas and the liver, which is obviously affected by too much alcohol.

Sagittarians are outgoing, honest, friendly and extremely fair-minded. They are social animals who appear optimistic and almost never reveal their problems and difficulties to others. Because of the need to keep up appearances, they are never able to be completely honest about their feelings and emotions. They love travelling, socializing, learning and teaching.

Capricorn on the Second House Cusp. The Saturnian influence on the second house indicates that Sagittarians must work hard for whatever they earn. As children, they may have been slow learners or had minor learning disabilities. A desire to supply their high standards of living will encourage frugality and an ability to invest wisely.

Aquarius on the Third House Cusp. With Saturn ruling this house, they may have had tense relationships with their siblings. Sagittarians often feel superior to others, which discourages mutual understanding or open lines of communication. They are serious students and are probably very talented writers.

Pisces on the Fourth House Cusp. As children, Sagittarians experienced domestic tranquillity and close ties with both their parents, especially the mother, who may have been artistic and religious. They search for perfection in their relationships and sometimes reside abroad for a good portion of their adult lives.

Aries on the Fifth House Cusp. Sagittarians find it very difficult committing themselves to a monogamous relationship. Aries, a barren sign, is on the fifth house cusp, so that Sagittarians may choose to start families when they are well into their thirties. Their children will be individualistic and often rebellious, and many arguments between parent and child will ensue.

Taurus on the Sixth House Cusp. Generally, the placement of Taurus in the sixth house describes robustness and resistance to illness. Sagittarians' sensitive areas, however, include the throat, neck, tonsils, facial muscles and the eyes. Gum disease is also very common. If tendencies towards excess and overindulgence pertaining to food, drinking and spending are tempered, it can lead to a balanced and healthy life.

Gemini on the Seventh House Cusp. Mercury-ruled Gemini occupying the seventh house of marriage indicates that their choice of partners is an intellectual rather than an emotional decision. Marriage is more likely to succeed if each partner respects the other's independence and common need to lead a busy life outside the home. Sagittarians must learn, however, to communicate feelings and assert their opinions so they are not misunderstood. They fear boredom and it is likely they will have more than one marriage.

Leo on the Ninth House Cusp. Sagittarians are apt to be lawyers, priests, journalists, linguists or teachers and may choose to reside abroad for a period of time. Their fathers were highly ambitious and successful and most probably the authority figures at home.

Virgo on the Tenth House Cusp. The aforementioned professions are corroborated by the placement of Mercury-ruled Virgo in the tenth house. Anything that involves the communication of ideas is ideal for Sagittarians. They will also succeed doing mathematics, research or highly detailed work. Sagittarians wish to be known and respected for their intellectual abilities as well as for their originality and inventiveness.

Libra on the Eleventh House Cusp. The eleventh house of Venus-ruled Libra provides these people with the propensity for meeting friends and maintaining those friendships for long periods of time. Since the eleventh house is ruled by Venus, many friendships will be with either women, artistic colleagues or with culturally reticent people who enjoy going to films, concerts and the theatre.

Scorpio on the Twelfth House Cusp. Scorpio's influence on the twelfth house indicates excessive spending in order to support expensive habits and lifestyles. Many conflicts with friends arise due to unsolicited advice which Sagittarians do not appreciate. Friends, however, care enough to continue to offer opinions and suggestions which most times go unheeded.

Makara (Capricorn) Lagna

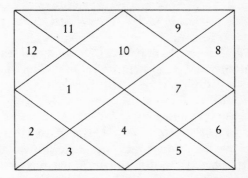

Weak in lower limbs, strength, will understand and follow when advised, indolent, religious, fortunate, wind disease . . .[19]

Saturn shows that one will be emaciated, weak and will grow slowly. Tall and slender. The face will be thin and oval and the nose will be long and the eyes deep set. Hair will be coarse.[20]

Health problems incurred by people with a Capricorn ascendant may be related to skin, bones, teeth, weak knees and, later in life, rheumatism and arthritis.

Capricornians are reserved and, like Taureans (also an earth sign), very rarely speak unless they have something significant to say. However, they are ambitious, serious, reliable and success is very important to them, sometimes overpowering everything else in life. They can also be ruthless and are capable of unscrupulous behaviour in order to succeed.

Aquarius on the Second House Cusp. Since the second house is ruled by the planet Saturn, early education will be rigid and structured. The occupancy of Aquarius indicates earning money through participation in social causes and group activities. Capricornians acquire income through hard work and tend to be frugal. They are often referred to as 'stingy' or 'penny-pinching'.

Pisces on the Third House Cusp. Interests in theosophy, law, philosophy, languages and political science are all related to the planet Jupiter as ruler of the third house. Capricornians also enjoy travelling and usually maintain a good relationship with their brothers and sisters.

Aries on the Fourth House Cusp. The family background, represented by Mars-ruled Aries, was most likely unharmonious. The parents may have argued a great deal and there may even have been the loss or separation of one parent early in life. The mother was most likely dynamic and opinionated as to how her children should lead their lives and most probably provoked much discord.

Taurus on the Fifth House Cusp. Venus-ruled Taurus occupying the fifth house indicates a passionate and jealous nature with a weakness for romantic liaisons. They should try to be more temperate and less jealous and possessive. Capricornians have conflicting attitudes towards disciplining their children. They tend to indulge and spoil the children when they are very young, but try to maintain their status as strict disciplinarians none the less. Since this is no easy task, they find the parenting role challenging to say the least.

Gemini on the Sixth House Cusp. Gemini occupying the sixth house indicates weakness in the corresponding body parts — arms and lungs. Their tendency to overwork may activate bronchial infection, tonsilitis or, at worst, pneumonia. They also have rather fragile nervous systems.

Cancer on the Seventh House Cusp. Capricornian males usually want to marry someone who is maternal while Capricornian females attract people looking for mother figures. Since the Moon-ruled Cancer occupies this house, the partner must represent someone who is 'good parental material' and who will provide domestic tranquillity. There will probably be more than one marriage or major relationship as the Moon personifies phases and/or changes.

Leo on the Eighth House Cusp. Capricornians' approach to business is intuitive and non-analytical. They seem to have a knack for achieving success in whatever areas their energies are directed. Relentless pursuit of prosperity enables them to marry equally ambitious and successful partners. If they follow their own instincts rather than the recommendations of outside advisers, their businesses will flourish.

Virgo on the Ninth House Cusp. Not only were their fathers extremely intellectual but their own capacity for accumulating knowledge is boundless. Capricornians love learning new languages and may be multi-lingual. They also lean towards degrees in psychology, chemistry, journalism or the law.

Libra on the Tenth House Cusp. Because of their aptitude for speaking and listening to others, Capricornians may utilize the influence of Libra in the tenth house in their careers as lawyers, salesmen, consultants or therapists. Their professions may also be connected to the arts, such as dancing, film-making, dress-making or jewellery-making. It may also just imply owning a boutique since Libra symbolizes clothes and jewellery.

Scorpio on the Eleventh House Cusp. With Mars-ruled Scorpio occupying the eleventh house, there will be many disagreements with friends and co-members of groups with whom they are involved. Due to their rigidity, Capricorns are impatient with other people whose ideas about life differ from their own. They are much more diplomatic with colleagues since they do not expect as much from them as they do from friends and families.

Sagittarius on the Twelfth House Cusp. Jupiter-ruled Sagittarius occupying the twelfth house is defined as expansion in the area this house represents: inner space, solitude and expenditures. Capricorns are deeply religious, and probably devote much of their time to humanitarian causes leaving little time for their families. In addition, they tend to donate too much money to causes although their resources seem to get replenished in the end.

Kumbha (Aquarius) Lagna

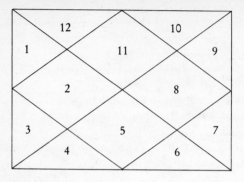

Commits sinful deeds secretly, does hindrance to others, means are limited, covetous and utilizes others' wealth, fond of perfumes and flowers . . .[21]

Aquarians are tall with full stature. They are strong, face is oval and complexion is fair. The signs of Venus, Taurus and Libra, and Aquarius produce beautiful children. Teeth may be defective and the hair has a brown shade.[22]

Aquarians are extremely highly strung and must temper their extreme mood changes. Due to these personality traits, their health concerns are heart ailments, circulatory weakness, water retention (especially around the ankles) and hypertension.

Aquarians are irritable, generous, serious, inflexible and active in social causes. They tend to be workaholics and must learn to relax. Although they are extremely humanitarian and concerned with the world at large, they are frequently inconsiderate to the people they love the most. Their eccentricities and extremes of mood make them difficult to understand, and their impatience with others does not always make them sympathetic friends.

Pisces on the Second House Cusp. Despite frequent mismanagement of finances, with Jupiter ruling the second house, there will still be steady income. Aquarians can be extravagant, spend money beyond their means and are guilty of being 'penny wise and pound foolish'.

Aries on the Third House Cusp. Aquarians are inventive, open-minded and inquisitive but equally argumentative and aggressive. By playing devil's advocate, they often invite an interesting exchange of opinions. They are good writers, journalists, broadcasters, researchers — professions where ideas must be conveyed to the public. Aquarians are known for their oratorical ability but have little capacity for listening. There may also be conflicts with neighbours and siblings due to the aggressive influence of Mars-ruled Aries.

Taurus on the Fourth House Cusp. Venus-ruled Taurus occupying the fourth house describes a home that is comfortably and luxuriously furnished. Their upbringings were most probably financially secure and their mothers were loving, attentive and the backbone of the family. Because Aquarians are social-minded, they frequently entertain and offer their homes as meeting areas for any 'ideologically sound' and politically aware group.

Gemini on the Fifth House Cusp. Classified as a barren sign, Gemini occupying the fifth house indicates that there will be a great deal of indecision as to whether to have children. When they do have children, however, they will probably have accomplished professional success. Aquarians are involved with so many activities outside of the home that they do not always devote as much time to their children as they should. The gap closes when their children mature and they can relate as equals rather than parent and child. Their children will be very precocious and highly intelligent.

Cancer on the Sixth House Cusp. Since Cancer rules the chest and stomach, there may be digestive problems and possible stomach ailments. These people must watch their diets since their digestive systems are extremely sensitive. Other illnesses they may be prone to are bronchitis, gallstones and asthma. Cancer signifies a tendency to retain water which, coupled with the swollen ankles symbolized by Aquarius, may lead to heart disease.

Leo on the Seventh House Cusp. Leo ruling the seventh house indicates that these people are extremely passionate and romantic. Aquarians are faithful and attentive lovers whose partners are independent and career-minded. Although there is mutual respect between Aquarians and their spouses, they are too possessive, too demanding and feel that their work is more important than that of their partners.

Virgo on the Eighth House Cusp. Due to their sharp and analytical minds, the spouses of Aquarians are good at handling finances and are extremely shrewd business people. They will make profitable investments but, because Mercury rules this house, incomes will tend to fluctuate.

Libra on the Ninth House Cusp. The ninth house, as represented by Venus-ruled Libra, indicates that there was a good relationship with the father who was good-natured and loving. Aquarians are likely to fall in love with well-educated and intelligent people. They make very good lawyers and teachers due to their eloquence and ability to express themselves lucidly.

Scorpio on the Tenth House Cusp. In their struggle to work for their political and social ideals, Aquarians are passionate, relentless and often intolerant of those who do not share their beliefs. Their work may include chemistry, research psychology, medicine, dentistry, law, or investigative journalism. Professions such as teaching and the law will reflect their philosophy of life and they are most probably active in at least one political or social organization in their spare time.

Sagittarius on the Eleventh House Cusp. The eleventh house, occupied by Jupiter-ruled Sagittarius, provides Aquarians with lively, high spirited and cheerful personalities. They have many friends and acquaintances and their magnanimity enables them to work well with people toward their goals of social and political reform. Since Jupiter rules both the second and eleventh houses, income may be derived by working with groups or teaching in a professional capacity.

Capricorn on the Twelfth House Cusp. Aquarians can overwork themselves to the point when they need periods of time for solitude and for meditation. Although they spend money foolishly from time to time, they are always conscious of attaining material security and will eventually buckle down and save wisely.

Meena (Pisces) Lagna

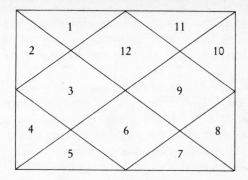

Drinks excess water, symmetrical and shining body, fond of his wife, learned, feels grateful for favours done to him, overcomes enemies, good eyes and is fortunate . . .[23]

Pisceans generally produce short people and will weigh as much as a tall person as they will be plump and the hands and feet will appear to be short and stout. The shoulders are muscular and spherical. The eyes will be big and protruding and the hair will be soft and silky.[24]

Since the lymphatic system — associated with this sign — is the body's defence against disease, Pisceans must consciously strive towards maintaining good health. This includes drinking eight glasses of water per day to cleanse their systems, curtailing late-night activities, and avoiding alcohol, fatty foods and drugs. Of course, active involvement in creative groups and activities helps to lessen the probability of involvement in bad habits. Their feet are weak and they have a tendency to retain water, the retention causing many Pisceans to be overweight.

Pisceans are imaginative, romantic, spiritual, good-natured and generous. They are very childlike and live within a world of their own creation. This enables them to work with children or to be involved with the arts like acting, dancing, painting or music. Sometimes their insecurity and lack of conviction, however, prevents them from being assertive and often results in manipulation by others.

Aries on the Second House Cusp. The influence of Mars-ruled Aries on the second house brings an enterprising

spirit and a challenge to begin new business ventures. If
one project should fail, they quickly move on to the next
one without a backward glance. However, they must be
cautious since there is a tendency towards impulsiveness
and poor judgment. They should, instead, listen to the
advice of financial advisers and/or friends more
knowledgeable in the area of finances.

Taurus on the Third House Cusp. Pisceans are slow
learners and are not particularly interested in memorizing
facts and figures. They are visual thinkers and use intuition,
images and colours the way others use logic and reasoning.
Since Venus rules the third house, they are soft-spoken,
tactful, diplomatic and have the ability to 'sweet talk'
others. Pisceans usually have good relationships with their
friends, neighbours and siblings.

Gemini on the Fourth House Cusp. Pisceans probably
spent a good portion of their childhoods frequently
changing residences due to the job fluctuations of one
parent. Their homes were stimulating centres of activity
where their parents entertained an interesting and diverse
circle of friends and acquaintances. As adults, Pisceans
attract creative people as friends, and trying to recreate
happy childhood experiences. They enjoy doing unusual
things and will travel at the 'drop of a hat'.

Cancer on the Fifth House Cusp. The fifth house,
occupied by Cancer, a fruitful sign, indicates a propensity
for having children at a young age and/or working with
children. Pisceans are extremely attentive parents who
devote themselves almost entirely to the emotional needs of
their children. As far as relationships are concerned, these
people are loyal and extremely tenacious once they find
someone to love who also returns their affections.

Leo on the Sixth House Cusp. Since the sixth house is
ruled by Leo, associated with the heart and spine, Pisceans
must watch their blood pressure, control hypertension, and
eat correctly to correct a tendency towards heart disease.
They may also be prone to stomach problems since Leo, in
Hindu astrology, rules the stomach. These difficulties can
be avoided, however, if Pisceans learn to modify their
excessive lifestyles.

Virgo on the Seventh House Cusp. A Piscean's selection
of spouse is dependent on a mutual ability to nourish each

other intellectually and romantically. The partner, represented by Virgo, is highly critical and fulfils the Piscean's need for someone from whom they can learn 'temperance'. Since Mercury, a changeable planet, rules the seventh house, Pisceans will most probably marry more than once.

Libra on the Eighth House Cusp. This placement indicates that the partner is not very adept at handling finances, and that both Pisceans and their spouses spend money extravagantly. There will be many opportunities for business partnerships and the probability of some type of patronage at some point in their lives.

Scorpio on the Ninth House Cusp. Pisceans are argumentative and do not willingly accept criticism. They dislike analysing situations and sometimes lack the ability to confront their negative emotions such as anger, hate and greed. There will be unresolved conflicts with the father, who probably could not communicate well with his children, though he cared very deeply.

Sagittarius on the Tenth House Cusp. Jupiter-ruled Sagittarius occupying the tenth house of profession is quite a fortunate placement. Pisceans have many work opportunities and must be cautious not to waste or overlook them. They usually need more discipline, however, in order to achieve their goals. Professional aspirations could include becoming a lawyer, banker, journalist, teacher or physician.

Capricorn on the Eleventh House Cusp. Pisceans have difficulty making friends easily and do not feel comfortable in crowds. They will be loyal, however, and their friendships will be lasting. Because they expect too much from other people — the result of the influence of Saturn-ruled Capricorn — they are very often disappointed.

Aquarius on the Twelfth House Cusp. Since Saturn-ruled Aquarius occupies the twelfth house, these people are dedicated to social or humanitarian causes. This common thread runs through all their activities from relationships to finances. Pisceans will donate their time and/or money to humanitarian organizations and pet charities.

This system of classifying and analysing each Rasi Chakra according to its Ascendant is only applicable using an equal house system. In horoscopes constructed with the unequal system — as in Western astrology — the number of degrees comprising the length of each house varies according to (a) the latitude of one's birth, and (b) the exact degree and minute of each Ascendant. Therefore, it is not always possible to determine the distribution of planetary rulers from the sign on the ascendant alone as it is in Hindu astrology.

Another purpose of these Ascendant combinations for Western astrologers is that of rectification. 'Rectification' is the term applied to the astrologer's adjustment of an estimated or unknown birth time usually based on (a) the sequence of events in a person's life, and (b) whether the signs occupying each house actually describe the corresponding personality traits.

Using Ascendant combinations for purposes of rectification is something that I have used from time to time in my own practice. A most recent example is a close friend who only knew that he was born sometime in the morning. I calculated the Ascendant for the earliest and latest possible times when he could have been born, and this produced three different Ascendants — Virgo, Libra and Scorpio. In the midst of reviewing the house descriptions for each of those three Ascendants, I realized that a description of the planetary rulers of a Virgo Ascendant was an almost accurate representation. He finally obtained his exact time of birth from his birth certificate and, sure enough, he had a Virgo Ascendant. Though this is certainly not a foolproof system, it has worked for me enough times over the years to merit consideration. It is important to realize that this system can only be used to determine the sign on the Ascendant and not the exact time of birth. It is also easier to rectify a chart when the approximate time of day is known so that the choices are narrowed down.

Chapter 6 will examine each planet's strength and weakness in its role as planetary ruler, and Chapter 7 will place those planets in their signs and houses.

6

DETERMINING STRENGTH AND WEAKNESS OF THE PLANETS AND HOUSES

Determining Planetary Strength

The first stage in interpreting an individual Rasi Chakra is to ascertain the strength or weakness of each planet according to its placements in the horoscope. While assessing planetary power it is important to keep in mind that each planet (a) embodies the house it rules, and (b) expresses that identity through the sign and house it occupies in the Rasi Chakra. The following steps illustrate the positions of the planets used to evaluate their strength and weakness:

Table 6.1. Determining planetary strength

Planets (Grahas)	Sign of rulership (Swakshetra)	Exaltation degree (Uchcha)	Fall degree (Neecha)	Moolatrikona degrees
Sun	Leo	10 Aries	10 Libra	1–20 Leo
Moon	Cancer	3 Taurus	3 Scorpio	3–30 Taurus
Mars	Aries, Scorpio	28 Capricorn	28 Cancer	1–12 Aries
Mercury	Gemini, Virgo	15 Virgo	15 Pisces	16–20 Virgo
Jupiter	Sagittarius, Pisces	5 Cancer	5 Capricorn	1–10 Sagittarius
Venus	Taurus, Libra	27 Pisces	27 Virgo	1–5 Libra
Saturn	Capricorn,	20 Libra	20 Aries	1–20 Aquarius

1. Determine Whether a Planet is in the Sign of Rulership, Exaltation, Debilitation (Fall) or Moolatrikona

Table 6.1 lists the planets, the zodiacal signs they rule, and the exact degree(s) where they are exalted, fallen or in their moolatrikona. With the exception of the moolatrikona, these possible relationships between a planet and its zodiacal sign — rulership, exaltation, and fall — are also utilized in Occidental astrology.

(a) *Rulership*. Each planet, except for the Sun and the Moon, rules two signs. The sign of rulership may be viewed as the constellation in which the planet operates most comfortably and whose attributes are shared by both the zodiacal sign and its ruling planet. For example, the characteristics of both Cancer and its planetary ruler — the Moon — are similar. The difference lies in the separate *functions* of the planets and the zodiacal signs, i.e. the planet is the subject while its zodiacal sign modifies the subject's behaviour and defines its activities. When there is dual rulership — two signs sharing the same planetary lord — the qualities of that planet are divided among both signs. An example is the way Aries and Scorpio maintain individual traits of the planet Mars, their shared ruling planet.

(b) *Exaltation and Fall*. In addition to the zodiacal sign it rules, each planet in the horoscope has its exact sign and degree of exaltation — where the planet is exceptionally strong and seems to shine — and its exact sign and degree of fall or debilitation — where the planet is exceptionally weak and can never really 'be himself'. As seen from Table 6.1, a planet's exaltation and fall are always opposing signs of the zodiac.

In Western astrology, it is the sign alone that defines exaltation and fall and not the degree(s) of the planet's location. Most contemporary Western astrologers, however, no longer implement the concepts of exaltation, fall and detriment (a separate category in Western astrology and the sign opposite the sign of rulership) in their horoscope interpretation since they refrain from categorizing planetary positions as *naturally* strong or weak.

(c) *Moolatrikona*. The moolatrikona, a concept unique to Hindu astrology, is very often the same sign as the planetary ruler and one of the most favourable positions for a planet to occupy. If a planet is in either the sign and degree of its exaltation or its moolatrikona, it receives supreme power and its most positive qualities will be exhibited by the person in the course of his/her life.

Table 6.2 Whether a Planet is Benefic, Neutral or Malefic

Benefic	Malefic	Neutral
Waxing Moon	Sun	Mercury
Venus	Waning Moon	
Jupiter	Mars	
	Saturn	
	Rahu	
	Kethu	

2. Determine Whether a Planet is Malefic, Benefic or Neutral

According to Table 6.2, the planets are categorized as either naturally benefic (beneficial), malefic (difficult)* or neutral. Many of these ancient classifications are easily explained as follows.

The Sun is malefic as its heat parches the land, ruins crops and leaves everyone with a general feeling of lethargy and fatigue. Shops and businesses close between the hours of noon and four o'clock when the Sun is in its strongest position directly overhead, and most Indians are eating and resting indoors before resuming work.

The Moon is waxing when it is 0–180° ahead of the Sun or up until the moment the Moon is full. It is waning during the period when it is 180–360° ahead of the Sun, the time elapsed between Full and New Moon. Because the intensity of illumination increases as it proceeds towards fullness each month, the waxing Moon is a benefic

---

* In the annals of Hindu astrology the word 'evil' is used to describe malefic influences. Throughout this book, however, I will substitute the words 'difficult', 'inauspicious' or any other words that imply the possibility of resolution.

influence. Conversely, during the half of the month when this luminary changes its position from full to new, the Moon's decreasing light does not encourage fecundation, a positive lunar principle. The waning Moon is, therefore, malefic.

Since Jupiter is the largest planet and Venus is the brightest and most beautiful, they are both benefic influences. Jupiter is known as the 'greater benefic' and Venus is called the 'lesser benefic'.

Mercury's character is changeable, for depending on its position in the horoscope, it can be benefic or malefic. If, for instance, Mercury shares the occupancy of a house with a benefic planet in the birth chart, its character will become beneficial. If Mercury is conjoined with a malefic, it will take on *that* quality.

Mars and Saturn have unattractive qualities such as aggression and depression, respectively, and are therefore considered malefic influences. Saturn, which has a ring around its circumference, projects a sense of restriction, one of its symbolic qualities.

Table 6.3 Satyacharya's list of individual benefics, malefics and neutrals. The house each planet rules within each Ascendant is listed next to that planet

Ascendant	Benefic	Malefic	Neutral
Aries	**Jupiter** (9 and 12) Sun (5) Mars (1 and 8)	Saturn (10 and 11) **Mercury** (3 and 6) Venus (2 and 7)	
Taurus	**Saturn** (9 and 10) Mercury (2 and 5) Mars (7 and 12) Sun (4)	Jupiter (8 and 11) Venus (1 and 6) Moon (3)	Venus* (1 and 6)
Gemini	Venus (5 and 12)	Mars (6 and 11) Jupiter (7 and 10) Sun (3)	Moon (2) Mercury (1 and 4)

* *Venus is both neutral and malefic with a Taurus Ascendant.*

Ascendant	Benefic	Malefic	Neutral
Cancer	Jupiter (6 and 9) **Mars** (5 and 10)	Venus (4 and 11) Mercury (3 and 12)	Saturn (6 and 7) Moon (1) Sun (2)
Leo	**Mars** (4 and 9) Sun (1)	Mercury (2 and 11) Venus (3 and 10)	Jupiter (5 and 8) Moon (12) Saturn (5 and 6)
Virgo	Venus (2 and 9)	Moon (11) Mars (3 and 8) Jupiter (4 and 7)	Saturn (4 and 5) Sun (12) Mercury (1 and 10)
Libra	**Saturn** (4 and 5) Mercury (9 and 12) Venus (1 and 8) Mars* (2 and 7)	Sun (11) Jupiter (3 and 6) Moon (10)	
Scorpio	**Moon** (9) Jupiter (2 and 5) Sun (10)	Mercury (8 and 11) Venus (7 and 12)	Mars (1 and 6) Saturn (2 and 3)
Sagittarius	Mars (5 and 12) Sun (9)	Venus (6 and 11) Saturn (2 and 3) Mercury (7 and 10)	Jupiter (1 and 4) Moon (8)
Capricorn	**Venus** (5 and 10) Mercury (6 and 9) Saturn (1 and 2)	**Mars** (4 and 11) Jupiter (3 and 12) Moon (7)	Sun (8)
Aquarius	Venus (4 and 9) Sun (7) Mars (3 and 10)	Jupiter (2 and 11) Moon (6)	Mercury (5 and 8)

* Mars is considered to be a weak benefic with a Libra Ascendant.

Ascendant	Benefic	Malefic	Neutral
Pisces	Moon (5)	Saturn	Jupiter
	Mars (2 and 9)	(10 and 11)	(1 and 10)
		Sun (6)	
		Venus	
		(3 and 8)	
		Mercury	
		(4 and 7)	

In addition to being either a 'natural' benefic, malefic or neutral planet (Table 6.2), a planet's categorization can change in accordance with the house it rules in an individual chart. The general principles are as follows:

1. Any planet ruling a Trikona house (the most auspicious) — 5th or 9th house — will become benefic.

2. Any natural malefic ruling a Kendra house — 1st, 4th, 7th and 10th — will become benefic. Any natural benefic ruling a Kendra house will become malefic unless the planet also owns the first house. (An example of this is a Sagittarius Ascendant where Jupiter, as ruler of the Ascendant, also rules the fourth house of Pisces. In this case, Jupiter is still benefic although it rules the fourth Kendra house.)

3. Any planet ruling one of the Upachaya houses — 3rd, 6th 10th, 11th — or one of the Dusthana houses — 6th, 8th, 12th — will become malefic. (The tenth house is considered to be an Upachaya house in this category and not a Kendra house. An example is a Libra Ascendant where the Moon, ruler of the tenth house, is classified as a malefic.)

Table 6.3 lists the planets the Hindu astrologer, Satyacharya, considered to be benefic, malefic and neutral for each of the 12 ascendants. Throughout the book I refer to planets as either *naturally* benefic, malefic or neutral (Table 6.2) or *individually* benefic, malefic or neutral (Table 6.3) These classifications are generally based on whether the planet rules an auspicious or inauspicious house according to the aforementioned three principles. Exceptions to these rules occur when a planet rules two houses of different values. In that case, the planet is often considered neutral. In other cases, even when one planet rules a Trikona house, it is very often considered benefic regardless of the rating of the other house. Because there are so many exceptions to these rules, I recommend referring directly to Table 6.3 instead of trying to calculate planetary rating for each ascendant according to their rulership of the houses. The following are two examples:

Fig 6.1 is a chart with a Taurus ascendant. Saturn rules Capricorn in the ninth house (a Trikona house) and Aquarius in the tenth house (a Kendra house). Since the ninth and tenth houses are both auspicious houses, Saturn — a natural malefic — becomes the most beneficial planet within the context of that horoscope according to Table 6.3.

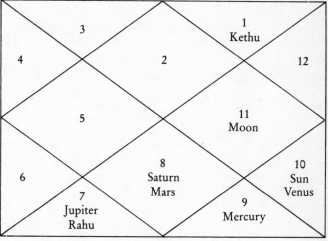

Fig 6.1   Matthew's Rasi Chakra

Another example is Fig 6.2, a chart with a Leo Ascendant. As ruler of both the ninth Trikona house and the fourth Kendra house, Mars — a natural malefic — transforms itself into that Ascendant's most benefic planet. Jupiter, on the other hand, rules the fifth house (a Trikona house) and the eighth house (an inauspicious Dusthana house). According to Satyacharya, this combination as ruler of both an auspicious house and an inauspicious house transforms Jupiter into a 'neutral' planet in this horoscope.

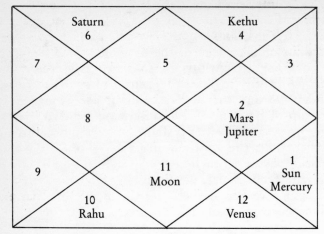

Fig 6.2 Jane's Rasi Chakra

Table 6.4 Satyacharya's list of natural friendship, enmity and neutrality between the planets[1]

Planets	Friend	Enemy	Neutral
Sun	Moon Jupiter Mars	Saturn Venus	Mercury
Moon	Sun Mercury		Venus Jupiter Mars Saturn
Mars	Sun Moon Jupiter	Mercury	Venus Saturn
Mercury	Sun Venus	Moon	Mars Jupiter Saturn
Jupiter	Sun Moon Mars	Mercury Venus	Saturn
Venus	Mercury Saturn	Sun Moon	Mars Jupiter
Saturn	Venus Mercury	Sun Moon Mars	Jupiter

3. Determining Planetary Friendship, Enmity and Neutrality

Natural friendship, enmity and neutrality between planets, another means of judging planetary strength, is an interesting concept that has no equivalent in Western astrology. Table 6.4 lists these definitive planetary relationships according to the astrologer Satyacharya.* These planetary relationships are used to define the affinity a particular planet has with (a) the ruler of the house that planet occupies, or with (b) another planet occupying the same house.

To illustrate the concept of friendship and enmity between planet and its house ruler, I like using the analogy of landlord and tenant. Every planet in the chart can be seen as the occupant, or guest, of the zodiacal house in which it is placed. The planetary ruler of that house is viewed as the landlord. When there is friendship between the occupant (planet) and the landlord (planetary ruler of the house), there will be excellent conditions surrounding the affairs of that house. A planet occupying a friendly house is empowered and the house will experience extreme good fortune. During its planetary period,** there will be success and a general sense of well-being. When there is neutrality between occupant and ruler, there is relative harmony. While there will be problems from time to time, they will not be without resolution. However, when the two planets — house occupant and house lord — are enemies, it is comparable to a tenant and landlord's inimical relationship or to having an unwanted guest in one's home. The situation within that house will most likely be tense and may result in a conflict of interests between the planet occupying that house and the planet ruling that house. The affairs represented by that house, i.e. second house = finances, third house = communications, etc., will be problematic with obstacles to overcome especially during that planet's period.

Effect of a planet occupying a friend's house in a nativity will be to make the owner thereof gain success. Through his

---

* Later Indian astrologers have also added Rahu and Kethu to this list but we will not use them here.
** Planetary periods will be discussed at length in Chapters 8 and 9.

friends in all his attempts, cultivate new friendships, possess
good sons, wife, wealth, corn and other fortunes and receive
help from all people . . . If a planet should occupy an
inimical sign the person concerned will have a base
disposition of mind. He will live in others' houses eating
their food. He will be utterly destitute and will always be
teased by enemies. Even a person who was originally his
friend will prove inimical to him in its planetary period.[2]

The relationship between two planets, however, is not
always reciprocated. As the most important heavenly body
in Indian mythology, the Moon has no enemies. According
to Table 6.4, Mercury is listed as a *friend* of the Moon,
whereas the Moon is listed as an *enemy* of Mercury. In
viewing landlord-tenant relations, however, the subject
referred to in the first column will be the occupying planet.
That means that when the Moon is the occupant of a
Mercury-ruled house, the Moon is situated in a friendly
house. Satyacharya's rule says that if two planets are friendly
one way and unfriendly another way, their relationship is
neutral. Mercury and the Moon would, therefore, be
considered to be neutral towards each other. Another
example is Venus and Saturn which are both neutral to the
Moon while the Moon is an enemy to both. In this case, the
Moon's enmity towards Venus and Saturn overpowers their
neutrality. Because of the neutral influence, however, their
inimical relationship is not as deadly as it would have been
had they been enemies from both directions.

4. Determining Aspects

Another way to determine the strength or weakness of a
planet is by assessing its relationship or aspect to another
planet. In Hindu astrology, aspects are calculated according
to the number of houses separating the two planets rather
than by the number of degrees separating them as in
Occidental astrology. The full aspect — two planets situated
opposite each other (seven signs/houses apart) — is the only
aspect utilized in this book. The conjunction — two or more
planets posited in the same house — will also be used in this
book though it is not classified by Hindu astrologers as an
'aspect' per se. Other aspects used by Hindus include three-
quarter aspects (two planets which are 4 and 8 houses apart

from each other with three-quarter strength), half aspects (two planets which are 5 and 9 houses apart with half strength), and quarter aspects (two planets which are 3 and 10 houses apart with quarter strength).

The full aspect is the classification assigned to two planets in opposing signs/houses. This principle also applies when one planet is posited at the beginning of one zodiacal sign and the aspecting planet is placed at the end of the opposing sign. An example is Fig 6.3 where Saturn is situated at 1° Leo in the sixth house and Venus is situated at 27° Aquarius in the twelfth house. The relationship between Venus and Saturn constitutes a full aspect since they occupy opposing houses and signs. This would not, however, be considered an opposition in Western astrology because, though they are in opposing signs, they are only 154° apart. An opposition in Western astrology must always be 180° apart with an orb on either side of 8° (anywhere from 172–188°).

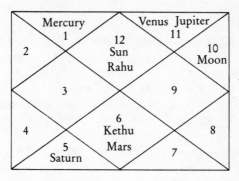

Fig 6.3 Steven's Rasi Chakra

In Hindu astrology, the full aspect — considered to have complete strength — is defined by the nature of the two planets forming the aspect. If Mars, for instance, receives an aspect from a benefic, then Mars and the affairs of the house it occupies will be greatly enhanced. If it is aspected by a malefic, Mars and the affairs of the house it occupies will be damaged. (In Western astrology, the opposition is almost always considered to be difficult with each planet trying to overwhelm the other.)

In addition to two planets aspecting each other, a planet always aspects its opposing house even if the house is unoccupied. This principle is especially significant when applied to planets in the seventh house which aspect the Lagna (first house). Since the Ascendant is the primary house of the zodiac from which the other houses emanate, any planet in the seventh house influences the person's health, appearance and entire outlook on life, everything the Lagna represents. To this end, a benefic planet in the seventh house enhances one's constitution, appearance and general well-being while a malefic planet in the seventh house adversely affects those same concerns.

An illustration of how aspects work can be found in Fig 6.2 (p. 154), the horoscope of Jane. Saturn in the second house receives a full aspect from Venus in the eighth house and vice versa. Since she has a Leo Ascendant, Venus is a malefic influence (See Table 6.3) and, therefore, does not have a positive effect on the affairs of the second house (the house of money and possessions), where Saturn is situated. In fact, Jane's life is consistently filled with financial ups and downs. Conversely, Saturn, a neutral planet in this chart, will not adversely affect Venus and the eighth house.

In this chart, the Lagna is aspected by the Moon in the seventh house so that Jane's appearance and personality are representative of the Moon rather than the Sun, which is the Ascendant ruler. Jane is emotional, moody and has a round face and full figure like the Moon (see the Moon's description on pp. 71–2).

5. Evaluating the House a Planet Occupies

A planet is said to be powerful when placed in an auspicious Trikona house (fifth or ninth) or an auspicious Kendra house (first, fourth, seventh or tenth). A planet does not have optimum influence, however, when placed in an inauspicious Dusthana house (sixth, eighth or twelfth). Though the remaining houses fall into various other categories used by the Hindus, we will consider the second, third, and eleventh houses as being somewhat neutral to their occupying planets.

6. Determining if a Planet is in its Vargottama Position

If a planet's zodiacal sign is identical to its corresponding Navamsa position, that planet is said to be placed in its Vargottama, a position of strength. Table 6.5 (abbreviated from Table 4.3) lists the degrees of each sign that share the same Navamsa sign and from its Vargottama.

Table 6.5 Vargottama positions

Degrees and sign		Navamsa
0.00– 3.20	Aries	Aries
13.20–16.40	Taurus	Taurus
26.40–30.00	Gemini	Gemini
0.00– 3.20	Cancer	Cancer
13.20–16.40	Leo	Leo
26.40–30.00	Virgo	Virgo
0.00– 3.20	Libra	Libra
13.20–16.40	Scorpio	Scorpio
26.40–30.00	Sagittarius	Sagittarius
0.00– 3.20	Capricorn	Capricorn
13.20–16.40	Aquarius	Aquarius
26.40–30.00	Pisces	Pisces

Shad Bala

In Hindu astrology, the term Shad Bala refers to the six sources from which a planet draws its strength — position, aspect, natural strength, motion, direction and time.

1. *Position (Sthanabala)* — According to their position in the horoscope (Sthanabala), the planets are listed in their ascending to descending order as follows:
   a. Planet in its exaltation } most powerful
   b. Planet in its moolatrikona } most powerful
   c. Planet in its rulership   — 3/4 power
   d. Situated in a friend's house   — 5/8 power
   e. Situated in a Trikona or Kendra house
                                       — 1/2 power

A planet situated in its Vargottama is also in a position of power, almost as strong in rank as a planet occupying its sign of rulership. A planet has *no* power when it is placed in its sign of debilitation, in the house of its enemy and/or in a Dusthana house.

2. *Aspect (Drigbala).* A planet becomes powerful when it is aspected by a benefic but loses its power when aspected by a malefic.

(Note: Only Sthanabala and Drigbala comprise the steps that will be used in this book to judge planetary strength and weakness.)

3. *Natural Strength (Naisargika Bala).* The natural strengths of the planets are as follows: (1) Rahu and Kethu; (2) The Sun; (3) The Moon; (4) Venus; (5) Jupiter; (6) Mercury; (7) Mars; (8) Saturn.

4. *Strength of Motion (Chestabala).* The Sun and the Moon are strong when placed in northern latitudes, meaning the signs of Capricorn, Aquarius, Pisces, Aries, Taurus and Gemini.

5. *Strength of Direction (Dikbala).* Mercury and Jupiter are strongest in the first house. The Moon and Venus are most powerful in the fourth house. Saturn displays the most strength in the seventh house. The Sun and Mars are at their best in the tenth house.

6. *Strength of Time (Kalabala).* The Moon, Mars and Saturn are strongest in the horoscopes of those born at night. The Sun, Jupiter and Venus are strongest in the horoscopes of those born during the day. Mercury, however, is equally strong at all times. Benefics have stronger results when placed in a horoscope where there is a waxing Moon, whereas malefics are stronger in a chart with a waning Moon.[3]

Shad Bala is a complicated system involving the assignation of numerical ratings to each planet in order to evaluate its influence in the horoscope. Rather than use this ancient method in its entirety, I have always worked with the six determinants of planetary strength and weakness outlined on pp. 151–162 which are based on Steps 1 and 2, position and aspect. This is another example of how ancient scriptural principles are successfully combined with modern interpretive techniques.

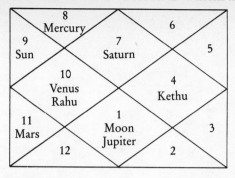

Fig 6.4 Annemarie's Rasi Chakra

The aforementioned steps used to determine planetary strength and weakness are exemplified in Annemarie's chart (Fig 6.4).

Step 1. Determine Whether a Planet is in the Sign of Rulership, Exaltation, Debilitation or Moolatrikona

Referring to Table 6.1, there are no planets in their rulership, debilitation, exaltation or moolatrikona in Annemarie's chart.

Step 2. Determine Whether a Planet is Malefic, Benefic or Neutral

Annemarie has a Libra Ascendant. From Table 6.3, we can list her planets, their roles as individually benefic, neutral or malefic, the houses they rule, and the houses they occupy. Mars, Mercury, Venus and Saturn are benefic influences while the Sun, the Moon and Jupiter, on the other hand, are malefic influences due to the houses they rule.

Planet	Qualities	House Ruled	House Occupied
Sun	Malefic	11th	3rd
Moon	Malefic	10th	7th
Mars	Benefic	2nd, 7th	5th
Mercury	Benefic	9th, 12th	2nd
Jupiter	Malefic	3rd, 6th	7th
Venus	Benefic	1st, 8th	4th
Saturn	Benefic	4th, 5th	1st

Step 3. Determining Planetary Friendship, Enmity and Neutrality

Annemarie's planets are listed according to the relationship the house occupant has to its house lord:

Occupying Planet	Sign	House	Ruler	Relationship
Sun	Sagittarius	3rd	Jupiter	Friend
The Moon	Aries	7th	Mars	Neutral
Mars	Aquarius	5th	Saturn	Neutral
Mercury	Scorpio	2nd	Mars	Neutral
Jupiter	Aries	7th	Mars	Friend
Venus	Capricorn	4th	Saturn	Friend
Saturn	Libra	1st	Venus	Friend

Annemarie is fortunate in that none of her planets fall into inimical houses. From this perspective, all her houses function well. Her planetary periods will also be relatively tranquil due to the friendly houses each of her planets occupy.

Step 4. Determining Aspects

In Annemarie's chart, Kethu in the tenth house is aspected by benefic Venus in the fourth house. The aspect from the 'planet of love' offsets the detrimental effects that Kethu might have on the tenth house and instead provides for the successful careers of both Annemarie and her father and for their harmonious relationship. On the other hand, malefic Kethu, which reciprocally aspects Venus, influences the difficult formative years and the relationship which exists between Annemarie and her mother. (Annemarie's early years were unstable due to the constant travelling of her parents.)

The other set of aspects in Annemarie's chart occurs between the Moon and Jupiter in the seventh house (malefics in this chart) and Saturn, the most beneficial planet according to Table 6.3. Because the first house is the domain of the appearance, the aspect from Jupiter and the Moon should indicate a full figure. But because Saturn, 'a thin and tall body',[4] is by far the most beneficial planet in this chart, its placement on the Ascendant is conducive to Annemarie's slender figure. Jupiter and the Moon, planets of excess aspecting the first house, do contribute to

Annemarie's indulgent personality and habits which affect her health and general well-being. Saturn's protection of the Ascendant, however, will prevent the consequences of excess that the Moon and Jupiter would otherwise bestow. In addition, Venus, as Ascendant ruler, adds its qualities of beauty to her physical appearance.

Step 5. Vargottama

The table below lists Annemarie's planets in Column A and their corresponding Navamsa signs in Column B. Referring to Table 6.5, Saturn is seen to be in its Vargottama position which, along with its exalted placement in Libra, should make Saturn one of the strongest planets in Annemarie's chart.

Column A		Column B
Annemarie's Planets		*Navamsa*
Sun	11 Sagittarius 20	Cancer
Moon	11 Aries 59	Cancer
Mars	21 Scorpio 1	Capricorn
Mercury	25 Capricorn 8	Leo
Jupiter	3 Aquarius 19	Libra
Venus	18 Aries 2	Virgo
Saturn	**2 Libra 46**	**Libra**
North Node	21 Capricorn 17	Cancer
South Node	21 Cancer 17	Capricorn
Ascendant	28 Libra 34	Gemini

Step 6. House Position

Mars is in the auspicious fifth house (a Trikona house) while Saturn, Venus, the Moon and Jupiter are placed in the first, fourth and seventh houses (auspicious Kendra houses). There are no planets in the sixth, eighth or twelfth houses.

To facilitate the judgment of strong and weak planets I have devised Table 6.6. Rather than provide a complicated numerical system (as the Hindus do) to rate planetary strength and weakness, this table illustrates the aforementioned six steps. This information may shed new light on horoscope interpretation for Western astrologers whose own assessment of planetary strength or weakness may give indecisive results.

Table 6.6 Determining Planetary Strength in Annemarie's Chart

	Sun	Moon	Mars	Mercury	Jupiter	Venus	Saturn	Rahu	Ketu
Strength									
Exaltation									
Moolatrikona									
Rulership									
In a friendly house	X		X		X	X	X		
In a Trikona or Kendra house		X			X	X	X	X	X
Aspected by a natural benefic		X			X				
Aspected by an individual benefic							X		
In its Vargottama			X	X		X	X		
Benefic planet in this Chart			X						
Weakness									
Fall									
Enemy's house									
In Dushtana					X				
Aspected by malefic		X			X				
Malefic planet in this Chart	X	X							

Each planet embodies the house it rules. In Annemarie's chart, Saturn, as ruler of the fourth house, represents her mother and her upbringing. Since Saturn has been determined to be a relatively well-placed planet, the mother tends to be a positive figure in Annemarie's life. The way the mother will express herself will be modified by the sign and house that Saturn is placed in (see Chapter 7).

Another way of using these planetary strengths and weaknesses is to see how they affect the houses they occupy. For instance, Saturn and Venus are overwhelmingly Annemarie's best planets, and so the affairs of the houses they occupy (first and fourth) will bring excellent results. Rahu and Kethu, unable to rule a planet/house, are also both well-placed in the fourth and tenth houses.

The first house, occupied by Saturn and ruled by Venus, emphasizes her personality, passion, position in life and her childhood — all positively endowed. The fourth and tenth houses are extremely powerful which means that the parents (represented by these two houses) were extremely compatible and successful. Other than the restlessness she felt growing up, Annemarie basically experienced harmonious familial relationships throughout her life (fourth house) and has always had various opportunities to further her career (tenth house). (Chapter 7 will continue to define the placements of the planets in their signs and their houses.)

According to this table, the Moon, Jupiter, and the Sun have an equal number of weak and strong points. This means that, based on the house occupancy of the planets alone, the third and the seventh house will not be coloured by positive *or* negative descriptions of the difficult planets whose weaknesses will be balanced by their strengths. As we delve further into horoscope interpretation based on other determinants such as house strength and yogas, these factors may be altered. By viewing this table, however, planetary strengths and weaknesses can be seen at first glance. This table clarifies the fact that it is not necessarily contradictory for a planet to be positive in one category and negative in another.

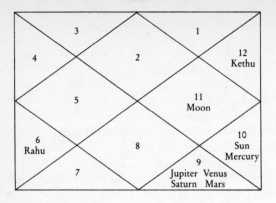

Fig 6.5 Barbara's Rasi Chakra

Barbara's chart (Fig. 6.5) will be analysed in the same manner according to the six steps for judging planetary strengths and weaknesses.

Step 1. Determine Whether a Planet is in the Sign of Rulership, Exaltation, Debilitation or Moolatrikona

In Barbara's chart, there are no planets in exaltation or debilitation. However, Jupiter is located at 1 Sagittarius 40, the sign of Jupiter's rulership and its moolatrikona. Since the rulership and moolatrikona are among the most powerful placements for a planet, Jupiter is strongly posited in this chart.

Step 2. Determine Whether a Planet is Malefic, Benefic or Neutral

With a Taurus Ascendant, Saturn, Mercury, Mars and the Sun are benefic planets. As natural malefics, the Sun, Mars and Saturn should be difficult influences in the chart, but in Barbara's chart they are benefic planets and enhance the houses they occupy. The Moon, Venus, and Jupiter — naturally benefic — are malefic influences here. Because Jupiter is in Sagittarius, however, the sign of its rulership and moolatrikona, its role as a malefic will be greatly reduced. This also applies to Venus, whose categorization as both a neutral and malefic planet decreases its negative influence.

Planet	Qualities	House Ruled	House Occupied
Sun	Benefic	4th	9th
Moon	Malefic	3rd	10th
Mars	Benefic	7th, 12th	8th
Mercury	Benefic	2nd, 5th	9th
Jupiter	Malefic	8th, 11th	8th
Venus	Neutral Malefic	1st, 6th	8th
Saturn	Benefic	9th, 10th	8th

Step 3. Determining Planetary Friendship, Enmity and Neutrality

Let us now repeat the process with Barbara's chart to see if there is friendship, enmity or neutrality between each planet and its house lord.

Occupying Planet	Sign	House	Ruler	Relationship
Sun	Capricorn	9th	Saturn	Enemy
The Moon	Aquarius	10th	Saturn	Neutral
Mars	Sagittarius	8th	Jupiter	Friend
Mercury	Capricorn	9th	Saturn	Neutral
Jupiter	Sagittarius	8th	Jupiter	In its Own House
Venus	Sagittarius	8th	Jupiter	Neutral
Saturn	Sagittarius	8th	Jupiter	Neutral

The Sun, occupying the Saturn-ruled ninth house, is the only planet placed in an enemy's house. This means that the Sun is not comfortable in the Saturn-ruled ninth house and will bring conflict to that area of life. Due to the Sun's role as a benefic in this chart (see Table 6.3) and its power by virtue of being placed in the auspicious ninth house, the effect of residing in an enemy's house is eased. (This is clearly seen in Table 6.6, showing strength and weakness.)

A description of the conflict the Sun (ruler of the fourth house) may face when placed in the house of its enemy Saturn (ruler of the ninth and tenth houses) may be explained as follows: The Sun — symbolic of the self and ruler of the fourth house representing the mother and the childhood — conflicts with Saturn which is (a) ruler of the ninth house representing higher education, religion, travel and the father; and (b) ruler of the tenth house, Barbara's career and the father's profession. Her father and mother have had many conflicts and their marriage hung in the balance on several occasions. Additionally, Barbara has had countless disagreements with her mother about career choices and lifestyles. Because the Sun is otherwise beneficial in this chart, the mother is a magnanimous figure and these situations were, therefore, resolved.

Step 4. Determining Whether There are Full Aspects
Barbara's chart shows no full aspects. However, because the eighth house contains four planets — Venus, Mars, Saturn and Jupiter — the second house receives a full aspect from each of those planets. For the most part, these planets are strong and Mars and Saturn, benefics in this chart, will especially endow the second house of finances.

Step 5. Vargottama
Barbara does not have any planets in their Vargottama position.

Step 6. House Position
The Sun and Mercury are in the ninth Trikona house and the Moon is in the tenth Kendra house. Saturn, Jupiter, Venus and Mars lose their power by being placed in the eighth Dusthana house.

It is clear from this rating system that Barbara's Mercury is strong because it is the only planet placed unequivocally in positive categories. Because it is placed in its moolatrikona and its rulership sign of Sagittarius, Jupiter is also a strong planet. Venus, on the other hand, is only placed in difficult categories. It does not receive any strong ratings and is considered both a neutral and a mild malefic with a Taurus Ascendant. Because the planets personify the houses they rule, the affairs of the Venus-ruled first and the sixth house are not always functioning to their optimum. Barbara's health (sixth house) may be fragile and she will have to heed those parts of the body ruled by Venus (eyes, kidneys) and by the sign of the sixth house, Libra (abdomen). These health problems may surface during the planetary periods ruled by Venus*or simply during times of emotional stress. Because Jupiter, Saturn and Mars, however, all occupy the same house, Venus is somewhat protected but not completely immune.

Determining House Strength

A house may receive strength if its occupant and house lord have a friendly relationship (as seen from Table 6.4). Another way to evaluate a house is to determine whether it receives a full aspect from a benefic or malefic planet. A third way is to see what type of planet — benefic, neutral or malefic — occupies that house. Though there are many categories of houses in Hindu astrology, the ones we will be working with are once again as follows:

Trikona houses (5 and 9) – the most auspicious houses
Kendra houses (1, 4, 7, 10) – auspicious houses
Upachaya houses (3, 6, 10, 11) – bothersome houses
Dusthana houses (6, 8 and 12) – difficult houses

As with the planets, the qualities of each house also change depending on the nature of the planet situated there. Generally speaking, the following principles are used to determine house strength when a naturally and individually benefic or malefic planet occupies that house:

1. A benefic planet occupying any house brings auspicious results to that house.
2. A malefic planet occupying a Kendra, Trikona or Dusthana house will ruin the environment of that house, causing adverse results.
3. A malefic planet occupying an Upachaya house, however, will bring excellent results to that house. The sixth house (classified as Dusthana and Upachaya) and the tenth houses (classified as Kendra and Upachaya) are considered Upachaya houses when this principle is applied. Therefore, a malefic occupying the sixth and tenth houses will enhance those houses rather than destroy them (Rule 2).

* Chapter 8 will further explore this theme.

Table 6.7. Determining Planetary Strength and Weakness

	Sun	Moon	Mars	Mercury	Jupiter	Venus	Saturn	Rahu	Kethu
Strength									
Exaltation									
Moolatrikona					X				
Rulership					X				
In a friendly house or its own house			X		X				
In a Trikona or Kendra house	X	X		X					
Aspected by a benefic									
In its Vargottama				X					
Benefic planet in this chart	X		X				X	X	
Weakness									
Debilitation	X								
Enemy's house									
In Dushtana			X			X	X		
Full aspect by malefic					X	X			
Malefic planet in this chart		X			X	X			

An example of Rule 3 is illustrated in Fig 6.3, 'Steven's' chart, with a Pisces Ascendant. Saturn, a malefic planet both naturally and individually, is placed in the sixth house. Because it is an Upachaya house, the sixth house, according to Rule 3, will be enhanced by Saturn and not damaged as it would have been had the sixth house been considered a Dusthana house.

If a house is occupied by a planet that is naturally benefic and individually malefic or vice versa, the effect on that house is somewhat altered. An example of this is Venus in the twelfth house from the same chart (Fig.6.3). According to Rule 1, Venus — as a natural benefic — enhances the twelfth house, an inauspicious Dusthana house. With a Pisces Ascendant, however, Venus is a malefic and, according to Rule 2, should ruin the affairs of the twelfth house. Because Venus is benefic one way and malefic the other, the effect is balanced and somewhat neutral.

Another example is Fig. 6.1, 'Matthew's' Rasi Chakra with a Taurus Ascendant and Saturn positioned in the fourth house. As a natural malefic, Saturn ruins the affairs of the fourth house (Rule 2). However, as an individual benefic, Saturn does not have any problematic effects on this house (Rule 1) and the outcome is one of balance (Rule 1).

The Sun is the only planet in Annemarie's chart which is both a natural and an individual malefic. Due to the malefic nature of the Sun, the third house, where the Sun is placed, loses some of its strength according to this rule. However, since none of the planets in Annemarie's chart are in inimical houses (Table 6.4), the house receives strength and decreases the severity of the Sun's influence. The third house represents siblings, short travels, communications and ability to learn. Since Annemarie is not an intellectual, she did indeed have learning difficulties in school. But due to her artistic talents and drive, it has not proved difficult for her to succeed. The other individual malefics in Annemarie's chart are the Moon and Jupiter, both naturally benefic planets. This means that the effects they have on houses will be, at worst, neutral. In Barbara's chart the individual malefics — the waxing Moon, Venus and Jupiter — are all naturally benefic, creating neutral effects on the houses they are placed in.

A confusing concept to grasp is the distinction between planetary strength and house strength. According to Rule 2 for determining house strength on p. 169, a malefic planet placed in a Kendra house will damage the affairs of that house. And yet according to Shad Bala, p. 159, a planet receives half power if it is placed in a Kendra house. This means that a malefic planet *receives* power from a benefic house and yet a benefic house is *ruined* by a malefic planet.

With so many planets in the eighth house, Barbara's chart is a perfect example of the contradictions between house strength and planetary strength. Each planet — Venus, Mars, Jupiter and Saturn — is weakened by its placement in the eighth Dusthana house. On the other hand, a benefic planet placed in the eighth house will bring good fortune to that house. Venus and Jupiter are naturally benefic and individually malefic while Mars and Saturn are individually benefic and naturally malefic. Their effects on the house are neutralized accordingly. Although the affairs of the eighth house will, therefore, be less devastating, the house still weakens the occupying planets by placement.

Raj Yogas

In the Rasi Chakra, the affairs of a house are also enhanced by the placement of a Raj Yoga in that house. Raj Yoga literally means 'royal union' since 'Raj' is Sanskrit for 'King' or 'royal' and 'Yoga' is Sanskrit for 'union'. 'Yoga' then, as it applies to the series of bodily postures and breathing exercises, literally means the 'union of body and soul'.

Raj Yogas are certain planetary combinations which create fortunate circumstances in one's life. It was written in the scriptures that anyone born with one of these planetary combinations would be endowed with qualities that would enable him or her to live like royalty. Translated into modern terminology, it means that this person could come from a family of substance which would provide countless opportunities throughout life. Raj Yogas also bring fortunate conditions to the area of life represented by (a) the house it occupies, and (b) the planets which make up the combination.

One of the best examples of Raj Yoga is the conjunction

of the rulers of the fifth house and ninth house, the two Trikona houses. The two planets that form Raj Yoga for each Ascendant are listed as follows:

Ascendants

Aries   — conjunction of Sun and Jupiter
Taurus   — conjunction of Mercury and Saturn
Gemini   — conjunction of Venus and Saturn
Cancer   — conjunction of Mars and Jupiter
Leo   — conjunction of Jupiter and Mars
Virgo   — conjunction of Saturn and Venus
Libra   — conjunction of Saturn and Mercury
Scorpio   — conjunction of Jupiter and the Moon
Sagittarius   — conjunction of Mars and the Sun
Capricorn   — conjunction of Venus and Mercury
Aquarius   — conjunction of Mercury and Venus
Pisces   — conjunction of the Moon and Mars

The affairs of any house containing the appropriate conjunction or Raj Yoga will benefit from this fortuitous placement. In Jane's horoscope (Fig 6.2), for example, there is Raj Yoga since Jupiter and Mars — rulers of the fifth and ninth houses, respectively — are conjunct in the tenth house under a Leo Ascendant. Not only will Jane's career soar (especially during the planetary periods and sub-periods of Mars and Jupiter) but her father will be a leader in his chosen field.

The Scriptures have assigned many planetary combinations to be known as Raj Yogas, many more than can be included in this book. The following are only a few examples.

Raj Yogas

1. Mars and Mercury occupying Second Bhava
2. Sun and Venus in Fourth House
    Mars, Saturn, Jupiter in tenth and eleventh from Lagna
    Moon aspected by Exalted planet or planet in Swakshetra (ruling sign) or full moon in Kendra
3. If Jupiter, Mercury, Venus or the Moon in the ninth house with aspects to friendly planets — native will be a great king worshipped like a deity by subjects.
4. Venus and Jupiter in Pisces. Saturn is exalted and in full aspect with Mars, Sun rises in Lagna with Aries.*

---

* For other listings of Raj Yogas, one is referred to *Brihat Jataka, Phaladeepika* or *Saravali.*

There are many other types of Yogas, or planetary combinations, that have significant effects when they appear in a Rasi Chakra. Though they are not mentioned here, they are all mentioned in the *Brihat Jataka*.

There are different ways to judge the strength of both a planet and a house and the use of one method alone is never sufficient. Even though this seems contradictory and unworkable, the two systems can actually work as checks and balances so that there is never any pronouncement until all aspects are considered. In the end, every factor in the horoscope must be carefully weighed. The following chapter takes the process of interpretation one step further by placing those planets in the signs and houses they occupy.

7

INTERPRETING THE PLANETS IN THE SIGNS AND HOUSES

As seen in the previous chapters, each planet personifies the house it rules in the Rasi Chakra. This means that the planet ruling the Ascendant is the indicator of health, personality, appearance and general approach to life; the planet ruling the sign occupying the second house represents finances; the planetary ruler of the sign of the third house indicates the nature of the siblings and describes the way one learns and communicates; the planet ruling the sign of the fourth house represents the mother and the childhood; etc.

Going one step further, the zodiacal sign where a planet is placed describes the manner in which the planet expresses itself while the house a planet occupies reveals the area of life in which that planet is expressed. The following positive and negative delineations represent the actions of each planet in both its sign and its house. Rather than use elaborate explanations, I have used key words and phrases — more commonly called 'cookbook definitions' — to describe these planetary actions. As usual, its positive or negative manifestation depends on the evaluation of each planet in the context of the Rasi Chakra.

With the exception of planetary rulership, exaltation, fall and moolatrikona, the zodiacal signs the planets occupy are less significant than their house positions. Even in one of these specialized instances, however, it is the degree or degrees of a planet which identifies it as being exalted, fallen or in its moolatrikona. It is important to remember — especially in Hindu astrology — that each and every factor must be carefully weighed before arriving at a definitive conclusion. Ultimately, the accuracy of the chart depends on the skill and experience of the astrologer to synthesize each element in the horoscope.

Note. The following definitions are taken from the scriptures and reworked into Western terminology. They should not, however, be confused with Western astrological definitions for the same combinations (though some may indeed be similar).

Planets in the signs

Sun
Aries (Exalted) and Scorpio: respected in one's field, well-off financially (if on exaltation degree, wealthy), aggressive, good worker, ambitious, may become a physician or surgeon, self-confident .

Taurus: financially secure, work may involve clothing, perfume, or other sensual and aesthetically pleasing items, skilled in the arts.

Gemini: communication skills, wealthy.

Cancer: independent, not financially well-off, will work for others.

Leo (Rulership and Moolatrikona): powerful, self-confident, aggressive, ambitious.

Virgo: skilled in writing and art, mathematically oriented, well-travelled.

Libra (Fall): tendency towards indulgence, instability, lack of self-confidence.

Sagittarius: religious, rich, independent, interested in medicine and sculpture.

Capricorn and Aquarius: will never be wealthy, will not live up to their potential, avaricious, possible ruthlessness.

Pisces: will earn money through water products, insecure.

Moon
Aries: round eyes, forgiving, fond of travel, sensual, financial instability, haughty and fickle.

Taurus (Exaltation and Moolatrikona): beautiful appearance, loyal friend, especially close to women, good appetite, interest in the arts.

Gemini and Virgo: fond of women, ability to communicate, sharp intellect, witty, beautiful features and sweet speech, skilled and fond of the arts, well-travelled.

Cancer (Rulership): influenced by women, loyal friend, learned in astrology, wealth, domestic happiness, close to one's mother.

Leo: temperamental, large cheeks, broad face, difficulty with women, holds grudges, mentally anxious, generous, principled, attached to mother.

Libra: religious, intelligent, philosophical, tall and thin, fond of travelling, wealthy.

Scorpio (Fall): broad eyes, mental instability, separated from family, ill as a child, law-abiding, does not express ideas clearly.

Sagittarius: long face and neck, generous, well-read, good communication skills.

Capricorn: family-minded, seeks appreciation and respect, works at a slow pace, likes to travel, powerful, can be ruthless.

Aquarius: tall and large-boned, can succeed and fail with the same intensity, attached to friendships, likes beautiful articles such as flowers, perfumes and fine materials.

Pisces: beautiful appearance, good salespeople, fair-minded, rich, well-educated.

Mars

Aries (Rulership and Moolatrikona) and Scorpio (Rulership): Respected position of authority or active in government affairs, fond of travel, sensual and sometimes indulgent, immense vitality.

Taurus and Libra: influenced by women, single-minded, sensual, enjoys aesthetically-pleasing items, shy, lazy.

Gemini and Virgo: bright appearance, helpful to others, skilled in music, fearless.

Cancer (Fall): may travel or live abroad, intelligent, can be self-centred, stomach troubles, unkempt appearance.

Sagittarius and Pisces: well-known and respected in chosen field, work for the government, will have adversaries, fearless.

Capricorn (Exaltation): wealthy, active in politics and social causes (perhaps government worker), leadership, good family background.

Aquarius: unhappy, poverty-stricken, travels, independent, dishonest.

Mercury
Aries and Scorpio: indulgent habits, argumentative, deceitful and dishonest ways.

Taurus and Libra: preacher, family-minded, capable of earning money, generous nature.

Gemini (Rulership): proud, learned in science and the arts, persuasive speech, fond of comfort.

Cancer: disliked by many, earns money through water-connected fields.

Leo: unstable character, will not succeed, generally difficult.

Virgo (Rulership, Exaltation and Moolatrikona): generous, well-educated, strong values, comfortable and patient, brilliant mind.

Sagittarius: respected by people in authority, scientific-minded, interested in law.

Capricorn and Aquarius: prefers to work for others, difficulties with money, sculptor, incurs debts.

Pisces (Fall): makes friends easily, open to others' views, lacks confidence, nervous and irritable.

Jupiter
Aries and Scorpio: financially well-off, leadership qualities, generous nature, patient, bright appearance, well-known in one's chosen field, happy domestic situation.

Taurus and Libra: strong constitution, lives comfortably, wealthy, many friends and acquaintances, generous and well-liked.

Gemini and Virgo: well-dressed, has an extensive wardrobe, may own more than one home, many friends and comfortable living conditions.

Cancer (Exaltation): likes beautiful things, blessed with good marriage and children, materially comfortable, intelligent.

Leo: executive abilities, likes taking charge, enjoys flattery and admiration, flair for the dramatic.

Sagittarius (Rulership and Moolatrikona) and Pisces (Rulership): enjoys positions of authority, religious-minded financial stability, comfortable.

Capricorn (Fall): allergies and other chronic ailments, unhappiness, inflexibility.

Aquarius: loyal friend, interested in astrology and other occult studies, financial stability and domestic happiness.

Venus

Aries and Scorpio: loss of property, conflicts with family, irresponsible and unsteady, extremely sensual and possessive.

Taurus (Rulership) and Libra (Rulership and Moolatrikona): wealth through powers of intelligence or artistic sensibilities, well-liked.

Gemini: position of responsibility and authority, financially well-established, fond of music.

Virgo (Fall): insecurity in relationships, accepts difficult tasks, unhappy in chosen profession.

Capricorn and Aquarius: well-liked, influenced by the opinions of women as well as a need to be appreciated by them.

Cancer: more than one marriage, timid, haughty and unhappy.

Leo: professional associations with women, devoted spouse.

Sagittarius: integrity, honesty, well-off financially.

Pisces (Exaltation): extravagant, artistic, likeable, well-educated, sensuous nature.

Saturn

Aries (Fall): foolish, has wanderlust, lonely.

Scorpio: often feels isolated and depressed, difficulty making friends, self-conscious.

Gemini or Virgo: unhappy, difficulty saving money.

Taurus: sensual and indulgent nature, usually marries more than once, difficulty accumulating money.

Libra (Exaltation): well-known in one's field, financial stability.

Cancer: difficult family life, may be estranged from mother, foolish.

Leo: must work hard for what one achieves, sadness.

Sagittarius or Pisces: loyal worker, saves money, domestic happiness.

Capricorn (Rulership) or Aquarius (Rulership and Moolatrikona): earns a good living, high status, intelligence, position of authority.

The following delineations illustrate the way the planets are likely to manifest in the houses of the Rasi Chakra.

Sun

First House: aggressive, impetuous, ambitious, proud, vitality, good health, impatient.

Second House: modest, learning problems, must work hard for one's money, financial ups and downs, difficulty expressing oneself.

Third House: intelligent, authoritative position, liberal, quarrels with siblings.

Fourth House: may work for the government or in another 'official' job, unhappy, difficult relationship with the mother.

Fifth House: intelligent, wealthy, difficulty with one's children, highly strung, risky for investments, indulgence in love affairs.

Sixth House: wealthy, vitality, concerned with health, enjoys helping others, service profession, good worker, successful career.

Seventh House: restlessness, difficulties with marriage which may take place later in life, strong sexuality.

Eighth House: difficulty in making friends, problematic relationship with the father, good health, poor eyesight.

Ninth House: difficulty with father, interested in the law, religion, philosophy, fair-minded, enjoys one's comfort, respected in one's field.

Tenth House: intelligence, wealth, fame, self-confident, leadership and success in one's chosen field.

Eleventh House: ambitious, reaches one's goals, is able to make money from wise investments.

Twelfth House: difficult relationship with the father, lack of wealth, may live abroad, lack of confidence, must work hard for achievements.

Moon

First House: strong constitution, enthusiasm, vacillating, nice-looking, works with the public, emotional and passionate.

Second House: financially well-off (even wealthy), educated, sensual, good family background.

Third House: good relationship with siblings, strong communication skills, artistic abilities, frugal.

Fourth House: happy, sensually indulgent, many

friendships, good relationship with the mother, generous and tolerant of others.

Fifth House: happiness through one's children, intelligent, love of sports and the arts, passionate and romantic.

Sixth House: difficult relationship with the mother and possibly with co-workers, stomach troubles, service profession.

Seventh House: beautiful, highly romantic and passionate, money through partner, may be married more than once but generally the marriages are successful unions.

Eighth House: little willpower, weak health, intelligence, difficulty with mother, lack of confidence.

Ninth House: prosperous, successful career, good relationship with father and children, generous, interested in religion.

Tenth House: ethical, well-liked, career involves helping others, good relationship with the mother and females in general.

Eleventh House: integrity, successful with children, wealth, realistic goals and ambition that helps realize them.

Twelfth House: reflective, lack of physical activity, emotional problems, difficulty making friends.

Mars

First House: adventurous, temperamental, aggressive, independent, assertive, accident-prone, physical prowess.

Second House: poor judge of character, difficulty learning, must work hard for success, short-tempered.

Third House: difficult relationships with siblings, adventurous, good communication skills.

Fourth House: loner, difficult relationship with mother, comfortable home, successful career.

Fifth House: impetuous, intelligent, highly strung, aggressive, work involves physical expression.

Sixth House: passionate, desire fulfilled through ambition and hard work, good earning power.

Seventh House: strong sexuality, argumentative nature, restless, difficulty with or separation from partner.

Eighth House: weak health, must work hard for one's money, strong sexuality.

Ninth House: difficulty with father, does not have many friends, great drive and ambition to get ahead, achieves recognition.

Tenth House: self-centred, highly ambitious, achieves career goals through sheer persistence.

Eleventh House: wealth, many ambitions will be realized, influential in the community, many friends who will help with career goals.

Twelfth House: lonely, strong sexuality, difficulties with siblings, must be careful not to incur debts.

Mercury

First House: sweet-speaking, sharp-witted, intelligent, generous, friendly, well-educated, charming.

Second House: wealth through one's own ingenuity, writer or poet, good communicator, well-educated.

Third House: risk-taker, business skills, good with communications and literary endeavours, good relationship with siblings, low physical energy.

Fourth House: educated, good conversationalist, travels frequently for both work and for pleasure, sociable, enjoys one's home.

Fifth House: inquisitive nature, good investments, generous, happiness through children, even-tempered.

Sixth House: interested in health matters, argumentative, restless nature.

Seventh House: intelligent, well-dressed, wealth through marriage partner.

Eighth House: gains fame and recognition, good health, benefits through finances of others, has difficulty learning because the mind is so restless.

Ninth House: well-educated, good earner, eloquent speaker, charming, interested in philosophy and religion.

Tenth House: successful career, well-respected in chosen field, learning ability, strength, intelligent, good speaker.

Eleventh House: successful with finances, friendships cultivated with intelligent and artistic people, honesty, happiness, wealthy.

Twelfth House: sorrowful, learning problems, lack of physical energy, weak nervous system and lack of confidence, frugal.

Jupiter

First House: good-looking, fortunate, strong constitution, luck through children, religious-minded.

Second House: talkative, lover of good food, educated,

earns a good living.

Third House: frugal, siblings are successful, good skills in the areas of communications and the arts.

Fourth House: enjoys extravagant lifestyle, happy, close relationship with family, successful career.

Fifth House: highly optimistic, good investments, talent with drama and money, political interests, happiness and fulfilment through one's children.

Sixth House: lethargy, can be excessive, good worker, charming.

Seventh House: friendly, popular, respected, generous and well-liked, good marriage.

Eighth House: not wealthy, good health, vitality, difficulty with career.

Ninth House: philosophical, religious and fair-minded, good teacher and well-educated, prosperous, happiness through children.

Tenth House: very ambitious, fulfils one's career goals and is well-known in one's field, fair-minded, position of leadership, interests are in the field of education, law, or government.

Eleventh House: well-off financially, initiates projects and works hard to fulfil goals, many opportunities, support of friends, good health.

Twelfth House: lethargy, inability to communicate, loner, problematic relationships.

Venus

First House: healthy, beautiful, happiness, strong constitution, passionate, extravagant.

Second House: likes material possessions and luxurious lifestyle, money is earned through artistic endeavours, extravagant.

Third House: loner, good relationship with siblings, talented in the arts.

Fourth House: comfortable home, likes clothes, art and luxuries, good relationship with mother, family-minded.

Fifth House: intelligent, artistic, romantic and sensual, financially stable, blessed with children.

Sixth House: many friends, work may involve the arts, gets along well with co-workers, good health.

Seventh House: many friends, fortunate in marriage and

other relationships, romantic nature, money through marriage partner.

Eighth House: strong constitution and good health, wealthy, happiness and money through partner, sensual nature.

Ninth House: prosperous, good relationships with marriage partner who may be foreign, many friends, enjoys children.

Tenth House: many fulfilling friendships, recognition through lucrative career, most likely in the arts.

Eleventh House: material comforts, financial stability, surrounds oneself with many friends especially women.

Twelfth House: sensual enjoyment, wealth, frugal yet enjoys spending money extravagantly.

Saturn

First House: emaciated, sorrowful, solemn, difficulties in childhood, health problems, delays, works hard, disciplined.

Second House: financial instability but comfortable later in life.

Third House: generous, good marriage, lack of physical activity, success comes through hard work and possibly late in life, may have difficulty with siblings.

Fourth House: unhappy, ill health in childhood, disciplined and serious, spends much time alone.

Fifth House: expresses oneself seriously, difficult relationships and difficulty with children, depressed, financial instability.

Sixth House: financially comfortable, highly ambitious and proficient in whatever one sets out to do.

Seventh House: difficult relationships with friends and with marriage partner, disciplined, may marry late in life to someone older.

Eighth House: one must overcome many obstacles in life, difficulty in communicating with others, argumentative personality.

Ninth House: solemn and religious, works hard for one's rewards, difficult relationship with family but especially with the father.

Tenth House: accepts challenges, recognition, fulfils ambition through perseverance and discipline.

Eleventh House: strong constitution, good income,

intelligent, leadership abilities and powerful figure within the community, influential friends.

Twelfth House: spends money rather foolishly, difficulty with studies, loner, not overly ambitious.

Rahu

First House: prone to headaches, wealth, strength, weak health, difficulties in marriage.

Second House: inability to express oneself clearly, tender-hearted, wealth, happiness.

Third House: proud, difficulty with siblings, strong-willed, good health, adventurous.

Fourth House: difficult relationship with the mother, lonely but happy most of the time none the less.

Fifth House: difficult relationships with children, intelligent but lacks confidence in abilities, problematic love affairs, stomach ailments.

Sixth House: misunderstood by others, ability to earn money through work, good health.

Seventh House: spends too much money on relationships, separation from loved ones, strong-willed.

Eighth House: difficulty with children, lack of domestic tranquillity, inability to handle one's finances, weak health.

Ninth House: argumentative, authoritative, active within the community, philosophical and religious-minded.

Tenth House: recognition by public through career, leadership qualities and ability to earn money, takes risks.

Eleventh House: prosperous, lucky with children, strong constitution, many powerful friends and influential within the community.

Twelfth House: spends money foolishly, spends a lot of time alone.

Kethu

First House: poor health, unhappy, difficulty in marriage, lack of confidence in one's abilities, instability.

Second House: difficulties in learning, financial instability, harsh speech quality.

Third House: strong constitution, financial know-how, fame, problematic relationship with brothers and sisters.

Fourth House: loss of property, may live and travel abroad, problematic relationship with mother.

Fifth House: difficulty with children, stomach disease, self-centred.

Sixth House: generous, fame, authority figure, can be excessive and jealous.

Seventh House: intestinal problems, difficulty in marriage and other relationships.

Eighth House: separations from friends and family, argumentative nature.

Ninth House: difficulty with father, must work hard to get past many obstacles.

Tenth House: energetic, takes risks, successful career.

Eleventh House: quite frugal, maternal nature, generous, successful in fulfilling goals.

Twelfth House: spendthrift, religious pursuits, loner.

Before presenting a closer examination of the horoscopes of Annemarie and Barbara, let's review the techniques that have been set out thus far for interpreting the Rasi Chakra. It must be emphasized that these techniques only represent an introduction to the variety of methodologies that may be used. Each astrologer will choose a personal style and method developed by years of experience to evaluate and synthesize each available factor in order to understand the entire Rasi Chakra. As stated in this section thus far, the principles are as follows:

(a) To examine the basic definitions of the planets, signs and houses (Chapter 4);

(b) To review the descriptions of the 12 possible Ascendant Combinations to see exactly how the zodiacal signs and planetary rulers associated with each house manifest in a particular Rasi Chakra (Chapter 5);

(c) To evaluate the strengths and weaknesses of each planet according to its placement in the horoscope (Chapter 6), and

(d) To define the way each planet — modified by its role as house ruler — is expressed through the sign and house placement (Chapter 7).

What follows are more extensive interpretations of Annemarie's and Barbara's charts. By applying the aforementioned principles, we will obtain information concerning their character traits, personality development, family backgrounds, attitudes towards marriage, children and career. The conclusions are by no means exhaustive or finite and, in the end, it is the free will of both Annemarie and Barbara which determines the way these traits ultimately manifest.

Annemarie

Let's begin with Annemarie by providing some background information about her life. Annemarie is a free-lance photographer who has regularly consulted me over the last 10 years. She was raised throughout Central and South America where her father, a diplomat for the Dutch Diplomatic Corps, met and married her Peruvian mother. Annemarie and her sisters attended international and American schools where their education was conducted in English. Their classmates — who came from all over the world — were children of ambassadors, foreign businessmen, journalists, international correspondents and visiting officials from other countries. Accordingly, Annemarie spoke three languages fluently — Spanish (with her mother, her sisters, maternal relatives and the community), English (at school and with her friends) and Dutch (with her father). Twenty years ago her family moved back to her father's native country, The Netherlands, where they all still reside.

To begin the process of interpretation there are two charts that must be listed for reference purposes. Table 7.1 lists: (a) each house; (b) occupying sign; (c) occupying planet (if any); (d) planetary ruler; and (e) the house in which that ruler is placed. Table 7.2, adapted from Satyacharya's Table in Chapter 6, lists which planets are benefic, malefic and neutral in a horoscope having a Libra Ascendant (as does Annemarie).

Table 7.1 Annemarie's planets by house and sign

House	Sign	Occupant	Ruler	House Occupied
First	Libra	Saturn	Venus	Fourth
Second	Scorpio	Mercury	Mars	Fifth
Third	Sagittarius	Sun	Jupiter	Seventh
Fourth	Capricorn	Venus, Kethu	Saturn	First
Fifth	Aquarius	Mars	Saturn	First
Sixth	Pisces		Jupiter	Seventh
Seventh	Aries	Moon, Jupiter	Mars	Fifth
Eighth	Taurus		Venus	Fourth
Ninth	Gemini		Mercury	Second
Tenth	Cancer	Rahu	Moon	Seventh
Eleventh	Leo		Sun	Third
Twelfth	Virgo		Mercury	Second

Table 7.2 Quality of Annemarie's planets based on her Libra Ascendant

Benefic	Malefic	Neutral
Saturn* (3 and 4)	Sun (11)	None
Mercury (9 and 12)	Jupiter (3 and 6)	
Venus (1 and 8)	Moon (10)	
Mars (2 and 7)		

The Rasi Chakra can be approached from many different angles. The descriptions which follow are listed in the order of the houses. Because many planets rule more than one house, some of the delineations overlap and will be described only once.

Lagna. Since Venus-ruled Libra occupies the first house of appearance, Annemarie is very attractive to the opposite sex and is, for both personal and professional reasons, very conscious of her public image. She is artistic, sensual but also has excessive habits and extravagant tastes due to the aspect the first house and its occupant, Saturn, receives from the Moon and Jupiter in the seventh house.

As ruler of the Lagna, Venus is the indicator of

---

* As stated in Chapter 6, Saturn is the strongest benefic in a chart with a Libra Ascendant.

Annemarie's personality and the key to her self-identification. Venus' occupancy of the fourth house indicates that her home environment is of utmost importance and many of her personality traits are revealed through the way her house is furnished and decorated. Through family connections and benefits attained from her varied background, she will be presented with artistic job opportunities that, taken advantage of, will allow her to succeed in most of her endeavours. She will also be quite fortunate in finding suitable living and studio space. Since Venus is conjoined with Kethu in the fourth house and is aspected by Rahu in the tenth house — both malefic influences — there is a conflict between enjoying the comforts of home (fourth house) and needing to be recognized professionally by both the public and by her peers (tenth house). This conflict is also illustrated by the differences both her mother (fourth house) and her father (tenth) experience with Annemarie concerning her lifestyle.

As the ruler of the eighth house of business and finances, Venus (an aesthetic planet) appropriately describes Annemarie's career as a photographer. It also signifies the creative partnership she maintained with her lover which successfully produced a series of greeting cards. Since the eighth house is not the best house for a planet to rule, Venus' placement in the fourth house creates tension with the mother and, in times of crisis, a tendency to withdraw from the world. In keeping with the full aspect Venus receives from malefic Rahu, the way in which Annemarie handles her business affairs will also be opposed by her parents. Because Venus, however, is a fairly well-rated planet in the chart, these family disagreements will not be disastrous — just the normal variance of opinions that commonly exist between family members.

In addition to the first house of Libra being examined in the light of Venus (its ruler), it must also be viewed through the eyes of Saturn — its occupant. Saturn is: (a) auspiciously placed in the first Kendra house; (b) exalted in the sign of Libra; (c) in its vargottama position; and (d) categorized as one of the most beneficial planets in a chart with a Libra Ascendant. In this particular horoscope,

Saturn's positive traits enhance rather than limit Annemarie's personality and general approach to life. These traits include discipline, integrity, seriousness, and goal-orientation — all of which assist Annemarie in the expression of her creativity. There will still be the expected self-consciousness, frugality and lack of physical vitality but they will not overpower the more positive aspects of Saturn. Because Saturn rules the fourth house, it is safe to say that Annemarie's mother was a very strong influence on her personality and general attitude and that Annemarie's combined home/studio (fourth house) is a place where she can work and which reflects her individuality (first house).

The fact that the ruler of the first house (Venus) is situated in the fourth house and (vice versa) the ruler of the fourth house (Saturn) is in the first house exemplifies the astrological concept of *receptivity*. The result, as we have seen, is a pronounced theme in Annemarie's life encompassing the interaction of these two houses (first and fourth) and signs (Libra and Capricorn).

Second House. The second house of Scorpio is ruled by Mars and, therefore, the nature of her finances and general productivity depends on this impetuous planet's position in the fifth house, a highly auspicious Trikona House. Since Annemarie is self-employed, she may depend too much on projects before they actually materialize and she may invest money in creative ventures which were idealistically conceived rather than realistically evaluated. Ultimately, she will be able to earn money through creative projects in conjunction with a romantic partner due to Mars' position as a benefic in this chart.

The second house, a neutral house, does not alter the nature of its occupant, Mercury, whose status in this horoscope is benefic. Since Mercury rules both the ninth and twelfth houses, travel (ninth house), higher education (twelfth house), research (twelfth house) and/or creativity (twelfth house) will help her to earn money.

Third House. As the ruler of the third house, Jupiter, an individual malefic in this chart, describes Annemarie's restless nature and adds to the difficulty she has in maintaining a long-term successful relationship (Jupiter in the seventh house). Its conjunction with the Moon in the seventh house also brings inconsistency to her relationships.

In accordance with the rule stating that 'a malefic planet occupying an Upachaya house brings excellent results to that house', the third house of Sagittarius is empowered by its occupancy of the Sun (ruler of the eleventh house). The most positive application of the Sun's position here is describing Annemarie as an independent and innovative thinker who has been able to maintain her career as a self-employed photographer. The Sun in the third house also defines the success of her sisters who are representative of the third house.

Fourth House. The fourth house has already been briefly discussed in Chapter 5 and on pp. 188-90 in connection with Saturn as ruler of the fourth house placed in the first house, and Venus as Ascendant ruler placed in the fourth house. Along with Venus, Kethu's placement in the fourth house is described as problematic for Annemarie's relationship with her mother, something that has already been seen. Conversely, Rahu's placement in the tenth house — accompanied by the full aspect from Venus — prompts Annemarie to take professional risks which work to her advantage. She has always been recognized by her peers and by the public as a unique talent and has always been able to earn a good living through her free-lance work.

Fifth House. As ruler of the fifth house, Saturn's benefic rating has already been discussed. Its position in the first house brings great success in life through her uniqueness and individuality.

The occupant of the fifth house, Mars, is naturally malefic and individually benefic. This means that its difficulties will be somewhat eased. Mars in Aquarius in the fifth house represents intelligence, impetuousness, aggression and a highly strung nature which may work to her disadvantage. It will also provide her with the exuberance and enthusiasm for numerous creative ventures. Its position in the fifth Trikona house will also bring her fortunate circumstances through love affairs and children. The occupancy of Aquarius and, especially the naturally malefic Mars, will give her ambivalent feelings about having children (the periods in which childbirth is most likely to occur will be discussed in more detail in Chapter 9).

Sixth House. The sixth house is occupied by the sign of Pisces which is ruled by Jupiter. As already stated in Chapter 5, this influence is one of work-related independence and, to this end, Annemarie has always remained self-employed. As the indicator of illness, Pisces contributes to her excessive and indulgent nature, the cause of any ailments she may have. Placed in the seventh house, Jupiter indicates that work will be with a partner or through the influence of her parents. The latter is due to Jupiter's conjunction with the Moon, ruler of the tenth house (father) and Jupiter's aspect by Saturn, ruler of the fourth house (mother). Because Jupiter is a malefic influence in this horoscope, there will probably be friction with partner and her parents due to the nature of her work. The sixth house has no occupants.

Seventh House. Mars, the ruler of the seventh house, has already been described through its role as ruler of the second house. As the ruler of the seventh house, Mars in the fifth house will probably indicate partnerships with people who share her participation in the arts and her passion for life.

The Moon and Jupiter, both occupants of the seventh house, are individually malefic planets and, therefore, further affect the situation of the partner. As previously discussed, the parents may have difficulties with the nature of Annemarie's relationships which are anything but secure. The aspect from Saturn, however, does eventually stabilize this part of Annemarie's life.

Eighth House. The occupancy of Venus-ruled Taurus in the eighth house lends Annemarie the love of collectables such as books, antiques, paintings, art objects, etc. Her need for companionship in addition to her need for financial stability may be reflected in her choice of marriage partner. (Venus, the eighth house ruler, has already been discussed in the section on the fourth house.)

Ninth House. As the ruler of the ninth house, Mercury and the sign it rules (Gemini) typify the father as an intellectual whose restless nature was satisfied through his role as both diplomat and international traveller. As a benefic in this chart, Mercury's position in the third house describes Annemarie's unique ability to make friends through travelling as well as her harmonious relationship with her sisters.

Tenth House. The ruler of the tenth house is the waxing Moon, naturally benefic but individually malefic. Placed in the seventh house and conjunct with Jupiter, individually malefic, the Moon brings a difficult influence to the seventh house. It indicates that Annemarie's partner may have conflicts with either Annemarie's career and/or her father — something that has already been hinted at.

Rahu's position in the tenth house reiterates her individualistic career and her ability to succeed and assert herself in her chosen field. The aspect Rahu receives from Venus in the fourth house shows that Annemarie's feeling for aesthetics and beauty is expressed through her career as a photographer. In addition her father's status, as represented by the tenth house, is blessed with the harmony that only Venus bestows.

Eleventh House. There are no planets occupying the eleventh house but the sign of Leo (whose natural ruler is the Sun) defines Annemarie's hopes, dreams, friendships and relationship to her community, everything represented by the eleventh house. With the individualistic Sun ruling this house, Annemarie's ambivalent attitude towards having children is reaffirmed. The placement of her natal Sun in the third house means that so many of her goals and ideals revolve around communication and mobility. Although she will have happy relationships with her sisters, there will also be normal sibling rivalry from time to time.

Twelfth House. As ruler of the ninth and twelfth houses, Mercury's placement in the second house has already been discussed. Even though it is inauspicious for a planet to rule the twelfth house — a Dusthana house — its rulership of the ninth house, however, contributes to Mercury's categorization as a benefic in this chart. Mercury-ruled Virgo lends Annemarie the ability to explore the art of photography which requires many solitary hours taking and developing photographs. Sometimes, however, Annemarie may get depressed and too self-deprecating due to the influence of Virgo in the twelfth house.

Barbara

The manner in which an astrologer broaches interpretation is highly personal and his/her style has usually developed through many years of experimenting with numerous methods. Analysing each house as we just did with Annemarie's chart is only one approach that can be used to interpret a chart. Beginning with a description of Barbara's upbringing and professional history, the following method summarizes some of the important aspects of her Rasi Chakra.

Barbara's family consists of her mother, father, and two older siblings whose comfortable home in the suburbs provided a typical American upbringing. Barbara was the youngest child, and felt alienated from the rest of her family. Even though she always had an outgoing personality she was basically insecure and restless. Her favourite pasttime always involved physical activities such as swimming, running and bicycle riding. At an early age, Barbara developed an independent streak which has enabled her to pursue a career and to make friends easily. For several years Barbara was a professional nurse and cared for terminally ill patients. She started out in a hospital and then transferred to a hospice, a more benevolent setting where terminal patients live out their remaining time with dignity in home-like surroundings. Additionally, she used alternative treatments for the terminally ill such as visualizations and affirmations, both positive reinforcement techniques. At present Barbara is a certified social worker specializing in counselling families who are dysfunctional (i.e. no longer functioning as a healthy family unit) due to the alcohol and/or drug abuse of one or more of its members.

As we begin to interpret Barbara's chart, the following tables will prove to be helpful.

Table 7.4 Quality of Barbara's Planets based on her Taurus Ascendant

Benefic	Malefic	Neutral
Saturn (9 and 10)	Jupiter (8 and 11)	Venus (1 and 6)*
Mercury (2 and 5)	Venus (1 and 6)	
Mars (7 and 12)	Moon (3)	
Sun (4)		

* Venus is considered to be neutral as well as malefic with a Taurus Ascendant

Table 7.3 Barbara's Planets by House and Sign

House	Sign	Occupant	Ruler	House Occupied
First	Taurus		Venus	Eighth
Second	Gemini		Mercury	Ninth
Third	Cancer		Moon	Tenth
Fourth	Leo		Sun	Ninth
Fifth	Virgo	Rahu	Mercury	Ninth
Sixth	Libra		Venus	Eighth
Seventh	Scorpio		Mars	Eighth
Eighth	Sagittarius	Venus, Mars Jupiter, Saturn	Jupiter	Eighth
Ninth	Capricorn	Sun, Mercury	Saturn	Eighth
Tenth	Aquarius	Moon	Saturn	Eighth
Eleventh	Pisces	Kethu	Jupiter	Eighth
Twelfth	Aries		Mars	Eighth

Using Barbara's chart, we'll approach interpretation from a slightly different point of view. As we have seen throughout this book Barbara's chart has a stellium (four or more planets) in the eighth house consisting of Venus, Mars, Jupiter and Saturn in Sagittarius. Because of the overwhelming influence the eighth house exerts on the Rasi Chakra, I'll begin the following synopsis of Barbara's chart by concentrating on each planet in the eighth house.

Mars. In its role as a natural malefic, Mars should ruin the affairs of the eighth house and, at the same time, be ruined by its placement in a Dusthana house. In Barbara's Rasi Chakra, however, Mars is not only individually benefic but works well in the eighth house due to its mutual friendship with Jupiter, the lord of the eighth house. Venus and Jupiter, the remaining eighth house planets, are, in fact, also friendly with Mars.

As ruler of Scorpio and the seventh house of partnership, Mars is indicative of Barbara's husband and the nature of their relationship. Because Scorpio is a passionate sign, it can be said that her marriage will be an exciting union which may present disagreements from time to time concerning money and mutual investments. Their partnership will, however, provide enough strength and happiness so that each crisis will be met head-on.

Mars' rulership of the twelfth house may mean that Barbara will have to temper her extravagant nature and aloof attitude towards money in order to satisfy her general need for financial security. Her Taurus Ascendant, however, keeps her in line and always ensures that she is provided with enough material comforts.

As the ruler of both the seventh and the twelfth houses, Mars' position in the eighth house describes her husband as emotional, hard-working and shrewd concerning investments and business ventures. Her husband will provide for his family and will ultimately be responsible for family finances. Because Mars is a passionate planet, Barbara has many emotional ups and downs which contribute to prolonged periods of listlessness. Though she also has stress-related digestive problems, Barbara has discovered that physical activity is an effective weapon to counter these and other potential ailments.

Jupiter. The ruler of the Sagittarian eighth house, Jupiter, is placed in its own sign and house. Though Jupiter is an individually malefic planet, Sagittarius is the sign of its rulership and moolatrikona, the two most fortunate placements for a planet. In addition, Jupiter's natural role as 'the greater benefic' tempers most of its malefic qualities.

Since Jupiter (the ruler of the eighth house of the partner's finances) is conjunct Mars (the ruler of the seventh house of partnership) their shared attitude towards financial security and sound investments is what Barbara and her husband, an accountant, have in common. Sagittarius' occupancy of the eighth house indicates that there will either be a legacy at some time or, more likely, endowments from either Barbara's parents and/or her husband's family.

Since Jupiter is also the ruler of the eleventh house, Barbara has the ability to become an excellent community organizer and fund-raiser for charitable and/or pet social causes. The eleventh house occupancy of Jupiter-ruled Pisces also contributes to Barbara's popularity and her penchant for working with groups who share her social and political ideals.

Venus. Because Venus is individually malefic and the only planet in Barbara's chart without a positive rating, Venus' role as a naturally benefic planet is somewhat diminished. The following definitions of Venus' influence in Barbara's Rasi Chakra, therefore, display the planet's more problematic sides.

To begin, Venus' rulership of the first house (appearance, personality, constitution) and the sixth house (health and work) indicates that her physical stamina is not always operating at its optimum level. Barbara has a tendency towards stomach troubles and poor eyesight (both Venus-ruled). When she is ill, Barbara — like most Taureans — tends to be stoical and rarely asks the people who love her for assistance. Because she distances herself during these times of need, it is difficult to recognize when she is ill or in pain.

The Taurus Ascendant endows her with a compulsive nature which sometimes results in mood swings and erratic behaviour. Her health may also be affected by her inability to balance these patterns of her personality. The Ascendant ruler, Venus, does, however, provide her with an attractive appearance and a sensual and indulgent nature, similar to the effects of a Libra Ascendant. As Ascendant ruler placed in the eighth house, Venus may be applied to Barbara's feelings of having insufficient power over her own destiny. Venus' role as sixth house ruler placed in the eighth house may indicate jealousy and power struggles between Barbara and her co-workers and/or supervisors.

Saturn. Saturn, individually benefic, is considered to be the most beneficial planet for a Taurus Ascendant. This stems from Saturn's rulership of two auspicious houses, the ninth Trikona house and the tenth Kendra house. Because of Saturn's rulership of these two houses which indicate the father and his professional status, Barbara's father was very successful in the publishing field. He was a hard worker and a model for discipline and responsibility.

Once Barbara forms an opinion, she is extremely inflexible and even those closest to her cannot penetrate her stubbornness. Conversely, Saturn-ruled Capricorn adds a serious and practical attitude towards her professional life while her patience and the ability to listen makes her an excellent teacher and counsellor. Aquarius' occupancy of the tenth house, representative of her career, corroborates the fact that she is a concerned social worker who takes the implications of her job quite seriously.

Saturn's position in the eighth house gives her a need to be financially secure but, at the same time, presents her with irrational fears of failure related to the pressures of everyday living. Taken to an extreme, these anxieties sometimes result in misunderstandings with friends due to differences of opinion and the inability to listen.

Though the eighth house tends to diminish the positive qualities of Saturn somewhat, its position as the most beneficial planet in this chart along with its friendly relationship with the house ruler (Jupiter) balances these ill effects. Although the planet does not function without difficulties, problematic areas may be resolved by calling on her reserve of Saturnian traits such as persistence and discipline. In fact, the only planet that does not receive any difficult marks at all (as seen from Chapter 6) is Mercury.

In general, the eighth house is more positively than negatively endowed. Because Mars and Saturn, natural malefics, are individually benefic with this Ascendant, the eighth house is not particularly damaged by them. Though Jupiter is individually malefic, its position in Sagittarius (the sign of its rulership and moolatrikona) offsets this effect. The only difficult planet is Venus and its individual malefic quality cannot overpower the effects of the rest of the planets occupying that house. The affairs of the eighth house — finances of the partner, business ventures, happiness through the partner — will, therefore, be enhanced rather than adversely affected.

Mercury. As one of the most positive planets in Barbara's horoscope and the ruler of Gemini, Mercury represents the affairs of the second house (finances and other material possessions) and the fifth house (creativity, romantic liaisons and children). Since there are no planets posited in the second house, its affairs will be judged primarily by Mercury's position in the horoscope. Because Mercury, an individual benefic, is placed in the auspicious ninth house, her financial situation will always be favourable. In addition, due to Mercury's conjunction with the individually benefic Sun (the ruler of the fourth house), there will always be substantial gifts from the family. These two placements corroborate the theme of financial well-being that has already been touched upon. When a theme or pattern repeats itself throughout the horoscope, it is almost guaranteed that it will be a dominant factor in the person's life.

Although there are no planets occupying the second house, its affairs are modified by the full aspect from each of the planets situated in its complementary eighth house which further defines its qualities. Due to these aspects, the implications of the second house are much more complex than that of an 'empty' house. Since the second house represents both finances and material possessions, the aspects the house receives from both benefic and malefic planets in the eighth house indicates that there will be great financial transitions throughout Barbara's life. Even though the indications are mostly positive (and we have already seen that finances will not be among Barbara's biggest problems), these aspects work as a system of checks and balances. In this sense, she must always work hard to attain her material and non-material goals. It also implies that, in addition to the gifts that she may receive throughout her life, she must always maintain a certain amount of control — if not autonomy — over her own finances.

As the lord of the fifth Trikona house placed in the ninth house (another Trikona house), Mercury endows Barbara's personality, her husband and their children with extremely favourable circumstances bordering on what some people refer to as 'luck'. To me, however, this simply means knowing how and when to surround oneself with the appropriate circumstances, and to recognize advantages and seize them.

Rahu and Kethu. To continue, Rahu's placement in the fifth house reiterates Barbara's stomach troubles and indicates that there will be difficulties either conceiving children or deciding on the appropriate time to have them. Another definition that applies to Barbara is her lack of confidence in her own unique abilities. Kethu's placement in the eleventh house, however, does not have a malefic influence but, instead, fosters an enabling situation in which Barbara can fulfil her goals.

The Moon. The waxing Moon, naturally benefic, is the ruler of the third Upachaya house and contributes to its categorization as an individually malefic planet. As the ruler of Cancer in the third house, the Moon describes her imaginative mind and ability to reflect upon what others have to say. Due to the nature of the Moon, however, Barbara is often insecure about the level of her intelligence and her aptitude for communicating ideas on a professional basis. The Moon also symbolizes her siblings and the emotional, familial bonds that tie them together.

The Moon is well-placed in the tenth house for several reasons:

1. As a natural benefic, the Waxing Moon enhances any house it occupies.
2. As an individual malefic, the Moon enhances the tenth house, which is considered, in this instance, to be an Upachaya House.
3. The Moon is a friend of Saturn, lord of the tenth house.

Since the third house represents Barbara's siblings this position is favourable for her sisters, who seem to have great professional ambitions. It also implies that Barbara will frequently travel for her work and that the desire she has to communicate with others will aid her career and help her to forge ahead. Other definitions for the placement of the Moon in the tenth house focus on her popularity, her involvement with helping others and working in a public service profession. The Moon, a symbol for femininity, also gives her an extremely close relationship with her mother and with women in general. This is, in fact, quite true of Barbara who gets along very well with her mother, mother-in-law, sisters and her many female friends.

Sun. The Sun is the ruler of the fourth Kendra house and is individually benefic and naturally malefic. Because the individualistic Sun represents the mother, the upbringing and the family, Barbara's tendency as a child was to spend time alone and to feel alienated from the rest of the family. Due to the Sun's placement in the ninth house, it also indicates that her mother is fortunate, a good teacher and, perhaps, a writer. The Sun's natural malevolence gives Barbara difficulty communicating with the father but since it rules the fourth house he was responsible for much of the comforts she had when she was growing up. The Sun conjunct Mercury, the ruler of the second house, shows that the mother is very responsible for

Barbara's attitude towards not only material security but the general way in which she has set up the structure of her life.

The preceding descriptions merely touch upon the Rasi Chakras of Annemarie and Barbara using the principles of interpretation mentioned in this section (Chapters 4–7). Like the multi-faceted parts of our personalities, the aspects of the Rasi Chakra are too numerous to mention in one horoscope reading. At each subsequent astrological consultation, another aspect of the personality unfolds in accordance with the timing of events in the person's life. Some characteristics do not manifest until much later and some traits can never be utilized. The method an astrologer uses to forecast the timing of events in a person's life is covered in the following section.

PART III
FORECASTING

8

HINDU PREDICTIVE ASTROLOGY: VIMSHODDHARI DASA SYSTEM

In addition to the Rasi Chakra, the Moon Chart and the Navamsa Chart, an equally important aspect of horoscope interpretation is the Hindu Dasa System, a method of prediction unique to India. At the heart of this system lie the 27 nakshatras — fixed star clusters — comprising the section of space known as the zodiacal belt (the 12 signs of the zodiac). Beginning at 0° of the actual constellation Aries, each of the 27 asterisms spans 13° 20' of the zodiac and corresponds to one of the nine planets (see Table 8.1).

The nakshatras are a fundamental feature of any lunar-based astrological system* and are known in Chinese astrology by the term 'lunar mansions'. The Moon, the most important heavenly body in Indian astrology and mythology, was regarded by most ancient cultures — including Sumer, Babylonia and China — as a god, not as a goddess. Because the Moon's cycle of 27–28 days correlates with the number of days in a woman's menstrual cycle, the Moon has mistakenly been considered by modern followers of ancient myth to be a feminine deity. There were, indeed, moon goddesses but they were either daughters of the Moon god — (the Semitic godesses Ishtar and the Sumerian Inanna) — or lovers and worshippers of the Moon — (the Greek Artemis and the Roman Diana). They were, however, never manifestations of the Moon itself which was considered to be male.

---

* Hindu astrology is a *soli-lunar system.* The Moon Chart and the Dasa system are based on the Moon while the construction of the Rasi Chakra is based on the Sun.

Table 8.1 Nakshatras According to Vimshoddhari Dasa

Nakshatras	Zodiacal position	Ruling planets	Planetary periods (in years)
1. Aswini	0♈ - 13♈20	Kethu	7
2. Bharani	13♈20 - 26♈40	Venus	20
3. Krittika	26♈40 - 10♉	Sun	6
4. Rohini	10♉ - 23♉20	Moon	10
5. Mrigsira	23♉20 - 6♊40	Mars	7
6. Ardra	6♊40 - 20♊	Rahu	18
7. Punarvasu	20♊ - 3♋20	Jupiter	16
8. Pushya	3♋20 - 16♋40	Saturn	19
9. Aslesha	16♋40 - 0♌	Mercury	17
10. Magha	0♌ - 13♌20	Kethu	7
11. Purvaphalguni	3♌20 - 26♌40	Venus	20
12. Uttraphalguni	26♌40 - 10♍	Sun	6
13. Hasta	10♍ - 23♍20	Moon	10
14. Chitra	23♍20 - 6♎40	Mars	7
15. Svati	6♎40 - 20♎	Rahu	18
16. Vishakha	20♎ - 3♏20	Jupiter	16
17. Anuradha	3♏20 - 16♏40	Saturn	19
18. Jyeshtha	16♏40 - 0♐	Mercury	17
19. Mula	0♐ - 13♐20	Kethu	7
20. Purvashadya	13♐20 - 26♐40	Venus	20
21. Uttrashadya	26♐40 - 10♑	Sun	6
22. Shravana	10♑ - 23♑20	Moon	10
23. Dhanishtha	23♑20 - 6♒40	Mars	7
24. Shatbisha	6♒40 - 20♒	Rahu	18
25. Purvaphadrapada	20♒ - 3♓20	Jupiter	16
26. Uttraphadrapada	3♓20 - 16♓40	Saturn	19
27. Revati	16♓40 - 0♈	Mercury	17

In Hindu mythology the Moon is very clearly a god and, according to legend, the 27 nakshatras — or lunar mansions — are his houses and resting places. According to still other stories, the Moon's 27 domiciles are personified as his amorous satellites (or wives) one for each day of the Moon's cycle. In this regard, several nakshatras have qualities very similar to the zodiacal signs they occupy or to one of the fixed stars contained within that particular sign. A perfect example is Rohini, the fourth constellation, known throughout Indian mythology as the Moon's favourite and most jealous wife.[1] Literally meaning 'red cow', Rohini spans 13^1/$_3$° of Taurus the Bull, the most possessive and most sensual sign of the zodiac. It's no wonder that the Moon's place of exaltation (where he feels most exhilarated) is Taurus, the very sign he loves so much.

Reflecting on my days as a student of Jyotish, I recall that my very first homework assignment was to memorize the names of the 27 nakshatras. Since they had to be recited in Sanskrit along with their foreign pronunciations (formed with different parts of the mouth than ours), it was not an easy task. When I finally learned their names in correct sequential order, I proudly recounted them to my teacher. At that moment, he knew I was a serious student of Hindu astrology.

The primary means of predicting cycles in Hindu astrology is the Vimshoddhari Dasa System — a system by which one's life is divided into nine planetary periods called Dasas. 'Dasa', Sanskrit for 'age', is an abbreviated form of the word, 'Mahadasa', whose prefix 'Maha' means 'great', as in Maha-rajah (great king) or Maha-rani (great queen). Vimshoddhari Dasa is comprised of 120 years, man's ultimate lifespan according to Hindu lore.* These 120 years are then divided into nine Dasas of unequal duration which, when listed sequentially, correspond to different Nakshatras (see Table 8.1). There is no apparent logic or mathematical reasoning behind the unequal division of Vimshoddhari Dasa. Many attempts, all unsuccessful, have been made by various astrologers to determine either numerically or philosophically why these periods are divided in this manner. In fact, one mathematician tried to prove this system's accuracy by basing it on Bode's Law but found this, too, provided no rationale.[2]

Of the numerous Dasa systems handed down by the Hindu sages, the three most commonly used are Ashtottari Dasa, Kalachakra Dasa, and Vimshoddhari Dasa — the system utilized throughout this book. The differences between the three systems lie in the number of years comprising the entire span of Mahadasas and the manner in which the individual planetary periods of each Dasa have been divided. Vimshoddhari Dasa, however, is by far the system of choice for most contemporary Hindu astrologers who have reaffirmed its accuracy mainly through trial and

* There is a common Yiddish expression, 'zolst leben biz a hindit'n tzwantzik yurn', translated as 'You should be so lucky and live to be 120 years'.

error. K.S. Krishnamurti, the late astrologer (whose books have guided much of my study), also maintains that Vimshoddhari Dasa is the most straightforward and accurate.

What follows is an illustration of the steps involved in calculating an individual's planetary periods according to Vimshoddhari Dasa. Annemarie's chart is the first example used to elucidate these steps. She was born 26 December 1952 at 5:50 a.m., Greenwich Mean Time. Her Sayana Moon position is 5 Taurus 5.

Step 1. Finding the Nakshatra of the Natal Moon
The initial step for calculating Vimshoddhari Dasa is to convert the Moon's Tropical (Sayana) position into its Sidereal (Nirayana) position. Although this computation was previously outlined in Chapter 2, let's review the process. Referring to Table 2.1 (pp. 52–3) the Ayanamsa for 1953 was 23° 6'. Subtracting this Ayanamsa from the Moon's Sayana position of 5 Taurus 5, the Moon's Nirayana position turns out to be 11 Aries 59.

The next step is to identify which Nakshatra the natal Moon occupied at the exact moment of birth. Table 8.1 indicates that, in addition to falling in the zodiacal sign of Aries, the Moon also falls in the first constellation of Aswini which runs from 0 to 13 Aries 20. This first Nakshatra corresponds to Kethu's Mahadasa which lasts seven years.

Step 2. Where the Birth Falls Within the Mahadasa
Now that we know that Annemarie was born in Kethu Mahadasa we must find out how many years, months and days of that Dasa preceded her birth and how much of it still remains. At the moment of birth the Moon was 11 Aries 59 and, according to Table 8.1, only 1°21' remained in Kethu's Dasa before the onset of the next constellation of Bharani and entrance into Venus Mahadasa. The following formula is used to see how many years of Kethu remain:

The number of years, months and days remaining in the Mahadasa will be proportionately equivalent to the difference between the exact degree the Moon occupies and the last degree of the constellation it is in.

Using minutes as the common denominator, the

following equations illustrate the above formula. Remember that each Nakshatra spans 13°20' (or 800') and in the equation for each horoscope that number remains constant.

$$\frac{\text{Difference in minutes between Moon degree and last degree of Nakshatra} \times \text{Years of Mahadasa}}{800' \text{ (total minutes in Nakshatra)}}$$

Let us now apply this formula to Annemarie's chart.

$$\frac{81}{800} \times 7 = 0.7$$

Eighty minutes are divided by 800 and then multiplied by 7 years, which gives us a total of 0.7. This decimal is a percentage of 365 1/4, the number of days in a year. Translating this into months and days we arrive at approximately 8 1/2 months or 8 months 15 days. From the time Annemarie was born on 26 December 1952, there were 8 months 15 days remaining in Kethu Dasa. Kethu Mahadasa, the first major period of Annemarie's life, lasted from the date of her birth, 26 December 1952 until 10 September 1953.

Step 3. Listing the Mahadasas to Follow

Table 8.2 Annemarie's Dasa Period: 26 December 1952 – 26 December 2072

	26 December 1952	
Kethu	+ 8 months, 15 days	= 26 December 1952– 10 September 1953
Venus	+ 20 Years	= 10 September 1953–10 September 1973
Sun	+ 6 Years	= 10 September 1973–10 September 1979
Moon	+ 10 Years	= 10 September 1973–10 September 1989
Mars	+ 7 Years	= 10 September 1989–10 September 1996
Rahu	+ 18 Years	= 10 September 1996–10 September 2014
Jupiter	+ 16 Years	= 10 September 2014–10 September 2030
Saturn	+ 19 Years	= 10 September 2030–10 September 2049
Mercury	+ 17 Years	= 10 September 2049–10 September 2066
Balance of Kethu	+ 6 years, 3 months, 15 days	= 10 September 2066–25 December 2072

This then adds up to the 120 years of Vimshoddhari Dasa.

Table 8.2 illustrates the sequence of Mahadasas in Annemarie's life. Going full circle, Vimshoddhari Dasa always begins and ends with the same planetary period (in this case it is Kethu) and will always total 120 years. Venus follows Kethu, adding another 20 years to the birth date. The Sun then follows Venus adding six more years, the Moon adds 10 more years, etc.

Vimshoddhari Dasa can be calculated using anyone's chart if the position of the Moon at birth is known. If the Moon's Nirayana position is already known, refer directly to the nakshatra table. If not, look up the Ayanamsa for the year of birth, and convert the Sayana position of the Moon into its Nirayana position. Then simply follow the mathematical formula in Step 2 to determine the major periods of a person's life. Although many of us use astrological software which can calculate Vimshoddhari Dasa within seconds, I feel it is important to review all the steps in order to understand the basis of the Dasa System.*

Another example is Barbara who was born on 30 January 1960 at 16:59 Greenwich Mean Time. Her Sayana Moon position is 12 Pisces 14.

Step 1. Finding the Nakshatra of the Natal Moon

As usual, convert the Moon's Sayana position into its equivalent Nirayana position. Table 2.1 indicates that in 1960 the Ayanamsa was 23°12'. Subtracting those numbers from Barbara's Sayana Moon position of 12 Pisces 14, as we did in Chapter 2, we arrive at 19 Aquarius 2. It is very clear from the nakshatra table that Barbara's Moon is situated in the 24th constellation, Shatbisha, which extends from 6.66–20° Aquarius and corresponds to Rahu Mahadasa lasting for 18 years.

---

* There are many available software packages and astrological services (see Appendix). Because of the absolute exactness the computer will give for the starting date of a planetary period, there may be a discrepancy of 2–3 days between this figure and the results obtained by manual calculations. For example, when Annemarie's chart is done by computer, her Dasa periods begin on 8 September rather than on 10 September.

Another discrepancy is due to the different Ayanamsas used. For example, the Ayanamsa of Krishnamurti (used in this book) and the Ayanamsa of Lahiri vary by 5 minutes and this difference leads to a discrepancy of up to one month for the start of a planetary period.

Step 2. Where the Birth Falls Within the Mahadasa

Although we know that Barbara was born in Rahu Mahadasa, we must learn exactly how many years, months and days of that Dasa have passed prior to her birth. According to Table 8.1, the constellation of Purva Phadrapada commences at 20° of Aquarius. With Barbara's Moon being positioned at 19 Aquarius 2, there are only 58' remaining in Shatbisha and Rahu Mahadasa. (In this case, because there is so little time remaining in the Mahadasa of her birth, it is not necessary to calculate *pre-natal time*.) In order to determine when Jupiter's Mahadasa will commence, the same formula is applied to Barbara's chart:

$$\frac{\text{Difference in minutes between Moon degree and last degree of Nakshatra} \times \text{Years of Mahadasa}}{800' \text{ (total minutes in Nakshatra)}}$$

$$\frac{58}{800} \times 18 = 1.3$$

Applying the above equation, we arrive at 1.3 years or exactly 1 year, 3 months, 20 days. In other words, the first major period of life, Rahu Mahadasa, lasts from 30 January 1960, the day of birth, until 20 May 1961 when Jupiter's Mahadasa begins.

Step 3. Listing the Mahadasas to Follow

We are now ready to list the Mahadasas which follow, beginning and ending with Rahu Mahadasa, bringing Vimshoddhari Dasa full circle. This, too, totals 120 years. The following table of Barbara's Dasa Period is based on the figures from Table 8.1.

Table 8.3. Barbara's Dasa Period: 30 January 1960 –
30 January 2080

	30 January 1960	
Rahu	+ 1 year 3 months,	
	20 days	= 20 May 1961
Jupiter	+ 16 years	= 20 May 1961–20 May 1977
Saturn	+ 19 years	= 20 May 1977–20 May 1996
Mercury	+ 17 years	= 20 May 1996–20 May 2013
Kethu	+ 7 years	= 20 May 2013–20 May 2020
Venus	+ 20 years	= 20 May 2020–20 May 2040
Sun	+ 6 years	= 20 May 2040–20 May 2046
Moon	+ 10 years	= 20 May 2046–20 May 2056
Mars	+ 7 years	= 20 May 2056–20 May 2063
Balance	+ 16 years, 8 months,	
of Rahu	10 days	= 30 May 2063–30 January 2080

Table 8.3 shows how Barbara's life is divided according to Vimshoddhari Dasa if she should live to be 120 years old.

It is clear from the previous two examples and from Table 8.1 that the number of years in each planetary period varies from 6 to 20 years. Since certain planetary periods last for quite a while, each Dasa is further divided into planetary sub-periods known as Bhukti Dasas for a more definitive and focused interpretation. Within the framework of each Mahadasa, there are nine Bhukties listed in the same sequential manner as the Mahadasas. Calculating the Bhukti Dasas is more intricate than calculating the Mahadasas as there are nine sub-periods within each of the nine major periods — each utilizing a different numerical formula. Table 8.4, therefore, consists of nine Tables. Each Mahadasa has its own set of figures indicating the manner in which the Bhukti Dasas are divided within the main period.

Referring to Table 8.4, it is clear that each major period begins with the Bhukti ruled by the same planet as the current Mahadasa. For instance, in the breakdown of Annemarie's present Moon Mahadasa, the initial Bhukti belongs to the Moon as well (see Table 8.5). The planets then follow in the same sequence as listed in Table 8.1. Mars Bhukti follows, then Rahu Bhukti, then Jupiter Bhukti, etc., all within the Moon's Mahadasa until the Moon's period ends with Sun Bhukti. Though it may not be

Table 8.4. Bhukti Dasas*

Dasa lord	Kethu mo.	Kethu d.	Venus mo.	Venus d.	Sun mo.	Sun d.	Moon mo.	Moon d.	Mars mo.	Mars d.	Rahu mo.	Rahu d.	Jupiter mo.	Jupiter d.	Saturn mo.	Saturn d.	Mercury mo.	Mercury d.
Kethu sub-period	4	27	40	0	3	18	10	0	4	27	32	12	25	18	36	3	28	27
Venus sub-period	14	0	12	0	6	0	7	0	12	18	28	24	30	12	32	9	11	27
Sun sub-period	4	6	20	0	4	6	18	0	11	6	34	6	27	6	13	9	34	0
Moon sub-period	7	0	14	0	10	24	16	0	13	9	30	18	11	6	38	0	10	6
Mars sub-period	4	27	36	0	9	18	19	0	11	27	12	18	32	0	11	12	17	0
Rahu sub-period	12	18	32	0	11	12	17	0	4	27	36	0	9	18	19	0	11	27
Jupiter sub-period	11	6	38	0	10	6	7	0	14	0	10	24	16	0	13	9	30	18
Saturn sub-period	13	9	34	0	4	6	20	0	4	6	18	0	11	6	34	6	27	6
Mercury sub-period	11	27	14	0	12	0	6	0	7	0	12	18	28	24	30	12	32	9
Total years of Dasa	7 yrs		20 yrs		6 yrs		10 yrs		7 yrs		18 yrs		16 yrs		19 yrs		17 yrs	

* Adapted from data provided in Casting the Horoscope, p. 92

obvious, there *is* a very definite formula used to arrive at the figures in Table 8.4. Even if most of us will be using a computer, it is still helpful to understand how Bhukties are calculated.

The major periods are proportionately divided into Bhukties the same way the 120 years of Vimshoddhari Dasa are divided into the nine Mahadasas. Using the Moon's Mahadasa, for example, the Mars Bhukti of Moon's Mahadasa is 7/120 multiplied by the 10 years of Moon's Dasa since there are 7 years in Mars Mahadasa, 120 years in the entire Vimshoddhari Dasa and 10 years in Moon's Mahadasa. Rahu is 18/120 multiplied by 10, Jupiter is 16/120 multiplied by 10, etc. If we actually took the time to calculate, the result would be the same as those shown in Table 8.4. The duration of Saturn's period will always be longest and the Sun's period will always be shortest — whether it is the Mahadasa, Bhukti Dasa or the sub-sub-period, the Antara Dasa.

Using the charts of Barbara and Annemarie, I have listed the Bhukti Dasas of their present Mahadasas beginning with Annemarie's. Before her present Mahadasa is divided into Bhukties we must first determine what proportion of the sub-period has passed as we did when we calculated the proportion of the Mahadasa which had passed at birth. Keeping in mind that Annemarie was born during Kethu's Mahadasa, refer to Table 8.4 to see in which Bhukti of Kethu's Mahadasa her birth falls. When she was born, a great portion of Kethu Dasa had passed, leaving 8 months 15 days before moving into Venus Mahadasa on 10 September 1953. It is apparent from Table 8.4 that Mercury Bhukti, the final Bhukti in Kethu's Dasa, lasts 11 months 27 days and was, therefore, in progress at the moment of birth.

The next complete Mahadasa is Venus and, according to Table 8.4, the Bhukti breakdown is listed in Table 8.5 as follows:

Table 8.5 Venus Mahadasa 10 September 1953 –
10 September 1973

Bhukties (taken directly from Table 8.4)

Venus	10 September 1953–10 January 1957	(+40 months)
Sun	10 January 1957–10 January 1958	(+12 months)
Moon	10 January 1958–10 September 1959	(+20 months)
Mars	10 September 1959–10 November 1960	(+14 months)
Rahu	10 November 1960–10 November 1963	(+36 months)
Jupiter	10 November 1963–10 July 1966	(+32 months)
Saturn	10 July 1966–10 September 1969	(+38 months)
Mercury	10 September 1969–10 July 1972	(+34 months)
Kethu	10 July 1972–10 September 1973	(+14 months)

The Sun's Mahadasa, which is next, is divided as follows:

Table 8.6 Sun Mahadasa 10 September 1973 – 10 September 1979

Bhukties (taken directly from Table 8.4)

Sun	10 September 1973–28 December 1973	(+3 months 18 days)
Moon	28 December 1973–28 June 1974	(+6 months)
Mars	28 June 1974–3 November 1974	(+4 months 6 days)
Rahu	3 November 1974–27 September 1975	(+10 months 24 days)
Jupiter	27 September 1975–15 July 1976	(+9 months 18 days)
Saturn	15 July 1976–27 June 1977	(+11 months 12 days)
Mercury	27 June 1977–3 May 1978	(+10 months 6 days)
Kethu	3 May 1978–9 September 1978	(+4 months 6 days)
Venus	9 September 1978–9 September 1979	(+12 months)

At the time of the writing of this book, Annemarie is in Moon Mahadasa which runs from 10 September 1979 until 10 September 1989. According to Table 8.4, the Bhukties are as follows:

Table 8.7 Moon Mahadasa 10 September 1979 –
10 September 1989

Bhukties (taken directly from Table 8.4)

Moon	10 September 1979–10 July 1980	(+10 months)
Mars	10 July 1980–10 February 1981	(+7 months)
Rahu	10 February 1981–10 August 1982	(+18 months)
Jupiter	10 August 1982–10 December 1983	(+16 months)
Saturn	10 December 1983–10 July 1985	(+19 months)
Mercury	10 July 1985–10 December 1986	(+17 months)
Kethu	10 December 1986–10 July 1987	(+7 months)
Venus	10 July 1987–10 March 1989	(+20 months)
Sun	10 March 1989–10 September 1989	(+6 months)

Mars Mahadasa, the Dasa Annemarie is currently in (at the time of publication) is listed as follows:

Table 8.8 Mars Mahadasa 11 September 1989 – 11 September 1996

Bhukties (taken directly from Table 8.4)

Mars	11 September 1989–7 February 1990	(+4 months 27 days)
Rahu	7 February 1990–25 February 1991	(+12 months 18 days)
Jupiter	25 February 1991–31 January 1992	(+11 months 6 days)
Saturn	31 January 1992–10 March 1993	(+13 months 9 days)
Mercury	10 March 1993–9 March 1994	(+11 months 27 days)
Kethu	9 March 1994–5 August 1994	(+4 months 27 days)
Venus	5 August 1994–5 October 1995	(+14 months)
Sun	5 October 1995–11 February 1996	(+4 months 6 days)
Moon	11 February 1996–11 September 1996	(+7 months)

Barbara's chart provides still another example. As we did with Annemarie's chart, we must first study her birth Mahadasa to see what portion has passed in order to divide the balance of the Mahadasa into Bhukties. Rahu Mahadasa, in which Barbara was born, had 1 year, 3 months, 20 days to run before Jupiter's Mahadasa began on 20 May 1961 and must be subdivided. In accordance with Table 8.4, her birth can be placed during Moon Bhukti with Mars Bhukti to follow. Subtracting the duration of Mars Bhukti (1 year 18 days) from the total remaining portion of Rahu Mahadasa (1 year 3 months 20 days) produces the difference of 3 months 2 days, the period of time left in Rahu Mahadasa Moon Bhukti and is shown below:

Rahu Mahadasa Moon Bhukti   30 January 1960–2 May 1960
Rahu Mahadasa Mars Bhukti   2 May 1960–20 May 1961

Table 8.9 Jupiter Mahadasa 20 May 1961–20 May 1977

Bhukties (taken directly from Table 8.4)

Jupiter	20 May 1961–7 July 1963	(+25 months 18 days)
Saturn	7 July 1963–19 January 1966	(+30 months 12 days)
Mercury	19 January 1966–25 April 1968	(+27 months 6 days)
Kethu	25 April 1968–1 May 1969	(+11 months 6 days)
Venus	1 May 1969–1 January 1972	(+32 months)
Sun	1 January 1972–19 October 1972	(+9 months 18 days)
Moon	20 September 1972–20 January 1974	(+16 months)
Mars	20 January 1974–27 December 1974	(+11 months 6 days)
Rahu	27 December 1974–18 May 1977	(+28 months 24 days)

Let's go one step further and divide the next two Dasas — Jupiter and Saturn — into Bhukti Dasas.

Table 8.10 displays Saturn's Mahadasa which started in her 17th year on 18 May 1977 and continues until 18 May 1996.

Table 8.10 Saturn Mahadasa 18 May 1977–18 May 1996

Bhukties (Taken directly from Table 8.4)

Saturn	18 May 1977–21 May 1980	(+36 months 3 days)
Mercury	21 May 1980–30 January 1983	(+32 months 9 days)
Kethu	30 January 1983–10 March 1984	(+13 months 9 days)
Venus	10 March 1984–10 May 1987	(+38 months)
Sun	10 May 1987–22 April 1988	(+11 months 12 days)
Moon	22 April 1988–22 November 1989	(+19 months)
Mars	22 November 1989–31 December 1990	(+13 months 9 days)
Rahu	31 December 1990–6 November 1993	(+34 months 6 days)
Jupiter	6 November 1993–18 May 1996	(+30 months 12 days)

If the astrologer wishes to divide each Bhukti Dasa into nine planetary periods, he would arrive at what is known as Antara Dasas — sub-sub-periods. These time periods are used:

1. to uncover trends or events in the Antara Dasa that may have gone unnoticed in a longer Bhukti period,
2. to emphasize trends which are repeated in both Bhukti and Antara Dasa and,
3. to supply additional information by introducing another planet's symbolic meaning to complete the picture.

For the purposes of this book, however, we will only be concerned with the Mahadasa and Bhukti Dasa. For those who wish to use Antara Dasas, Table 8.11 lists the sub-sub-periods within each Bhukti Dasa.

The Hindu Dasa System is used to forecast planetary cycles the same way that Western astrologers use secondary and solar arc progressions.* Common to both progressions and the Dasa system is the fact that they are both defined

* Progressions are calculated much differently from the Dasa Periods. Secondary Progressions and Solar Arc Progressions represent the symbolic movement of the planets by counting either one day for one year from the birth date or approximately one degree for one year from the birth date.

by the interaction of two planets and by what those two planets symbolically represent. The major difference between these two systems is the fact that we are not always under the influence of a major planetary configuration by progression. By adhering to the Dasa System, however, we are under the influence of a planetary period at all times.

In addition to employing the Dasa System, Hindu astrologers also use transiting planets and the Moon's nakshatra position for prognostication of trends and cycles:

(A) Transits (as defined by Western astrology) are the aspects formed between a planet's present position and another planet in the birth chart. For example, if Venus is posited at 26° of Sagittarius in the natal chart, then Saturn — when located at the very same degree — is said to be transiting natal Venus. Saturn will continue to transit Venus as long as it is within a one degree orb (between 25 and 27° of Sagittarius). In Hindu astrology, however, Saturn is considered to be transiting natal Venus the entire 2½ years it passes through the sign and house of Sagittarius. Within the system of Indian transits, it is the zodiacal sign through which the planet passes that is important and not its degree.

(B) Because it takes only one month for the Moon to travel through the entire zodiac, Eastern astrologers use its transits for short-term prediction, i.e. the best time to start a project, buy a house, sign a legal document or even test-drive a car. The exact time the Moon is placed in either an auspicious or inauspicious nakshatra (classifications that are not mentioned in this book) will determine if the astrologer gives the red or green light. Western astrologers work with the zodiacal sign of the transiting Moon for short-term prediction and transits and progressions of the other planets for long-term prediction; Indian astrologers use the Moon's nakshatra position for short-term and the Hindu Dasa System for long-term predictions.

This chapter was devoted to Vimshoddhari Dasa — the major system used for predicting trends and cycles. In the following chapter I will use the charts of Annemarie and Barbara to illustrate how the Dasa System is used to interpret these trends and cycles.

Table 8.10 Antara Dasas (adapted from data provided in Hindu Dasa System, *pp. 205–18)*

Sun Bhukti

1. Sun Antara

	M	D
Sun	0	5
Moon	0	9
Mars	0	6
Rahu	0	16
Jupiter	0	14
Saturn	0	17
Mercury	0	15
Kethu	0	6
Venus	0	18
Total	3	18

2. Moon Antara

	M	D
Moon	0	15
Mars	0	10
Rahu	0	27
Jupiter	0	24
Saturn	0	28
Mercury	0	25
Kethu	0	10
Venus	1	0
Sun	0	9
Total	6	0

3. Mars Antara

	M	D
Mars	0	17
Rahu	0	18
Jupiter	0	16
Saturn	0	9
Mercury	0	17
Kethu	0	7
Venus	0	21
Sun	0	6
Moon	0	10
Total	4	6

4. Rahu Antara

	M	D
Rahu	1	18
Jupiter	1	13
Saturn	1	21
Mercury	1	15
Kethu	0	18
Venus	1	24
Sun	0	16
Moon	0	27
Mars	0	18
Total	10	24

5. Jupiter Antara

	M	D
Jupiter	1	8
Saturn	1	15
Mercury	1	10
Kethu	0	16
Venus	1	18
Sun	0	14
Moon	0	24
Mars	0	16
Rahu	1	13
Total	9	18

6. Saturn Antara

	M	D
Saturn	1	24
Mercury	1	18
Kethu	0	19
Venus	1	27
Sun	0	17
Moon	0	28
Mars	0	19
Rahu	1	21
Jupiter	1	15
Total	11	12

7. Mercury Antara

	M	D
Mercury	1	13
Kethu	0	17
Venus	1	21
Sun	0	15
Moon	0	25
Mars	0	17
Rahu	1	15
Jupiter	1	10
Saturn	1	18
Total	10	6

8. Kethu Antara

	M	D
Kethu	0	7
Venus	0	21
Sun	2	6
Moon	0	10
Mars	0	7
Rahu	0	18
Jupiter	0	16
Saturn	0	19
Mercury	0	17
Total	4	6

9. Venus Antara

	M	D
Venus	2	0
Sun	0	18
Moon	1	0
Mars	0	21
Rahu	1	24
Jupiter	1	18
Saturn	1	27
Mercury	1	21
Kethu	0	21
Total	12	0

Moon Bhukti

1. Moon Antara

	M	D
Moon	0	25
Mars	0	17
Rahu	1	15
Jupiter	1	10
Saturn	1	17
Mercury	1	12
Kethu	0	17
Venus	1	20
Sun	0	15
Total	10	0

2. Mars Antara

	M	D
Mars	0	12
Rahu	1	1
Jupiter	0	28
Saturn	1	3
Mercury	0	29
Kethu	0	12
Venus	1	5
Sun	0	10
Moon	0	17
Total	7	0

3. Rahu Antara

	M	D
Rahu	2	21
Jupiter	2	12
Saturn	2	25
Mercury	2	16
Kethu	1	1
Venus	3	0
Sun	0	27
Moon	1	15
Mars	1	1
Total	18	0

4. Jupiter Antara

	M	D
Jupiter	2	4
Saturn	2	16
Mercury	2	8
Kethu	0	28
Venus	2	20
Sun	0	24
Moon	1	10
Mars	0	28
Rahu	2	12
Total	16	0

5. Saturn Antara

	M	D
Saturn	3	0
Mercury	2	20
Kethu	1	3
Venus	3	5
Sun	0	28
Moon	1	17
Mars	1	3
Rahu	2	25
Jupiter	2	16
Total	19	0

6. Mercury Antara

	M	D
Mercury	2	12
Kethu	0	29
Venus	2	25
Sun	0	25
Moon	1	12
Mars	0	29
Rahu	2	16
Jupiter	2	8
Saturn	2	20
Total	17	0

7. Kethu Antara

	M	D
Kethu	0	12
Venus	1	5
Sun	0	10
Moon	0	17
Mars	0	12
Rahu	1	1
Jupiter	0	28
Saturn	1	3
Mercury	0	29
Total	7	0

8. Venus Antara

	M	D
Venus	3	10
Sun	1	0
Moon	1	20
Mars	1	5
Rahu	3	0
Jupiter	2	20
Saturn	3	5
Mercury	2	25
Kethu	1	5
Total	20	0

9. Sun Antara

	M	D
Sun	0	9
Moon	0	15
Mars	0	10
Rahu	0	27
Jupiter	0	24
Saturn	0	28
Mercury	0	25
Kethu	0	10
Venus	1	0
Total	6	0

Mars Bhukti

1. Mars Antara	M	D
Mars	0	8
Rahu	0	22
Jupiter	0	19
Saturn	0	23
Mercury	0	20
Kethu	0	8
Venus	0	24
Sun	0	7
Moon	0	12
Total	4	27

2. Rahu Antara	M	D
Rahu	1	26
Jupiter	1	20
Saturn	1	29
Mercury	1	23
Kethu	0	22
Venus	2	3
Sun	0	18
Moon	1	1
Mars	0	22
Total	12	18

3. Jupiter Antara	M	D
Jupiter	1	14
Saturn	1	23
Mercury	1	17
Kethu	0	19
Venus	2	26
Sun	0	16
Moon	0	28
Mars	0	19
Rahu	1	20
Total	11	6

4. Saturn Antara	M	D
Saturn	2	3
Mercury	1	26
Kethu	0	23
Venus	2	6
Sun	0	19
Moon	1	3
Mars	0	23
Rahu	1	29
Jupiter	1	23
Total	13	9

5. Mercury Antara	M	D
Mercury	1	20
Kethu	0	20
Venus	1	29
Sun	0	17
Moon	0	29
Mars	0	20
Rahu	1	23
Jupiter	1	17
Saturn	1	26
Total	11	27

6. Kethu Antara	M	D
Kethu	0	8
Venus	0	24
Sun	0	7
Moon	0	12
Mars	0	8
Rahu	0	22
Jupiter	0	19
Saturn	0	23
Mercury	0	20
Total	4	27

7. Venus Antara	M	D
Venus	2	10
Sun	0	21
Moon	1	5
Mars	0	24
Rahu	2	3
Jupiter	1	26
Saturn	2	6
Mercury	1	29
Kethu	0	24
Total	14	0

8. Sun Antara	M	D
Sun	6	6
Moon	0	10
Mars	0	7
Rahu	0	18
Saturn	0	19
Saturn	0	19
Mercury	0	17
Kethu	0	7
Venus	0	21
Total	4	6

9. Moon Antara	M	D
Moon	0	17
Mars	0	12
Rahu	1	1
Jupiter	0	28
Saturn	1	3
Mercury	0	29
Kethu	0	12
Venus	1	5
Sun	0	10
Total	7	0

Rahu Bhukti

1. Rahu Antara

	M	D
Rahu	4	25
Jupiter	4	9
Saturn	5	3
Mercury	4	17
Kethu	1	26
Venus	5	12
Sun	1	18
Moon	2	21
Mars	1	26
Total	32	12

2. Jupiter Antara

	M	D
Jupiter	3	25
Saturn	4	16
Mercury	4	2
Kethu	1	20
Venus	2	24
Sun	1	13
Moon	2	12
Mars	1	20
Rahu	4	9
Total	28	24

3. Saturn Antara

	M	D
Saturn	5	12
Mercury	4	25
Kethu	1	29
Venus	5	21
Sun	1	21
Moon	2	25
Mars	1	29
Rahu	5	3
Jupiter	4	16
Total	34	6

4. Mercury Antara

	M	D
Mercury	4	10
Kethu	1	23
Venus	5	3
Sun	1	15
Moon	2	16
Mars	1	23
Rahu	4	17
Jupiter	4	2
Saturn	4	25
Total	30	18

5. Kethu Antara

	M	D
Kethu	0	22
Venus	0	3
Sun	0	18
Moon	1	1
Mars	0	22
Rahu	1	26
Jupiter	1	20
Saturn	1	29
Mercury	1	23
Total	12	18

6. Venus Antara

	M	D
Venus	6	0
Sun	1	24
Moon	3	0
Mars	2	3
Rahu	5	12
Jupiter	4	24
Saturn	5	21
Mercury	5	3
Kethu	2	3
Total	26	0

7. Sun Antara

	M	D
Sun	0	16
Moon	0	27
Mars	0	18
Rahu	1	18
Jupiter	1	13
Saturn	1	21
Mercury	1	15
Kethu	0	18
Venus	1	24
Total	10	24

8. Moon Antara

	M	D
Moon	1	15
Mars	1	1
Rahu	2	21
Jupiter	2	12
Saturn	2	25
Mercury	2	16
Kethu	1	1
Venus	3	0
Sun	0	27
Total	18	0

9. Mars Antara

	M	D
Mars	0	22
Rahu	1	26
Jupiter	1	20
Saturn	1	29
Mercury	1	23
Kethu	0	22
Venus	2	3
Sun	0	18
Moon	1	1
Total	12	18

Jupiter Bhukti

1. Jupiter Antara	M	D
Jupiter	8	12
Saturn	4	1
Mercury	3	18
Kethu	1	14
Venus	4	8
Sun	1	8
Moon	2	4
Mars	1	14
Rahu	3	25
Total	25	18

2. Saturn Antara	M	D
Saturn	4	24
Mercury	4	9
Kethu	1	23
Venus	5	2
Sun	1	15
Moon	2	16
Mars	1	23
Rahu	4	16
Jupiter	4	1
Total	30	12

3. Mercury Antara	M	D
Mercury	3	25
Kethu	1	17
Venus	4	16
Sun	1	10
Moon`	2	8
Mars	1	17
Rahu	4	2
Jupiter	3	18
Saturn	4	9
Total	27	6

4. Kethu Antara	M	D
Kethu	0	19
Venus	1	26
Sun	0	16
Moon	0	28
Mars	0	10
Rahu	1	20
Jupiter	1	14
Saturn	1	23
Mercury	1	17
Total	11	6

5. Venus Antara	M	D
Venus	5	10
Sun	1	18
Moon	2	20
Mars	1	26
Rahu	4	24
Jupiter	4	8
Saturn	5	2
Mercury	4	16
Kethu	1	26
Total	32	0

6. Sun Antara	M	D
Sun	0	14
Moon	0	24
M ars	0	16
Rahu	1	13
Jupiter	1	8
Saturn	1	15
Mercury	1	10
Kethu	0	16
Venus`	1	18
Total	9	8

7. Moon Antara	M	D
Moon	1	10
Mars	0	28
Rahu	2	12
Jupiter	2	4
Saturn	2	16
Mercury	2	8
Kethu	0	28
Venus	2	20
Sun	0	24
Total	16	0

8. Mars Antara	M	D
Mars	0	19
Rahu	1	20
Jupiter	1	14
Saturn	1	23
Mercury	1	17
Kethu	0	19
Venus	1	26
Sun	0	16
Moon	0	28
Total	11	6

9. Rahu Antara	M	D
Rahu	4	9
Jupiter	3	25
Saturn	4	16
Mercury	4	2
Kethu	1	20
Venus	4	24
Sun	1	13
Moon	2	12
Mars	1	20
Total	28	24

Saturn Bhukti

1. Saturn Antara

	M	D
Saturn	5	21
Mercury	5	3
Kethu	2	3
Venus	6	0
Sun	1	24
Moon	3	0
Mars	2	3
Rahu	5	12
Jupiter	4	24
Total	36	3

2. Mercury Antara

	M	D
Mercury	4	17
Kethu	1	26
Venus	5	11
Sun	1	18
Moon	2	20
Mars	1	26
Rahu	4	25
Jupiter	4	9
Saturn	5	3
Total	32	9

3. Kethu Antara

	M	D
Kethu	0	23
Venus	2	6
Sun	0	19
Moon	1	3
Mars	0	23
Rahu	1	29
Jupiter	1	23
Saturn	2	3
Mercury	1	26
Total	13	9

4. Venus Antara

	M	D
Venus	6	10
Sun	1	27
Moon	3	5
Mars	2	6
Rahu	5	21
Jupiter	5	2
Saturn	6	0
Mercury	4	11
Kethu	2	6
Total	38	0

5. Sun Antara

	M	D
Sun	0	17
Moon	0	28
Mars	0	19
Rahu	1	21
Jupiter	1	15
Saturn	1	24
Mercury	1	18
Kethu	0	19
Venus	1	27
Total	11	12

6. Moon Antara

	M	D
Moon	1	17
Mars	1	3
Rahu	2	25
Jupiter	2	16
Saturn	3	0
Mercury	2	20
Kethu	1	3
Venus	3	5
Sun	0	28
Total	19	0

7. Mars Antara

	M	D
Mars	0	23
Rahu	1	29
Jupiter	1	23
Saturn	2	3
Mercury	1	26
Kethu	0	23
Venus	2	6
Sun	0	9
Moon	1	3
Total	13	9

8. Rahu Antara

	M	D
Rahu	5	3
Jupiter	4	16
Saturn	5	12
Mercury	4	25
Kethu	1	29
Venus	5	21
Sun	1	21
Moon	2	25
Mars	1	29
Total	34	6

9. Jupiter Antara

	M	D
Jupiter	4	1
Saturn	4	24
Mercury	4	9
Kethu	1	23
Venus	5	2
Sun	1	15
Moon	2	16
Mars	1	23
Rahu	4	16
Total	30	12

Mercury Bhukti

1. Mercury Antara	M	D
Mercury	4	2
Kethu	1	20
Venus	4	24
Sun	1	13
Moon	2	12
Mars	1	20
Rahu	4	10
Jupiter	3	25
Saturn	4	17
Total	28	27

2. Kethu Antara	M	D
Kethu	0	20
Venus	1	29
Sun	0	17
Moon	0	29
Mars	0	20
Rahu	1	23
Jupiter	1	17
Saturn	1	26
Mercury	1	20
Total	11	27

3. Venus Antara	M	D
Venus	5	20
Sun	1	21
Moon	2	25
Mars	1	29
Rahu	5	3
Jupiter	4	16
Saturn	5	11
Mercury	4	23
Kethu	1	29
Total	34	0

4. Sun Antara	M	D
Sun	0	15
Moon	0	25
Mars	0	17
Rahu	1	15
Jupiter	1	10
Saturn	1	18
Mercury	1	13
Kethu	0	17
Venus	1	21
Total	10	6

5. Moon Antara	M	D
Moon	1	12
Mars	0	29
Rahu	2	16
Jupiter	2	8
Saturn	2	20
Mercury	2	12
Kethu	0	29
Venus	2	25
Sun	0	25
Total	17	0

6. Mars Antara	M	D
Mars	0	20
Rahu	1	23
Jupiter	1	17
Saturn	1	26
Mercury	1	20
Kethu	0	20
Venus	1	29
Sun	0	17
Moon	0	29
Total	11	27

7. Rahu Antara	M	D
Rahu	4	17
Jupiter	4	2
Saturn	4	25
Mercury	4	10
Kethu	1	23
Venus	5	3
Sun	1	15
Moon	2	16
Mars	1	23
Total	30	18

8. Jupiter Antara	M	D
Jupiter	3	18
Saturn	4	9
Mercury	3	25
Kethu	1	17
Venus	4	16
Sun	1	10
Moon	2	8
Mars	1	17
Rahu	4	2
Total	27	6

9. Saturn Antara	M	D
Saturn	5	3
Mercury	4	17
Kethu	1	26
Venus	5	11
Sun	1	18
Moon	2	20
Mars	1	26
Rahu	4	25
Jupiter	4	9
Total	32	9

Kethu Bhukti

1. Kethu Antara

	M	D
Kethu	0	8
Venus	0	24
Sun	0	7
Moon	0	12
Mars	0	8
Rahu	0	22
Jupiter	0	19
Saturn	0	23
Mercury	0	20
Total	4	27

2. Venus Antara

	M	D
Venus	2	10
Sun	0	21
Moon	1	5
Mars	0	24
Rahu	2	3
Jupiter	1	26
Saturn	2	6
Mercury	1	29
Kethu	1	24
Total	14	0

3. Sun Antara

	M	D
Sun	0	6
Moon	0	10
Mars	0	7
Rahu	0	18
Jupiter	0	16
Saturn	0	19
Mercury	0	17
Kethu	0	7
Venus	0	21
Total	4	6

4. Moon Antara

	M	D
Moon	0	17
Mars	0	12
Rahu	1	1
Jupiter	0	28
Saturn	1	3
Mercury	0	29
Kethu	0	12
Venus	1	5
Sun	0	10
Total	7	0

5. Mars Antara

	M	D
Mars	0	8
Rahu	0	22
Jupiter	0	19
Saturn	0	23
Mercury	0	20
Kethu	0	8
Venus	0	24
Sun	0	7
Moon	0	12
Total	4	27

6. Rahu Antara

	M	D
Rahu	1	26
Jupiter	1	20
Saturn	1	29
Mercury	1	23
Kethu	0	22
Venus	2	3
Sun	0	18
Moon	1	1
Mars	0	22
Total	12	18

7. Jupiter Antara

	M	D
Jupiter	1	14
Saturn	1	23
Mercury	1	17
Kethu	0	19
Venus	1	26
Sun	0	16
Moon	0	28
Mars	0	19
Rahu	1	20
Total	11	6

8. Saturn Antara

	M	D
Saturn	2	3
Mercury	1	26
Kethu	0	23
Venus	2	6
Sun	0	19
Moon	1	3
Mars	0	23
Rahu	1	29
Jupiter	1	23
Total	13	9

9. Mercury Antara

	M	D
Mercury	1	20
Kethu	1	20
Venus	1	29
Sun	0	17
Moon	0	29
Mars	0	20
Rahu	1	23
Jupiter	1	17
Saturn	1	26
Total	11	27

Venus Bhukti

1. Venus Antara	M	D
Venus	6	20
Sun	2	0
Moon	3	10
Mars	2	10
Rahu	6	0
Jupiter	5	10
Saturn	6	10
Mercury	5	20
Kethu	2	10
Total	40	0

2. Sun Antara	M	D
Sun `	0	18
Moon	1	0
Mars	0	21
Rahu	1	24
Jupiter	1	18
Saturn	1	27
Mercury	1	21
Kethu	0	21
Venus	2	0
Total	12	0

3. Moon Antara	M	D
Moon	1	20
Mars	1	5
Rahu	3	0
Jupiter	2	20
Saturn	3	5
Mercury	2	25
Kethu	1	5
Venus	3	10
Sun	1	0
Total	20	0

4. Mars Antara	M	D
Mars	0	24
Rahu	2	3
Jupiter	1	26
Saturn	2	6
Mercury	1	29
Kethu	0	24
Venus	2	10
Sun	0	21
Moon	1	5
Total	14	0

5. Rahu Antara	M	D
Rahu	5	12
Jupiter	4	24
Saturn	5	21
Mercury	5	3
Kethu	2	3
Venus	6	0
Sun	1	24
Moon`	3	0
Mars	2	3
Total	36	0

6. Jupiter Antara	M	D
Jupiter	4	8
Saturn	5	2
Mercury	4	16
Kethu	1	26
Venus	5	10
Sun	1	18
Moon	2	20
Mars	1	26
Rahu	4	24
Total	32	0

7. Saturn Antara	M	D
Saturn	6	0
Mercury	5	11
Kethu	2	6
Venus	6	10
Sun	1	27
Moon	3	5
Mars	2	6
Rahu	5	21
Jupiter	5	2
Total	38	0

8. Mercury Antara	M	D
Mercury	4	24
Kethu	1	29
Venus	5	20
Sun	1	21
Moon	2	25
Marts	1	29
Rahu	5	3
Jupiter	4	16
Saturn	1	11
Total	34	0

9. Kethu Antara	M	D
Kethu	0	24
Venus	2	10
Sun	0	21
Moon	1	5
Mars	0	24
Rahu	2	3
Jupiter	1	26
Saturn	2	6
Mercury	1	29
Total	14	0

9

INTERPRETING THE DASAS AND BHUKTIES

Eastern and Western forecasting techniques (Hindu dasa system vs. transits and progressions) are as dissimilar in their methodologies as they are in their mathematical calculations. Rather than predict actual events, contemporary Western astrologers tend to describe future trends and behaviour patterns which occur and recur throughout life. They encourage their clients to make their own choices based on a thorough understanding of the self (i.e. horoscope) and an awareness of their planetary life cycles (transits and progressions).

The task of the Hindu astrologer, whose religion dictates an acceptance of fate and a belief in reincarnation, is to tell his* clients what life has in store for them and to advise them accordingly. Within the confines of Hinduism, an astrologer's clients do not have freedom of choice, and his recommendations will be based on the timing of events rather than on an understanding of their significance. This approach, of course, eliminates the Rasi Chakra as a means of self-knowledge or as a reflection of inner motivations — functions of the horoscope in the West.

In order to facilitate the accuracy of his lifetime predictions, the Hindu astrologer employs the Vimshoddhari Dasa System. Traditionally, his first task is to calculate whether his client will live to an early, middle or late age. Since it is not only impossible but unethical for a Western astrologer to predict death, I do not include this subject in my discussion of Dasa and Bhukti periods (or

---

* Due to the fact that among Hindus an astrologer is always a man, I have used the pronoun 'he' throughout this book. In the West, however, most astrologers tend to be women.

anywhere in this book, for that matter). There are, however, several chapters in many of the ancient astrological texts devoted to the determination of life expectancy which I advise using cautiously, if at all. Since these texts were written in an era when there was little medical knowledge, the application of principles regarding illness and death to Western, or even, Indian horoscopy will be false and misleading.

In analysing the Mahadasas and Bhukti Dasas of Annemarie and Barbara, I have included only those traditional interpretations which are either relevant or can be translated into modern terminology.

Mahadasa Rulers

The favoured method for assessing each Mahadasa is to evaluate the strength of its planetary ruler according to the complicated numerical ratings of Shad Bala (which was discussed in Chapter 6). The planets with the highest number of points represent the most beneficial Dasas and the planets with the lowest ratings represent the least favourable periods. For those who regard astrology fatalistically, the numerical rating system merits consideration since there is nothing to intuit or judge. In general, however, it is too archaic and too event-oriented for the Westerner to profit by.

Instead of determining whether the Dasa will bring either 'good' or 'bad' results, I advocate defining the quality of each Mahadasa by its planetary ruler's (a) general description, and (b) individual significance.

Mahadasas: General Issues

The following descriptions emphasize the issues which will be important during each Mahadasa (based on the general definitions of each planetary ruler; see Chapter 4).

Sun Mahadasa. During the Dasa of Sun there will be involvement with public life and the focus will be on the career, travel, education, acquisition of land and money.

The affairs of the house the Sun rules and/or occupies in the birth chart will be emphasized in this period.

If the Sun occupies the sixth, eighth or twelfth house in the birth chart or is otherwise poorly placed, there may be loss of position, illnesses related to the eyes or teeth and difficulties with the father or anything inherited from the father.

Moon Mahadasa. If the Moon is well-placed in the Natal Chart, this Mahadasa will be fortunate for one's mother, partner, and children. It is a good time to begin a new business or commercial venture, attain literary success and achieve relative harmony.

If the Moon is not well-placed in the horoscope, there may be vacillation as to professional ventures, emotional ups-and-downs and misunderstandings between friends and relatives. The sign and house position of the Moon will also affect these issues.

Mars Mahadasa. With Mars well-placed in the birth chart, there will be the opportunity to apply strong will, action and determination to any project undertaken. Health will be excellent and this will be a perfect time to develop an exercise programme or engage in a sport or hobby involving physical skills. It may be a time for travel or any other new enterprise or adventure. Friends will be helpful during this time.

Conversely, a poorly placed Mars will bring fevers, colds, chronic ailments and accidents if one is not careful. During this period, there may be marital problems, misunderstandings between friends and colleagues and general impatience and argumentativeness. There may be restlessness and independence that could lead to changing jobs and/or residences.

Rahu Mahadasa. Even though Rahu is considered to be a terrible malefic, it may still be well-placed in the horoscope. In Annemarie's chart we have already seen that Rahu was positively placed in a kendra house and received a full aspect from Venus. If Rahu is positively positioned in the chart, Rahu Mahadasa will set up conditions where the native may be successful, acquire money and travel frequently. Otherwise, during Rahu Mahadasa one may expect professional setbacks, loss of work or friends and the possible breakup of a marriage.

Jupiter Mahadasa. Jupiter's Dasa will often become a period of excess. If it is well-placed, one will attract people, general luck and harmony, marriage and the births of children, and success in one's chosen profession. One may also become interested during this period in Jupiterian subjects like the law, philosophy, theology and teaching. If Jupiter is well-aspected in the horoscope, there will be unlimited success and prosperity in this period.

If, however, Jupiter is not well-placed there will be extravagance, greed and laziness which may result in the loss of one's opportunities, job or finances.

Saturn Mahadasa. If Saturn is well-placed, this period may bring the success one has worked so hard to achieve. Saturn's period may also bring the results of any action that was previously begun in another period. This only comes, however, through continued patience and efforts.

If Saturn is poorly placed or aspected, then there will be illness, depression and loneliness during this Mahadasa. There may also be obstacles that are sometimes beyond one's immediate control or jurisdiction.

Mercury Mahadasa. Mercury's period brings a time of changing residences, jobs or partners. It is especially a time when people can develop an interest in returning to school or pursuing degrees. They may begin businesses or start careers in writing, communications, accounting or sales. If it is well-placed, Mercury Dasa will bring success to business ventures and the person can expand horizons through writing, reading and travelling. One may even begin seeing a therapist or participating in other activities that lead toward self-understanding.

If Mercury is not well-placed, there will be a period of depression, anxiety, pessimism, disappointments and delay in business ventures.

Kethu Mahadasa. Kethu Mahadasa, like complementary Rahu's period, tends to stifle the activity of the native (though this will be reversed if all indications for Kethu in the chart are beneficial). If it is well-placed, the period of Kethu is accompanied by a great promotion at work or the acquisition of a job that will lead to career opportunities. It may also be a time of spiritual awareness and meditation.

If it is ill-placed, whichever natal house is occupied by

Kethu will suffer dramatically. There may be monetary and personal losses as well as sadness and alienation which result in the need to withdraw.

Venus Mahadasa. It is obvious that in addition to influencing whatever Venus represents in the birth chart, this period will be one that focuses on love and its attainment. Relationships are perfected and sought after, and may range from marriage to friendship to siblings to colleagues — anything where there is camaraderie. If it is well-placed, there tend to be successful relationships, acquisitions, travels, births of children, and generally harmonious times when one's social life is fulfilling.

If it is ill-placed, Venus Mahadasa will be a period where the native may spend too much money, be taken advantage of and have quarrels with friends. There may also be serious disagreements with members of the family.

Mahadasas: Planetary Rulers and Houses

The significant issues which may arise during a particular Mahadasa are also determined by the individual meaning of its planetary ruler, i.e. the house(s) it occupies and rules in the Rasi Chakra. The relative strength and weakness of each planet determines whether the issues at stake during these periods will reap rewards or present difficulties. The following represent some of the concerns of the Dasa whose planetary lord rules or occupies.

Lagna — professional and personal fulfilment, adjustments to health and appearance.

Second House — addition to the family, earning power, eloquence in speech, early educational matters.

Third House — brothers and sisters, risk-taking, recognition for efforts, travel, literary efforts, change.

Fourth House — family matters, mother, acquisition of land or purchase of home, promotion.

Fifth House — children, indulgence, creative projects, sports.

Sixth House — health, daily job, service to others, domestic animals.

Seventh House — marriage, contracts, forming partnerships.

Eighth House — debts, quarrels with friends, anxiety,

partner's finances, business ventures, investments, interpersonal relationships.

Ninth House — prosperity, higher education, travel, publishing, rewards for one's efforts, timely opportunities.

Tenth House — complete undertakings, professional success or failure, father, political concerns.

Eleventh House — happiness, prosperity, ideals and goals fulfilled, community service, social concerns.

Twelfth House — extravagances, isolation, alienation, foreign travel, spiritual practice, research.

In addition to determining life expectancy, one of the most important functions of the Dasa System for the Hindu astrologer has traditionally been to see which periods are most conducive for marriage and/or childbearing. As unofficial matchmaker, the Hindu astrologer is responsible for (1) advising about the best time for marriage to take place; and (2) approving prospective brides and grooms for their families. It is therefore never certain whether most marriages would have indeed occurred on the predicted dates had they not been arranged by the astrologer himself (see Chapter 10).

According to the *Phaladeepika*, marriage may take place during the Dasa of one of the following planets:*

1. Planet in the seventh house
2. Planet aspecting the seventh house**
3. Planet owning the seventh house
4. When lord of Lagna transits the seventh house[1]

It is also common for the Hindu astrologer to arrange a marriage during whichever of the aforementioned Dasas is conducive for childbirth. He has a wide span of years from which to choose this date because so many Hindu women marry when still in their teens to men at least ten years

---

* There are many other indications for suitable Dasas in which marriage may take place — too numerous to mention here — which involve more complicated calculations. This is just a cross-section of the most popularly used choices.

** Although I only use the full aspect for determining strength or weakness in Chapter 6, this rule also refers to the weaker aspects which include three-quarter-aspect (four and eight houses apart); half-aspect (five and nine houses apart); and quarter-aspect (three and ten houses apart).

older than they are who are ready to settle down. According to the *Phaladeepika*, birth of a child may be expected during the Dasa of one of the following planets:

1. Lord of Lagna
2. Lord of the seventh house
3. Lord of the fifth house
4. Jupiter
5. Planet aspecting the fifth house or occupying the fifth house[2]

Though this method of calculation is still practised in India, any attempt to predict pregnancy and the birth of a child is extremely difficult in the East as well as in the West. Due to sophisticated methods of birth control and the added possibility to choose legalized abortions, most contemporary women — Hindu and Western — have mastery over their biological destinies. Even if the exact moment of conception and pregnancy could be predicted, the use of birth control prevents their occurrence. Conversely, due to advances in corrective surgery and an infinite variety of fertilization techniques available to promote pregnancies, it is no longer possible to predict conception based on our natural cycles.

Because the timing of these Hindu traditions cannot be applied to Western horoscope delineation, I recommend using the Hindu Dasa System to suggest, rather than predict, various periods which may be conducive for marriage and childbirth. What is most reliable, however, is applying common sense and logic to planetary indications.

Bhukti Rulers

Like the Mahadasa Ruler, the planetary ruler of each Bhukti is also judged according to its general definitions (pp. 229–32) and to its placement in the Rasi Chakra according to:

1. The house it rules
2. The house it occupies
3. Its relative strength or weakness

The planetary ruler of each Bhukti is also judged according to its relation to the Dasa Lord in the following ways:

4. The Bhukti Lord is either friend, enemy or neutral to the Dasa Ruler

5. By placing the Dasa Lord as Ascendant, the new house
    the planet occupies is evaluated*

The remainder of this chapter will be devoted to describing
the Dasa and Bhukti periods of Annemarie and Barbara. As
with the interpretation of the Rasi Chakra (Chapter 7), it is
easier to judge these time periods retrospectively to discern
the astrological basis of events. Because freedom of choice
in the West virtually precludes the ability to make accurate
predictions, the expected effects of each period according
to the Hindu Dasa System may not coincide with the
actual course of events. The issues at hand during each
period usually, however, correlate with those of its
planetary ruler.

Annemarie

The following is a step-by-step description of the trends
and cycles in Annemarie's life according to the Hindu Dasa
System (see Table 9.1). I was introduced to Annemarie by a
mutual friend in 1978 shortly before the beginning of the
Moon's Mahadasa in September 1979. Over the next several
years we occasionally met at various functions, and we
became increasingly interested in the other's skills and
talents. After some time, we began to exchange services —
she provided me with slides I needed for a workshop I was
leading and I rendered advice based on her horoscope. As
our relationship continued, she began to consult me
professionally about once a year. The focus of the readings
were the subjects that concerned her the most: her
fluctuating romantic liaisons and the nature of her career
which was on the rise.

   Although Annemarie has been a photographer for the
last 15 years, it wasn't until 1980 that her work was
publicly recognized and she gained well-earned respect
from her peers. She has travelled to London, Lisbon and
Buenos Aires where her photographs have been exhibited
to critical acclaim. At present she is compiling a book of
her photographic studies (appropriately entitled *Life
Studies*) which is based on an ongoing photographic series

---

* This is the same type of chart as we drew up for the Moon Chart by placing
another planet in the Ascendant position.

Table 9.1 Annemarie's Dasas 26 December 1952 –
26 December 2072 (see Chapter 8 for method of calculation).

	26 December 1952	
Kethu	+ 8 months	= 26 December 1952–10 September 1953
	15 days	
Venus	+ 20 Years	= 10 September 1953–10 September 1973
Sun	+ 6 Years	= 10 September 1973–10 September 1979
Moon	+ 10 Years	= 10 September 1979–10 September 1989
Mars	+ 7 Years	= 10 September 1989–10 September 1996
Rahu	+ 18 Years	= 10 September 1996–10 September 2014
Jupiter	+ 16 Years	= 10 September 2014–10 September 2030
Saturn	+ 19 Years	= 10 September 2030–10 September 2049
Mercury	+ 17 Years	= 10 September 2049–10 September 2066
Balance	+ 6 years, 3 months	
of Kethu	15 days	= 10 September 2066–25 December 2072

Venus Mahadasa (10 September 1953 – 10 September 1973)

Bhukties

Venus	10 September 1953–10 January 1957	(+40 months)
Sun	10 January 1957–10 January 1958	(+12 months)
Moon	10 January 1958–10 September 1959	(+20 months)
Mars	10 September 1959–10 November 1960	(+14 months)
Rahu	10 November 1960–10 November 1963	(+36 months)
Jupiter	10 November 1963–10 July 1966	(+32 months)
Saturn	10 July 1966–10 September 1969	(+38 months)
Mercury	10 September 1969–10 July 1972	(+34 months)
Kethu	10 July 1972–10 September 1973	(+14 months)

Sun Mahadasa (10 September 1973 – 10 September 1979)

Bhukties

Sun	10 September 1973–28 December 1973	(+3 months 18 days)
Moon	28 December 1973–28 June 1974	(+6 months)
Mars	28 June 1974–3 November 1974	(+4 months 6 days)
Rahu	3 November 1974–27 September 1975	(+10 months 24 days)
Jupiter	27 September 1975–15 July 1976	(+9 months 18 days)
Saturn	15 July 1976–27 June 1977	(+11 months 12 days)
Mercury	27 June 1977–3 May 1978	(+10 months 6 days)
Kethu	3 May 1978–9 September 1978	(+4 months 6 days)
Venus	9 September 1978–9 September 1979	(+12 months)

Moon Mahadasa (10 September 1979 – 10 September 1989)

Bhukties

Moon	10 September 1979–10 July 1980	(+10 months)
Mars	10 July 1980–10 February 1981	(+7 months)
Rahu	10 February 1981–10 August 1982	(+18 months)
Jupiter	10 August 1982–10 December 1983	(+16 months)
Saturn	10 December 1983–10 July 1985	(+19 months)
Mercury	10 July 1985–10 December 1986	(+17 months)
Kethu	10 December 1986–10 July 1987	(+7 months)
Venus	10 July 1987–10 March 1989	(+20 months)
Sun	10 March 1989–10 September 1989	(+6 months)

Mars Mahadasa (11 September 1989 – 11 September 1996)

Bhukties

Mars	11 September 1989–7 February 1990	(+4 months 27 days)
Rahu	7 February 1990–25 February 1991	(+12 months 18 days)
Jupiter	25 February 1991–31 January 1992	(+11 months 6 days)
Saturn	31 January 1992–10 March 1993	(+13 months 9 days)
Mercury	10 March 1993–9 March 1994	(+11 months 27 days)
Kethu	9 March 1994–5 August 1994	(+4 months 27 days)
Venus	5 August 1994–5 October 1995	(+14 months)
Sun	5 October 1995–11 February 1996	(+4 months 6 days)
Moon	11 February 1996–11 September 1996	(+7 months)

---

of the same name. With hindsight, let's review the ten-year period of the Moon's Mahadasa using some of the interpretive techniques previously discussed.

Moon Mahadasa (1979–1989)

In general the Moon's period provides an emphasis on business and on familial relationships. During her Moon's Mahadasa, Annemarie had several relationship changes as well as professional successes which enhanced her reputation as a free-lance photographer.

In Annemarie's Rasi Chakra, the Moon is the ruler of the tenth house and is placed in the seventh house — both Kendra houses. The Moon's Mahadasa should, therefore, bring a concentration on Annemarie's career (tenth house) and countless opportunities for success through both professional and romantic partnerships (seventh house). Fame is, therefore, almost guaranteed during this period since the tenth house — one of the three 'working' houses

— relates to public recognition rather than to earning money (second house) or developing skills (sixth house). The aspect the Moon receives from Saturn (the planet of work) in the first house, however, indicates that Annemarie must work hard to attain her professional goals. The Moon is also conjoined in the seventh house with Jupiter, naturally benefic and individually malefic, whose influence may cause opportunities to be overlooked or even wasted.

Bhukti Dasas

Now let us continue by focusing on each Bhukti Dasa as calculated in the previous chapter. It is important to note that in Annemarie's situation each Bhukti ruler will have a good relationship with the Mahadasa ruler because the Moon has no enemies. Throughout any disappointing period, the Mahadasa will always be relatively successful because of the Moon's positive relationship with the ruler of each of the sub-periods.

Fig 9.1 is an illustration of Annemarie's 'Dasa as Ruler' chart with the sign of the Dasa Ruler — the Moon in Aries — situated in the Ascendant position. The following

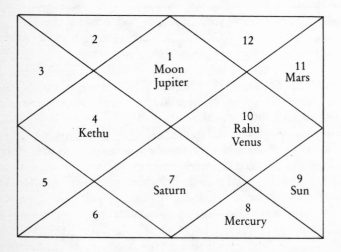

Fig 9.1 Annemarie's Rasi Chakra when Dasa ruler is placed in the Lagna position.

descriptions of the Bhukti periods of Annemarie further demonstrate this principle.

Moon Mahadasa Moon Bhukti (1 September 1979 – 1 July 1980)

The first Bhukti of each Mahadasa always shares its planetary lord with the Dasa ruler and is generally considered inauspicious. Because the Moon is naturally benefic with no enemies, its individual malevolence will be tempered.

The Moon Bhukti reflects the same concerns as the Moon Mahadasa: the seventh house of partnership and the tenth house of career orientation. According to Annemarie, at this time there was indeed tension with her live-in relationship although her career was, in fact, on the rise.

Moon Mahadasa Mars Bhukti (1 July 1980 – 1 February 1981)

Natally, Mars is placed in the fifth house and rules both the second house (Scorpio) and the seventh house (Aries). If Annemarie was more traditional, the interpretation might be, 'marry someone with money during this period.' Instead, as the ruler of the second and seventh houses, Mars provides the opportunity to earn money through the formation of a partnership and the fifth house indicates that the partnership is likely to be a romantic one. On the more negative side, however, it also implies a time of impulsive spending or financial risk-taking. In the 'Moon as Dasa' chart, Mars is situated in the eleventh house of hopes and ideals.

In this period, Annemarie and her lover, also a photographer, formed an artistic partnership producing and marketing a series of greeting cards and erotic postcards for which Annemarie was not only photographer but often the model. Due to Mars' influence, however, this venture was challenging and creative but also involved a great amount of financial speculation. As it turned out, the business itself lost money but the artistic end of the project was enormously successful. Annemarie and her lover suddenly became a couple 'known around town' and acquired a following of fans and colleagues who believed in the future of their work. They were asked to 'show' at exhibitions and co-authored a book. Additionally, their photographs appeared in international publications. Although the partnership revitalized their relationship temporarily, they would eventually go their separate ways during the next sub-period of Rahu.

Moon Mahadasa Rahu Bhukti (1 February 1981 – 1 August 1982)

A glimpse of the natal chart shows that Rahu is in the fourth house and it is conjoined with Venus. As Rahu cannot rule a particular house, its influence is considered to be that of the fourth house (the house it occupies natally) and the tenth house (the house it is placed in according to the Moon chart). A malefic planet by nature, Rahu's difficult effect is greatly reduced since it occupies a Kendra house and is aspected by Venus.

Annemarie's relationship with her partner/lover ended during Rahu's Bhukti and she went through a period of depression when she doubted her ability to be independently creative. She literally spent most of her time at home (fourth house) rethinking her career (tenth house), and contemplated the direction her work should take to maintain the prestige she'd acquired during the previous period of Mars. Annemarie reassessed her work and discontinued the self-portraits which comprised a significant portion of what she'd done in conjunction with her ex-partner. She also experimented with new photographic techniques and subject matter aimed at cultivating a 'more humanistic and less self-centred approach to her work'.

Moon Mahadasa Jupiter Bhukti (1 August 1982 – 1 December 1983)

As the ruler of the natal third and sixth houses (inauspicious houses), Jupiter (naturally benefic and individually malefic) is aspected by Saturn (naturally malefic and individually benefic) and brings mixed influences — both beneficial and detrimental. It was during this period that the more problematic face of Jupiter reared its ugly head and, along with the fame and recognition she acquired during this period, came the carelessness and tendency towards excess that Jupiter so easily brings. Ignoring health and work (sixth house) led to the excessive spending that would have its consequences later on during Saturn Bhukti.

Since Jupiter is conjunct the waxing Moon in the natal seventh house and situated in the first house of the Moon chart (both Kendra houses), the period was not completely inauspicious. In fact, as we saw from Annemarie's Rasi Chakra, there are no planets that are totally malefic. That factor will influence our interpretation of the Mahadasas and Bhukti Dasas such that no period will be considered completely detrimental.

Moon Mahadasa Saturn Bhukti (1 December 1983 – 1 July 1985)

In Annemarie's natal horoscope, Saturn's auspiciousness is seen through its exalted position in Libra in the first house, rulership of both the fourth Kendra house and the fifth Trikona house, and its placement in its Vargottama. Most importantly, Saturn (a natural malefic) is situated in the seventh house from the Dasa Ruler — the Moon — and, accordingly, Saturn's Bhukti should be a period pertaining to partnerships and other seventh-house concerns.

In this period, a new relationship came into Annemarie's life. Because the indulgent Moon and Jupiter both aspect Saturn and because Saturn is in Libra, this union had many excesses, passions and other insurmountable obstacles. Though it ended rather abruptly, Annemarie still considered it to be a worthwhile learning experience.

The seventh house is also an indicator of legal matters and, therefore, problems resulting from unpaid taxes surfaced during this period. These financial difficulties had been incurred during the excessive and careless period of the previous Jupiter Bhukti. Because of the beneficial nature of Saturn, however, these problems were resolved. It was also in this Saturn period that Annemarie applied for a government grant to further her *Life Studies* photography project.

Moon Mahadasa Mercury Bhukti (1 July 1985 –
1 December 1986)

In her natal chart, Mercury is in Scorpio in the second house, the house of finances. It is also eighth from the Moon making the affairs of the eighth sign/house — life and death, occult studies, matters of the body and money from other sources — equally important during this period. Mercury also rules the natal ninth and twelfth houses making it individually benefic although somewhat weakened by its association with the second and eighth houses.

It was in this period that Annemarie actually received the subsidy (second house) she had applied for. Her *Life Studies* project (eighth and ninth house) included portraits of people related to one another in various ways, i.e. sisters, brothers, mother and daughter, mother and son, etc. The project culminated in an exhibition during the autumn of 1986 and is the subject of a book to be published in 1990.

As the ruler of the ninth and twelfth placed in the second house, Mercury Bhukti also involves generating revenue from either educational studies, working abroad or from research projects, and Annemarie was indeed hired to teach a few short courses. Despite her professional accomplishments, however, this was not a successful time for relationships and there was personal unhappiness with Mercury in Scorpio in the second house, the eighth house from the Moon.

Moon Mahadasa Kethu Bhukti (1 December 1986 –
1 July 1987)

As two natural malefics, Rahu and Kethu should always be the least favourable periods in any Mahadasa. But the placements of Rahu and Kethu both natally as well as in the chart of the Dasa ruler are auspicious. Kethu, natally placed in the tenth, is in the fourth house from the Moon, and is aspected by Venus, tenth house from the Moon. Kethu is likely to be a slightly better period than Rahu — especially for her career — because of the *full* aspect it receives from Venus. Since it is in the fourth house from the Moon, it could also have an effect on the parents, and indeed her father became ill during this time.

In February 1987, during Kethu's period, Annemarie consulted me to ascertain if the time was right to buy a home she'd seen which was a photographer's dream as it combined an art studio and living space. She was considering the possibility of renting the house with her current lover and later taking advantage of the option to buy. The house would be vacant in September 1987, during the sub-period of Venus. Her main concern was whether changing homes at that moment was in her best interest and what the ramifications would be if she proceeded. It is no wonder that, with the emphasis on the fourth and tenth houses, she should find a house which combined living and working space in Kethu's period. I advised her that a new home/work space accompanied by a stable relationship would certainly be an appropriate beginning for the Venus period.

I advised Annemarie that, based on how the approaching Venus Bhukti appeared to me at the time of the consultation (February 1987), moving should be beneficial if it took place during that Bhukti (1 July 1987 – 1 March 1989) which was to follow the present sub-period of Kethu.

During this same consultation Annemarie wanted to know if it was possible to predict when she might have a baby. By applying the rules set out in the beginning of the chapter, it is quite possible, in theory, to determine which Dasa and Sub-Dasa periods would be most auspicious for Annemarie to give birth. Let's see how a Hindu astrologer might attempt to answer Annemarie's question. Apart from determining Annemarie's fertility and the likelihood of a relatively easy pregnancy (based on the fifth and seventh house), the first step would be to calculate which Dasas fall between the ages of 15 and 50 — the absolute maximum number of years during which a woman may conceive a child. According to Table 9.1, this period would encompass the Dasas between 1967–2002; these are the Dasas of Venus, the Sun, the Moon, Mars and Rahu.

The next step would be to determine which of those years fit the description according to the guidelines of the *Phaladeepika* (p.234). Applying this to Annemarie's chart, the Dasas in which she is likely to give birth are as follows:

1. Lord of Lagna — Venus Mahadasa
2. Lord of the seventh house — Mars Mahadasa
3. Lord of the fifth house — Saturn Mahadasa
4. Jupiter Mahadasa
5. As the occupying planet of the fifth house — Mars
   Mahadasa

Since the Dasas of Jupiter and Saturn take place after the age of 50, Venus and Mars Mahadasa would be the two periods most feasible for having a baby. Venus Mahadasa lasted until 1973 when Annemarie was 21 years old. Had Annemarie been a typical young Hindu woman, it would not have been unusual for the astrologer to arrange a marriage so that she could, indeed, give birth before Venus Mahadasa ended. For Westerners, it may seem relatively young to marry and have children before the age of 21, but within the Hindu community in India it is still quite common. Since Annemarie's Venus Mahadasa has already passed, the most likely period for childbearing — using the Hindu Dasa System — would be any Mars Bhukti or Mars Mahadasa beginning in 1989 and ending in 1996, between the ages of 36 and 43. I advised Annemarie that, according to the Hindu Dasa System, it is possible that she could have a baby during Mars Mahadasa. Because Mars Mahadasa coincidentally spans her 36th–43rd year, she will either have a child during this time or not at all, according to the Dasa System and her fertility cycle.

Moon Mahadasa Venus Bhukti (1 July 1987 –
1 March 1989)
This brings us to her present Venus Bhukti. Venus is the lord of the first house (the area of self and the personality) and the eighth house (business affairs). She has been very much in demand to appear at functions and/or to exhibit her photography and, in addition, the business of promoting and selling her work has also take up a great deal of time. Her highly sexual and passionate nature, due to Venus' rulership of the natal first and eighth houses, has been tested in Venus' sub-period.

Venus is situated in the fourth house of the natal chart (home) and it is the tenth house from the Moon (career). During September–December 1987, Annemarie was simultaneously exhibiting her photographs in Lisbon,

Portugal and London. With her reputation soaring, Annemarie was then invited to exhibit in Buenos Aires. Her reputation as a photographer continued to soar throughout Venus Bhukti; however the aspects natal Venus receives from Rahu and Kethu always keeps her on her toes and prevents her from becoming over-confident. She still has a bit of conflict regarding fourth- and tenth-house matters, and must learn to strike a balance between her career and her relationship — a difficult task, as both take place in her home.

In September 1987, Annemarie rented the house she found during Kethu's sub-period, thus unifying her home and career. Her primary concern during this period was to maintain the professional standards which would enable her to buy the dream house.* She applied for an additional subsidy to increase the number of photographs in her *Life Studies* series and has contracted to produce a book from this series. If her plans materialize, the book will be published during the sub-period of the Sun. According to the weight of the Bhukties, I feel that on a professional level the period of the Sun will be her most successful during Moon Mahadasa.

Moon Mahadasa Sun Bhukti (1 March 1989 – 1 September 1989)

Her Sun is in Sagittarius in the third house and is in the ninth house from the Moon. It rules the eleventh house and, like Mercury, is friendly to the Moon. In the Sun's sub-period Annemarie may have many offers to travel and may even reside abroad for a time. Because the Sun occupies the ninth house (Trikona) from the Moon, I anticipate it will be one of her most beneficial and productive periods to date.

Barbara

The following is a step-by-step interpretation of the trends and cycles in Barbara's life according to the Hindu Dasa System (see Table 9.2) When she first consulted me in

* At the time of writing, March 1989, she was still trying to finance the purchase.

1984, Barbara was contemplating a career change from nursing and, to this end, was enrolled in a graduate programme to become a certified social worker. Her first

Table 9.2 Barbara's Dasa Period 30 January 1960 – 30 January 2080

	30 January 1960		
Rahu	+ 1 year 3 months 20 days	=	20 May 1961
Jupiter	+ 16 years	=	20 May 1977
Saturn	+ 19 years	=	20 May 1996
Mercury	+ 17 years	=	20 May 2013
Kethu	+ 7 years	=	20 May 2020
Venus	+ 20 years	=	20 May 2040
Sun	+ 6 years	=	20 May 2046
Moon	+ 10 years	=	20 May 2056
Mars	+ 7 years	=	20 May 2063
Balance of Rahu	+ 16 years 8 months 10 days	=	30 January 2080

Jupiter Mahadasa (20 May 1961 – 20 May 1977)

Bhukties

Jupiter	20 May 1961–7 July 1963	(+25 months 18 days)
Saturn	7 July 1963–19 January 1966	(+30 months 12 days)
Mercury	19 January 1966–25 April 1968	(+27 months 6 days)
Kethu	25 April 1968–1 May 1969	(+11 months 6 days)
Venus	1 May 1969–1 January 1972	(+32 months)
Sun	1 January 1972–19 October 1972	(+9 months 18 days)
Moon	20 September 1972–20 January 1974	(+16 months)
Mars	20 January 1974–27 December 1974	(+11 months 6 days)
Rahu	27 December 1974–18 May 1977	(+28 months 24 days)

Saturn Mahadasa (18 May 1977 – 18 May 1996)

Bhukties

Saturn	18 May 1977–21 May 1980	(+36 months 3 days)
Mercury	21 May 1980–30 January 1983	(+32 months 9 days)
Kethu	30 January 1983–10 March 1984	(+13 months 9 days)
Venus	10 March 1984–10 May 1987	(+38 months)
Sun	10 May 1987–22 April 1988	(+11 months 12 days)
Moon	22 April 1988–22 November 1989	(+19 months)
Mars	22 November 1989–31 December 1990	(+13 months 9 days)
Rahu	31 December 1990–6 November 1993	(+34 months 6 days)
Jupiter	6 November 1993–18 May 1996	(+30 months 12 days)

job in this field was working in a treatment facility for teenage drug addicts providing individual therapy and group counselling. Presently, she is employed by an out-patient treatment centre to counsel and instruct recovered alcohol and substance abusers.

Before analysing her present Saturn Mahadasa which comprises the 19 years between 1977 and 1996, let us quickly assess her previous Jupiter Mahadasa which spanned 1961 until 1977 (Barbara was 1–17 years old). Ruling this youthful period, Jupiter indicates a time of education and friendships. Jupiter is the ruler of the eighth and the eleventh houses, and is placed in the eighth house.* Although Jupiter is individually malefic, it is naturally benefic and extremely well-placed in Sagittarius, its sign of rulership and moolatrikona. These very powerful positions balance the despair and pessimism resulting from the influence of the eighth house.

Barbara had a very stable and loving upbringing. However, sometime during puberty she developed an inferiority complex stemming from the fact that her height was under average, and she was also the youngest in a family of achievers. During her adolescence, she became preoccupied with death and first showed what became a chronic tendency towards melancholia and depression. Throughout Jupiter Mahadasa until she was 17, she felt alienated most of the time. Though adolescence is very often a period of confusion and estrangement from family who don't ever seem to 'understand', some teenagers suffer varying degrees of depression while others do not suffer at all. We cannot, therefore, attribute Barbara's moods only to adolescence but must assume that it was partially due to the enormous influence of the eighth house — the realm of matters concerning life and death, anxiety and chronic illness.

During this time, a significant concern was her height since, due to a hormonal imbalance, she was much shorter than most girls her age and was worried she would not grow. A Hindu astrologer assured Barbara that there

* Since Jupiter Mahadasa occurred during this youthful period in Barbara's life, it is unlikely that many of the descriptions attached to the eighth and eleventh houses would have manifested.

would be a great change when Saturn's Mahadasa began. Jupiter, he explained, both ruled and was placed in the inauspicious eighth house and was surrounded by two malefics, Saturn and Mars. Saturn, on the other hand, was individually a very benefic planet and ruled two auspicious houses, the ninth and the tenth. Just as the astrologer predicted, during the early period of Saturn's Mahadasa, Barbara grew three inches and her hormonal imbalance vastly improved.

One of the more fascinating facets of the Hindu Dasa System is the uncanny timing of events that sometimes cannot be explained by using progressions or transits. This does not mean, however, that either system is foolproof since we are, in the end, masters of our own fates.

Let us now review Saturn's Mahadasa until the present. As we have just seen, Saturn in Barbara's chart is a beneficial planet. In addition to Saturn ruling the ninth and tenth houses in the natal chart, it is situated in the eighth house. With all of Barbara's planets relating to the eighth, ninth and tenth houses, the emphasis of this Dasa will be on business partnerships, inter-personal relationships, depression, chronic illness, higher education, travel, and profession — things that are foremost between the ages of 17 and 36. Saturn's position in the eighth house ensures that, throughout all this activity, there will be always be

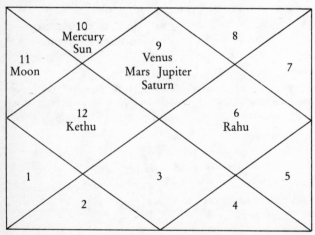

Fig 9.2 Barbara's Rasi Chakra when Dasa Ruler is placed in the Lagna position.

intermittent periods of worry, anxiety and general melancholia.

The following interpretation of the Bhukti Dasas enables us to pinpoint more specifically when these issues will be most significant. It is important to remember that Saturn's friends are Venus and Mercury; the enemy is the Sun; and Moon, Mars and Jupiter are neutral to Saturn. Fig 9.2 is Barbara's 'Dasa as Ruler' chart with Saturn in Sagittarius placed in the Ascendant position and all of her planets concentrated in the first three houses.

Saturn Mahadasa Saturn Bhukti (18 May 1977 – 21 May 1980)

Though the first sub-period of any Dasa is always considered detrimental, Saturn's rulership of the ninth and tenth houses lends its positive influence. As already stated, however, the murky background of the eighth house forever seems to be standing in the way of achieving total success and/or happiness. During this Bhukti, her father received a promotion which changed the entire course of his professional life. Because Barbara was young, she could not experience the tenth house as her own profession but only that of her father's.

It was in this period that Barbara attended college (ninth house) and took the first steps toward selecting a career. Before finally deciding on nursing, she attended three universities in an attempt to resolve which school would best serve her professional needs.

It was also in this period that she experienced her first 'mature' relationship which lasted from her teenage years into early adulthood. Although she no longer suffered from an inferiority complex or insecurity, there were still the periodic bouts with depression which still plague her today. Additionally, the deaths of members of the family had a profound effect on her (Saturn in the eighth). With four planets natally placed in the eighth house, death will always surround her, one way or another; even her work with drug addicts is shadowed by the risk of their attempts at suicide and possible overdose.

Saturn Mahadasa Mercury Bhukti (21 May 1980 –
30 January 1983)

Natally, Mercury is placed in the ninth house, a Trikona house and it rules the second house and the fifth house, also a Trikona house. Because Mercury is friendly to Saturn, individually benefic and is not placed in any negative categories, Mercury Bhukti was an extremely beneficial time. It is conjoined with the Sun, however, which is individually malefic and the ruler of the natal fourth house. Decisions made during this Mercury Bhukti were opposed by her mother (fourth house), who especially disapproved of the relationship she was having.

Since Mercury occupies the second house from Saturn, and rules both the second and fifth houses, many of these decisions concerned the establishment of a secure financial base (second house), and an affirmation of individuality (fifth house). In conjunction with Mercury which represents intellectual pursuits and the attainments of degrees, this period saw college graduation, her first trip abroad and her first nursing job. She started looking for her own apartment and ended the relationship which had begun in Saturn's Bhukti. Looking at Mercury as representative of financial success and professional satisfaction, I would safely say that during Mercury's Mahadasa, between the ages of 36 and 53, Barbara will probably reach her financial peak and fulfil many of her personal and professional goals.

Saturn Mahadasa Kethu Bhukti (30 January 1983 –
10 March 1984)

Natally, Kethu is in the eleventh house — group activities, hopes and dreams — and it is in the fourth house from Saturn. In this period Barbara moved into her own apartment (fourth house), the location of which was strongly opposed by her parents. Her mother voiced concern over Barbara's lifestyle and found it generally difficult adjusting to her youngest daughter's independence. By living in a centrally located and affordable apartment (fourth house), Barbara became an active member of the neighbourhood by participating in community-sponsored activities for artists and writers (eleventh house). She had a beneficial job change but due to the depressive influence of

Kethu, she spent many lonely hours adjusting to living alone.

Saturn Mahadasa Venus Bhukti (10 March 1984 – 10 May 1987)

Venus is not in a position of strength in the natal chart. Though it is naturally benefic, its rulership of the first and sixth houses define it as individually malefic (though considered to be a 'feeble' malefic). It is placed in the eighth house and is in the first house from Saturn. As already discussed in Chapter 7, Barbara's afflicted Venus indicates a tendency towards precarious mental and physical health. Barbara had to contend with lingering illnesses, allergies, and continued depression during this period.

As sixth house ruler, Venus Bhukti was also a time of extremely hard work, constant self-examination, and a reorientation of her skills. Barbara returned to school to earn a Master's degree in social work which enabled her to switch professions. Another sixth house matter — domestic animals — reared its head in the form of the death of a beloved pet. The first house, ruled by Venus, is the eighth house (death) from the sixth house (pets).

In its favour, Venus in her chart is a friend to Saturn and shares the eighth house. Due to Venus' mundane meaning as indicator of love and partnership, Barbara met her husband during this Bhukti.

Saturn Mahadasa Sun Bhukti (10 May 1987 – 22 April 1988)

In the Rasi Chakra, the Sun is placed in the ninth house (a Trikona house) and is classified as a benefic planet due to its rulership of the fourth house. The concentration on higher education (ninth house) shone through as Barbara obtained her Master's degree in social work in June 1987 and subsequently began her first job as a certified social worker. The Sun is placed in the second house from Saturn and describes her ability to earn money professionally with a practical eye towards the future. During this Bhukti, she also solidified her relationship with her boyfriend; they rented an apartment together and made plans to marry.

The Sun is an enemy of Saturn which indicates that this

period still had its pitfalls. Although living with her boyfriend was certainly a move in the right direction, Barbara's eighth house would not allow her to adjust easily to yet another change in her life. The pressures of her first job as a case worker responsible for the welfare of her many clients, along with sharing a small apartment caused her a great deal of stress and anxiety. This period was, however, pivotal for her personal growth and did, indeed, prepare her for the pressures of her profession and the positive and negative facets of married life.

Saturn Mahadasa Moon Bhukti (22 April 1988 – 22 November 1989)

As of this writing, Barbara is in the midst of the Bhukti of the Moon — Saturn's enemy — which occupies the third house from Saturn. In the Rasi Chakra, the Moon, individually malefic, is the ruler of the third house and it is placed in Aquarius in the tenth house, a Kendra house and an Upachaya house. This position strengthens the affairs of the tenth house due to its occupancy by the Moon (see pp. 169–72).)

Because there is an emphasis on the third house, this period has been a very busy time for her siblings. During the Moon's Bhukti, her oldest sister dissolved a live-in relationship, moved into her own apartment and switched careers. Her other sister married and she and her husband are presently trying to purchase a house. Due to the Moon's individually malefic influence on the tenth house, Barbara changed her job within the social work profession and, as of this writing, is very unhappy and frustrated with her new position which she will probably leave before the Bhukti is over. The Moon in the tenth house brought changes with her father's job as well who, as of this writing, announced that he was opting for early retirement.

Since the influence of the third house represents a change in her living situation, it is not altogether surprising that Barbara was married in August 1989 (still part of the Moon's Bhukti). Let's see how those guidelines for prediction of marriage (p.233) apply to Barbara's decision. The Dasas of the following planets indicate possible times for marriage:

1. Planet in the seventh house — None

2. Planet aspecting the seventh house
    a. No full aspect
    b. No 3/4 aspect
    c. 1/2 aspect — Rahu
    d. 1/4 aspect — Kethu and the Moon
3. Planet owning the seventh house — Mars
4. When lord of Lagna transits the seventh house —
    whenever Venus transits Scorpio

The present Saturn Mahadasa does not fit into any of these categories. Therefore, these planets must be used to describe the Bhukti Dasas. Since the natal Moon occupies the tenth house, it is considered to aspect the seventh house with a quarter-aspect (tenth house from the tenth house) and fits the description under Step 2. Because the quarter-aspect is weak, however, the following Mars Bhukti — the planet ruling the seventh house — seems like the most predictable time for a Hindu astrologer to arrange marriage. Ironically, Barbara recently told me that she had originally planned her wedding for November 1989 (Mars Bhukti) but, due to unforeseen circumstances changed it to August. Although marriage is still difficult to predict in the West due to the incidence of couples living together without actually 'tying the knot', these guidelines do often indicate the planetary Dasa or Bhukti in which an actual wedding takes place.

Saturn Mahadasa Mars Bhukti (22 November 1989 –
31 December 1990)
Natally, Mars is placed in the eighth house, an inauspicious house, and rules the seventh and twelfth. Due to Mars' position as an individual benefic in the Rasi Chakra, this period should relieve some of the tensions and pressures of the Moon's period. It is still, however, an enemy of Saturn which means there will be obstacles regarding education and career (the domains of Saturn in Barbara's chart).

Because the seventh house is ruled by Mars, I had thought that Barbara would marry during this Bhukti. It is possible that during this period, she will actually experience 'married life' and begin making definite long-term plans and moves. Because Mars rules the twelfth house, I have cautioned her to pay more attention to her expenditures and to avoid bouts of depression due to the influence of the introspective and sometimes alienating twelfth house.

Because I make a point of not venturing more than a year or two ahead, I do not want to continue second-guessing the remaining years of Saturn's Mahadasa. In general, however, it should continue to bring new educational opportunities which will be applied towards professional advancement.

As I already mentioned, I believe that Mercury's Dasa — spanning the ages of 36–53 — will be her most financially successful and emotionally fulfilling. Recently she asked me if I could speculate on which period might be the best time for having children. According to the *Phaladeepika*, conception will take place during the Dasa of one of the following planets:

1. Lord of Lagna — Venus Mahadasa
2. Lord of the seventh house — Mars Mahadasa
3. Lord of the fifth house — Mercury Mahadasa
4. Jupiter Mahadasa
5. As the occupying planet of the fifth house — Rahu Mahadasa

Because Saturn and Mercury's Mahadasa cover the years between 17 and 53, pregnancy must take place during one of these two periods. According to the aforementioned indications for childbirth, Saturn's Dasa is not mentioned but Mercury, lord of the fifth house, is mentioned. I would guess that Barbara will be professionally secure when she is in her mid-thirties and most likely to begin a family at that time.

This chapter should have served as a way of seeing that there are many factors in determining which issues are important during a particular period. As with interpretation, it is always clearer when viewing it with hindsight. Most importantly, the Dasa System works well as a supplement to our own progressions and transits. I would not, however, substitute the Dasa System as a definitive means of forecasting. For example, Hindu texts interpret Rahu and Kethu periods as malefic, almost ominous.* I would concur with these observations because even when Rahu and Kethu are well-placed in the Rasi Chakra, their periods bring obstacles, and projects are often unable to get off the ground. As soon as these periods do conclude, however, renewed energy emerges and projects will usually be carried to fruition.

A case in point is the horoscope of a woman whose Rahu Mahadasa lasted from 1971 until June 1988. She had a series of relationships that did not work out for one reason or another. I anticipated that once Rahu's period ended and Jupiter's began, she might meet someone with whom she could have a lasting relationship. In the summer of 1988 when Jupiter's Mahadasa began, she started dating someone and in June 1989 they were married. In Western astrology, the changeover from one planetary period to the next is comparable to the movement of the progressed Moon (or another progressed or transiting planet) through the twelfth house. Once that planet crosses the Ascendant, the difficulties seem to lift and events progress smoothly.

The following chapter will discuss the influence and authority of the Hindu astrologer, and will illustrate how his insights and decision-making abilities affect everyone in the community.

---

* One rationale for this categorization is Rahu and Kethu's lack of assignment to house rulership; they can, therefore, never become individually benefic due to house rulership.

10
THE ROLE OF THE ASTROLOGER

A book about Hindu astrology would be incomplete without a more definitive description of the Hindu astrologer and the invaluable services he provides. His influential and multi-functional role of therapist, medical practitioner and — at times — priest has earned him the utmost praise and respect within the Hindu Community.

In order to maintain a commercial practice, an astrologer must possess a university degree in Jyotish — a complicated study of the precise mathematical and astronomical principles of the heavenly bodies — sometimes taking up to eight years to complete. Although he may never use every facet of this study, the astrologer must none the less know them all, while, as a devout Hindu, must have the ability to transmit the spiritual implications of a horoscope to his clientele. When the Jyotish degree is obtained, he must apprentice for many years before opening his own practice in order to gain first-hand experience in applying the astronomical principles to the art of interpretation. Since it is common for professions to be handed down through generations of families, he usually serves his apprenticeship in the practice or shop of his father, uncle or other relative before sharing or taking over the business — work he has been geared for since childhood.

It is quite usual to have a chart constructed by an astrologer when a child is born. During the time I studied with my second teacher, the practising astrologer Deoki Nandan Shastri, I was present on many occasions when parents brought their children to his office for horoscope readings — a common practice in India tantamount to a check-up at the paediatrician's in the West. The horoscope is usually presented to the parents in multi-page booklet form and always includes the Rasi Chakra, the Moon Chart, the Navamsa Chart and the planetary periods of Vimshoddhari Dasa (the inclusion of other Shodasavarga charts is optional). These drawings and diagrams are accompanied by long, hand-written explanations of character traits, learning capabilities, parental descriptions, possible illness(es), the profession one is most suited for (though many times it is that of the father), the most suitable marriage partner, and a general summary as to how the child's life will proceed. Also included are prognostications for auspicious and inauspicious periods, and times most conducive for education, marriage, children, residence and/or travel. The information is then relayed orally and is followed by a question-and-answer session when parents may ask anything they wish to about the destiny of their child. Until the child weds, it is very common for the astrologer to advise the parents about eating habits, behaviour patterns, upbringing, education, or any phase affecting the formative years.

Since a great majority of Hindus have had their charts constructed at birth, throughout their lives they usually consult the same astrologer who guides them medically and developmentally much like a general practitioner or family doctor. The astrologer is almost always acquainted with the entire family whose horoscopes he has also constructed. Since he is usually knowledgeable in medicine and child psychology, he is also very often called upon by doctors and teachers to render a second opinion. Medical astrology is a very important branch of Hindu astrology and practised by astrologers in varying degrees. By assessing the planets in terms of their physical correspondences, the astrologer can easily see which part or parts of the body are weak and the periods during which they will be most problematic. The astrologer may suggest that a gemstone or amulet be worn close to the affected part of the body in order to revive it. He may also suggest wearing a charm to improve the general constitution and ward off disease and 'evil spirits', and can provide certain tinctures or recommend the use of various medicinal and herbal remedies.

Though there are a wide variety of reasons why people pay an astrologer an office visit, his advice is most often sought when making major long-term decisions (i.e. change of residence, choosing a career, marriage, etc.) and short-term decisions (one's business, the signing of a document, the purchase of a car or house, etc.) If the client so requests, the astrologer may even choose the precise moment when an event should take place based on the nakshatra the Moon occupies and the nature of any transiting planets. If the client requires short-term counsel or needs to chat, a visit is possible without an appointment. Though his advice is based on precise mathematical calculations, his real ability to counsel is predicated on an unselfish concern for others, objective insight and experiential wisdom. Because so many people heed the astrologer's advice regarding major decisions, it is difficult to judge whether Hindu predictive techniques actually work as accurately as Hindu astrologers insist they do.

An example is the story of Shiva, an Indian friend of mine whose business takes him to Europe several times a year. Since Shiva lives in Benares (where I studied Hindu astrology), I asked him to give my regards to Shastri, my astrology teacher, when in India. Although Shiva's horoscope was drawn up at birth, he had not as an adult consulted an astrologer and saw this as a perfect opportunity to do so. At their first meeting my friend enquired whether it would be feasible to expand his import/export business in Western Europe. He was advised only to repeat a certain mantra each morning and wear a gemstone around his neck 24 hours a day. After following my teacher's advice for two weeks, Shiva returned to see him and was then encouraged to proceed with the business. He was warned, however, to start slowly, patiently and frugally and was told that within five years, business would soar. Shiva heeded the astrologer's advice and began by importing a limited supply of Indian artefacts and selling them to many different storekeepers. Now, 10 years later, he operates three of his own extremely successful shops located in two different countries and is looking forward to opening another one. Due to many family responsibilities in the East and his business in the West, Shiva travels back and forth between Europe and

India at least four times a year. Once or twice a year, however, if he has a very important decision to make, or if he simply needs someone to converse with, Shiva returns to Shastri for advice. It is very probable that Shiva's excellent business instincts brought him the success that he enjoys today. His humility, however, dictates that credit for his success be partially given to the wearing of the amulet, the singing of the mantra and the advice and blessing of my teacher/his astrologer.

In addition to the astrologer's position in the community as general seer, confidante, and therapist, he is also the source of sacred knowledge. In ancient times the astrologer believed he had a direct line to the gods, that his words had a divine source, that he was an intermediary who transmitted sacred teachings. Although there are some religious gurus in India who teach meditative techniques and others who profess to have the ability to heal and power to bless, it is the astrologer who, like the priest or rabbi, provides non-judgemental and wise counsel. His astrological sessions are, at times, 'confessionals' furnishing comfort, hope and encouragement in bleaker moments. Unlike his Western counterpart, the Hindu astrologer serves the community and is available for advice whenever needed. Modern young Hindus do not always visit an astrologer for accurate lifelong prediction as their parents did. Instead they seek him for unbiased advice, or simply to discuss their problems. If they leave less burdened, their visit was worthwhile.

Perhaps the astrologer's most significant duty towards his community is sanctioning marriages, still mostly pre-arranged by the parents and one of the most important decisions a woman and man must make. As is the case with many contemporary religions and cultures whose ancient traditions are still practised, Hindu matrimony is not merely the marriage of two individuals but the union of two families. More often than not, it is part of a business merger or other profitable exchange in which each family, as a result of the wedding, receives something the other needs. If a business transaction is not the criterion, the parents will seek out a prospective son or daughter-in-law from a family of appropriate caste who will be a good provider for their children and grandchildren. To ensure her financial security and happiness, the bride's family still presents their prospective son-in-law with the traditional dowry — 'the money, goods, or estate* that a woman brings to her husband in marriage'.[1]

Families who do not have prospective partners in mind must search for another family with whom to unite. Sometimes they may consult an astrologer who will advise them as to profession, age, caste, and even in which direction to search. If the daughter or son's chart reveals that the marriage partner lives to the east, the astrologer advises them to search in places located east of the child's birthplace. If the west is indicated, they are advised to look west of the birthplace. The search for a suitable marriage partner may take place by word of mouth, business or family connections or by means of a newspaper advertisement, a very common practice in India.

Fig 10.1 is a reproduction of several authentic advertisements from the Sunday edition of *The Hindu*, an English-language newspaper written for and read by educated Indians. (Advertisements are also placed in Indian-language newspapers.) An ad is placed by the family of both the prospective bride or groom, and contains a description of the son or daughter as well as specific requirements which pertain to age, caste, family background, education level, and profession. It is evident from these newspaper clippings that the birth information is also sometimes requested in order to determine character, family background and to ensure that the Dasa cycles of both parties coincide. In addition, the request for birth information is also a means of providing information about each family's relationship to astrology. Anyone who responds to an advertisement requesting birth information has probably been informed by an astrologer that it is the right period in which to marry. Once the family receives the information by mail, it is brought to their astrologer who will draw up the prospective mate's chart.

By comparing the two Navamsa charts, the divisions of their Dasas and other interpretive techniques, he will be able to ascertain whether the couple will be compatible and which may be the problematic areas. If the astrologer

---

* This may also consist of land, animals or a business offer from her father.

BRIDEGROOMS WANTED

Vathima Bharadwaja Maham, 22/160 M.C.A., L & T. employed, beautiful. Subsect acceptable. Decent marriage. Reply horoscope Box No. 4710, C/o THE HINDU, Madras-600002.

Alliance invited for good-looking Kammawar Naidu Graduate, 29/166/1100, State Government employed. Send horoscope family details Box No. 4478, C/o THE HINDU, Madras-600002.

Alliance from Iyer widower/ divorcee employed in Central Bank around 42 years for Iyer girl Vadama Kousika Barani divorcee no children aged 37 employed Central Govt. earning 2500. Reply with horoscope. Box No. 4694, C/o THE HINDU, Madras-600002.

Well educated and well placed groom around 38 years for a Garga double graduate Vadama girl, Chitrai. Send horoscope with biodata to Box. No. 4714, C/o THE HINDU, Madras-600002.

Saiva Vellala Pillai Doctor 24/156 cm slim fair non-veg seeks good alliance Doctor, Engineer same caste Mudaliar respectable family. Reply with horoscope Box No. 4722, C/o THE HINDU, Madras-600002.

Alliance for Srivatsa Vadama Avittam, Iyer girl. B. Tech., 22/163, from professionally qualified well settled boys of respectable family. Reply with horoscope to Box No. 4526, C/o THE HINDU, Madras-600002.

BRIDES WANTED

USA Greencard M.S. Engineer, 28/172, only son affluent

Srivaishnavite Iyengar family seeks Iyengar/Iyer/Telugu brahmin, below 23, beautiful tall accomplished well educated bride. Send horoscope. Box No. 7358, C/o THE HINDU, Madras 600002.

Wanted Graduate girl with transferable employment for graduate, Kousika Rohini, insurance employed, Tamil Iyer Boy, 28/170. Write details with horoscope. Box No. 7353, C/o THE HINDU, Madras-600002.

Telugu Yadava fair complexion girl, below 22 for boy, M. Com. 26/170 cm doing business. Reply with horoscope Box No. 4497, C/o THE HINDU, Madras-600002.

Alliance for Graduate, Brahacharanam, Kashyapa Aayilyam, 34/170/2500 Kerala Iyer employed in Multinational Co., in Bangalore from employed girls. Send horoscope. Box No. BA6217, C/o THE HINDU, Bangalore-560001.

Vaadyama Boy, Bharathwaja Gothram, Swathi, PUC, 30 age, 165 cms, only son, fair, well to do, self employed, defective vision but not blind, requires fair good looking plus Two, sincere, accommodative, respectable, home loving girl. Subsect no bar. Reply with horoscope: M. Ramamurthi, 40, I Main Road, CIT Colony, Mylapore, Madras-600004.

Alliance sought for well built, Propertied, Mudaliar groom, B.Sc., F.I.I.I. officer in General Insurance, 27/180/4000 with Chevvai Dosham from Pretty tall homely, intelligent, graduate/postgraduate Mudaiar girls, Reply Bio-data horoscope Box No. 4276, C/o THE HINDU, Madras-600002.

Fig 10.1 Matrimonial advertisements taken from The Hindu, *Sunday 16 April 1989.*

sanctifies the union, the family informs the other family who may then take the two charts to their own astrologer. If approved, the families will plan the wedding whose exact time and place may be arranged by the astrologer.

On the other hand, if the astrologer discourages the union, the families may either seek a second opinion or dissolve the match and resume their search — depending, of course, on how much value they place on the astrologer's opinion. If the family cannot find a suitable partner, the astrologer may assume the role of matchmaker by contacting families who, in his opinion, will 'pass the acid test'. Once a candidate is found, chart analysis begins anew.

Because marriage is such an important decision to be made, the astrologer tells the family how he feels about a possible union in no uncertain terms. If he approves, his enthusiasm is boundless. If, however, he feels strongly that the marriage will bring disastrous results, he adamantly orders a rejection of the proposal. I observed a few of these consultations with disappointed families, and although I could not understand the literal words of the ensuing conversation, the flailing and waving of the astrologer's arms and the defiant, commanding tone displayed his disapproval. It also illustrates the power he wields over lives, a quality which, ironically, endears him to the Hindu community.

The more educated, younger generations of Indians do not always have their marriages pre-arranged. They may decide to marry for love and not for practical purposes — but still would like the union sanctioned. To this end, they may visit an astrologer to please their parents or to hear his opinion about what may be encountered should the marriage take place. They may not necessarily take his advice but will, none the less, listen to what he says. (Most Western astrologers do not advise two people whether they should be together but, instead, point out what they have in common along with difficulties which may arise.)

Often, when my astrology lesson was over, I lingered on in my teacher's one-room storefront office to witness a typical day. People strolled in and out continually without appointments seeking advice on marriage prospects, business, children or were there to pick up a horoscope which had been prepared in advance. Though they conversed in Hindi (the language commonly spoken in Benares), by observing facial expressions, hand movements, and by the tone of their voices, I was able to follow the outline of their conversation. Sometimes, shop owners, colleagues and friends came by and would all sit cross-legged on the carpeted floor drinking tea and conversing intellectually or discussing neighbourhood gossip. At other times, there were serious Jyotish students who, like myself, were there to listen to consultations in an effort to experience first-hand the application of astrological theory to horoscope interpretation.

Although an astrologer's office will reflect his individuality, there are certain objects which remain constant. What I remember most about Pandit Shastri's office was that there were books in every corner of the room, not only about astrology but about healing rituals, medicine, child development and other related subjects. As an example of his devotion, there was a miniature altar upon which stood a photo of his spiritual guru or patron god/goddess, flowers and burning incense. Covering the walls were murals and photos of various mythical gods, goddesses and astrological and Vedic sages, all of which illustrate the extent to which spirituality and religion are tied to the study of astrology. Most importantly, somewhere in most every astrologer's room or office, there is a photograph or reproduction of the elephant-god, Ganesh — who guards the realm of secret knowledge, including astrology — one of the highest forms of knowledge that the gods and goddesses are said to have bestowed upon the earth.

NOTES

Chapter One

1. Cumont, *Astrology Among the Greeks and Romans*, pp. 7–8
2. *Report of the Calendar Reform Committee*, p. 188
3. Table 1.1 is taken directly from *Report of the Calendar Reform Committee, Chronological Table*
4. Information taken from classifications as set forth in the *Report of the Calendar Reform Committee*
5. Kublin, *India*, p. 35
6. McIntosh, *Ibid.*, p.43
7. McIntosh, *Astrologers and their Creed*, p. 49
8. Sharma, *Astrology and Jyotirvidya*. p. 13
9. McIntosh, *op. cit.*, p. 49
10. Raman, *Planetary Influences on Human Affairs*, pp. 29–30
11. *Ibid.*, p. 29
12. *Report of the Calendar Reform Committee*, p. 283
13. *Ibid.*, p. 235
14. Table 1.3 along with the explanation is taken directly from *Report of the Calendar Reform Committee*, Table 8, p. 193
15. *Ibid.*, pp. 238-239
16. *Ibid.*, p. 221
17. Raman, *op. cit.*, p. 24 and p. 34
18. Raman, *op. cit.*, p. 21
19. *Report of the Calendar Reform Committee*, p. 2
20. Chakravarty, *Origin and Development of Indian Calendrical Science*, p. 49
21. *Report of the Calendar Reform Committee*, p. 8
22. Chakravarty, *op. cit.*, pp. 56–57
23. *Ibid.*, p. 57

Chapter Two

1. Baigent, Campion and Harvey, *Mundane Astrology*, p. 124
2. *Ibid.*, p. 124
3. Krishnamurti, *Casting the Horoscope*, p. 58
4. *Ibid.*, p. 57

Chapter Three

1. Kannan, *Fundamentals of Hindu Astrology*, p. 300
2. Addey, *Harmonics in Astrology*, p. 101
3. *Ibid.*, p. 13
4. *Ibid.*, p. 90

Chapter Four

1. *Phaladeepika*, Adhyaya 2, Sloka 1, p. 11
2. *Brihat Jataka*, p. 19, Ch. 2, Line 8
3. *Phaladeepika*, Adhyaya 2, Sloka 8, p. 14
4. *Ibid.* Adhyaya 2, Sloka 2, p. 11
5. *Brihat Jataka*, p. 19, Ch. 2, Line 8.
6. *Phaladeepika*, Adhyaya 2, Sloka 9, p. 14
7. *Ibid.*, Adhyaya 2, Sloka 3, p. 12
8. *Brihat Jataka*, p. 19, Ch. 2, Line 9
9. *Phaladeepika*, Adhyaya 2, Sloka 10, p. 15
10. *Ibid.*, Adhyaya 2, Sloka 4, p. 12
11. *Brihat Jataka*, p. 20, Ch. 2, Line 9
12. *Phaladeepika*, Adhyaya 2, Sloka 11, p. 15
13. *Ibid.*, Adhyaya 2, Sloka 5, p. 13
14. *Brihat Jataka*, p. 20, Ch. 2, Line 10
15. *Phaladeepika*, Adhyaya 2, Sloka 12, p. 15
16. Monier-Williams, *A Sanskrit–English Dictionary*, p. 359
17. *Phaladeepika*, Adhyaya 2, Sloka 6, p. 13
18. *Brihat Jataka*, p. 20, Ch. 2, Line 10
19. *Phaladeepika*, Adhyaya 2, Sloka 13, p. 16
20. *Ibid.*, Adhyaya 2, Sloka 7, p. 13
21. *Brihat Jataka*, p. 20, Ch. 2, Line 11
22. *Phaladeepika*, Adhyaya 2, Sloka 14, p. 16
23. *Ibid.*, Adhyaya 2
24. *Ibid.*, Adhyaya 2
25. Kalyana Varma, *Saravali*, p. 22
26. *Ibid.*, p. 43
27. *Phaladeepika*, Adhyaya 1, Sloka 10, p. 6
28. *Ibid.*, Adhyaya 1, Sloka 10, p. 6

29. *Ibid.*, Adhyaya 1, Sloka 11–12, p. 7
30. *Ibid.*, Adhyaya 1, Sloka 11–12, p. 7
31. *Ibid.*, Adhyaya 1, Sloka 11–12, p. 7
32. *Ibid.*, Adhyaya 1, Sloka 13, p. 7
33. *Ibid.*, Adhyaya 1, Sloka 13, p. 7
34. *Ibid.*, Adhyaya 1, Sloka 14, p. 8
35. *Ibid.*, Adhyaya 1, Sloka 14, p. 8
36. *Ibid.*, Adhyaya 1, Sloka 15, p. 9
37. *Ibid.*, Adhyaya 1, Sloka 15, p. 9
38. *Ibid.*, Adhyaya 1, Sloka 16, p. 9
39. Kalyana Varma, *op. cit.*, p. 35

Chapter Five

1. *Phaladeepika*, Adhyaya 9, Sloka 1, p. 124
2. Krishnamurti, *Fundamental Principles of Astrology*, p. 73
3. *Phaladeepika*, Adhyaya 9, Sloka 2, p. 124
4. Krishnamurti, *op. cit.*, p. 78
5. *Phaladeepika*, Adhyaya 9, Sloka 3, p. 125
6. Krishnamurti, *op. cit.*, p. 87–8
7. *Phaladeepika*, Adhyaya 9, Sloka 4, p. 125
8. Krishnamurti, *op. cit.*, p. 97
9. *Phaladeepika*, Adhyaya 9, Sloka 5, p. 125
10. Krishnamurti, *op. cit.*, p. 105
11. *Phaladeepika*, Adhyaya 9, Sloka 6, p. 126
12. Krishnamurti, *op. cit.*, p. 116
13. *Phaladeepika*, Adhyaya 9, Sloka 7, p. 126
14. Krishnamurti, *op. cit.*, p. 127
15. *Phaladeepika*, Adhyaya 9, Sloka 8, p. 126
16. Krishnamurti, *op. cit.*, p. 135
17. *Phaladeepika*, Adhyaya 9, Sloka 9, p. 127
18. Krishnamurti, *op. cit.*, p. 143
19. *Phaladeepika*, Adhyaya 9, Sloka 10, p. 127
20. Krishnamurti, *op. cit.*, p. 150
21. *Phaladeepika*, Adhyaya 9, Sloka 11, p. 127
22. Krishnamurti, *op. cit.*, p. 160
23. *Phaladeepika*, Adhyaya 9, Sloka 12, p. 128
24. Krishnamurti, *op. cit.*, p. 170

Chapter Six

1. *Brihat Jataka*, commentary on p. 23
2. *Phaladeepika*, Adhyaya 10, Sloka 16
3. Krishnamurti, *op. cit.*, p. 24
4. *Brihat Jataka*, Ch. 2, Line 11, p. 20

Chapter Eight

1. O'Flaherty, *Hindu Myths*, p. 351
2. Inglis, *Hindu Dasa System*, pp. 8–9

Chapter Nine

1. *Phaladeepika*, Adhyaya 10, Sloka 13, p. 137
2. *Ibid.*, Adhyaya 12, Sloka 25, p. 159

Chapter Ten

1. *Webster's Ninth New Collegiate Dictionary*, p. 379

BIBLIOGRAPHY

John Addey, *Harmonics in Astrology* (L.N. Fowler & Co., Ltd., 1976).

Michael Baigent, Nicholas Campion and Charles Harvey *Mundane Astrology* (Aquarian Press, 1984).

James T. Braha, *Ancient Hindu Astrology for the Modern Western Astrologer* (Hermetician Press, 1986).

W.G. de Burgh, *The Legacy of the Ancient World* (Penguin Books, 1947) (Originally published by MacDonald & Evans, 1923).

Apurba Kumar Chakravarty, *Origin and Development of Indian Calendrical Science* (Published by R.K. Maitra on behalf of 'Indian Studies Past and Present', 1975).

Council of Scientific and Industrial Research, *Report of the Calendar Reform Committee* (Government of India Publications, New Delhi, 1955).

Franz Cumont, *Astrology and Religion Among the Greeks and Romans* (Dover Publications, 1960).

Grace Inglis, *Hindu Dasa System* (Sagar Publications, 1973).

Kalyana Varma, *Saravali*, translated and commentary by R. Santhanam (two volume set Ranjan Publications, 1983).

S. Kannan, *Fundamentals of Hindu Astrology* (Sagar Publications, 1981).

K.S. Krishnamurti, *Casting the Horoscope*, Volume I Mahabala, 1971).

K.S. Krishnamurti, *Fundamental Principles of Astrology*, Volume II (Mahabala, 1971).

Hyman Kublin, *India* (Houghton Miflin, 1968).

Christopher McIntosh, *Astrologers and their Creed* (Century Hutchinson Publishing Group Ltd; originally published by Frederick A. Praeger, 1969).

Mantreswar, *Phaladeepika*, Fifth Edition, translated by V. Subrahmanya Sastry (K. Subrahmanyam, 1981).

Jeff Mayo, *The Astrologer's Astronomical Handbook* (L.N. Fowler, 1965).

Sir Monier Monier-Williams, *A Sanskrit-English Dictionary: Etymologically and Philologically Arranged* (Clarendon Press, 1899).

Wendy O'Flaherty (trans.), *Hindu Myths: A Sourcebook Translated from the Sanskrit* (Penguin Books, 1975).

W.M. O'Neil, *Time and the Calendars* (Sydney University Press, 1973).

B.V. Raman, *Planetary Influences on Human Behavior* (IBH Prakashana, 1982).

B.V. Raman, *Three Hundred Important Combinations*, Ninth edition (IBH Prakashana, 1983).

B.V. Raman, *Graha and Bhava Balas*

Wolfgang Alexander Schocken, *The Calculated Confusion of Calendars* (Vantage Press, 1976).

Viswantath Deva Sharma, *Astrology and Jyotirvidya: The Fundamental Principles and the Systems of Prognosis* (Viswa Jyotirvid Samgha, 1973).

Anthony Philip Stone, *Hindu Astrology: Myths, Symbols and Realities* (Select Books, 1981).

Vaharamihira, *Brihat Jataka*, translated by Usha & Shashi (Sagar Publications, 1985).

Derek Walters, *Chinese Astrology* (Aquarian Press, 1987).

Diane Wolkstein and Samuel Noah Kramer, *Inanna: Queen of Heaven and Earth* (Harper and Row, 1983).

GLOSSARY

Antara Dasa One of nine planetary sub-sub-periods into which a Bhukti Dasa is divided

Autumn Equinox The opposite point of the vernal equinox; 21 or 22 September; the first day of autumn and the first degree of Libra when there are an equal number of daylight and nighttime hours

Ayanamsa The numerical difference in degrees and minutes between the *actual* 0° Aries and the equinoctial point, the Tropical Zodiac's *symbolic* 0° Aries

Benefic A naturally auspicious planet, i.e. Venus, Jupiter, waxing Moon

Bhava Sanskrit for one of the 12 houses or arbitrary divisions of the zodiac

Bhukti One of nine planetary sub-periods into which a Mahadasa is divided

Budha Sanskrit for Mercury

Caste One of the five socio-economic classes based on the deeds and actions of the previous life into which a Hindu is born

Chandra Sanskrit for the Moon

Dasa an abbreviated form of Mahadasa

Dhanus Sanskrit for Sagittarius

Dharma One's mission or predetermined work that is supposed to be carried out in this lifetime based on one's caste and partly on one's horoscope

Dreccan One third of a zodiacal sign

Dusthana House Sixth, eighth or twelfth house and considered to be inauspicious

Equinoctial Point See Vernal Equinox

Grahas Sanskrit for 'rotating bodies' and including the Sun, Moon, planets and Moon's Nodes

Guru Sanskrit for the planet Jupiter; literally meaning 'one who transmits knowledge'

Harmonics System of degree divisional charts founded by John Addey

Hinduism Religion of four-fifths of the population of India

Hora One half of a zodiacal sign

Jyotish The discipline of Hindu astrology comprising mathematical, astronomical and interpretive principles

Kanya Sanskrit for Virgo

Karma Accumulated actions from former lifetimes that help to create one's present

Kataka Sanskrit for Cancer

Kendra House First, fourth, seventh or tenth house and considered to be auspicious

Kethu Sanskrit for Dragon's tail or South Node

Kuja Sanskrit for Mars

Kumbha Sanskrit for Aquarius

Lagna Sanskrit for Ascendant

Mahadasa One of nine major planetary periods

Makara Sanskrit for Capricorn

Malefic A naturally inauspicious planet, i.e. Mars, Saturn, Sun, waning Moon

Mantra Sacred song that is recited as part of one's daily prayers

Meena Sanskrit for Pisces

Mesha Sanskrit for Aries

Mithuna Sanskrit for Gemini

Moolatrikona A set of degrees within a zodiacal sign considered to be the most favourable position for a certain planet to occupy

Nakshatra One of the 27 asterisms or fixed star clusters which each span 13°20' of the zodiacal belt

Navamsa One ninth of a zodiacal sign

Neecha Degree and sign of planetary fall

Nirayana Zodiac Sidereal Zodiac based on actual position of the constellations of the zodiac

Occidental Astrology Western Astrology

Panchamsa One fifth of a zodiacal sign

Precession of the Equinoxes The retrograde movement of the equinoctial point (and, therefore, the four cardinal points) through the constellations of the zodiac

Rahu Sanskrit for Dragon's Head or North Node

Raj Yoga Sanskrit for 'royal union'; Raj Yogas are certain planetary combinations which create fortunate circumstances in one's life

Rasi Sanskrit for one of the 12 signs of the zodiac

Rasi Chakra Sanskrit for 'zodiacal wheel'; Rasi Chakra is the horoscope itself

Ravi Sanskrit for Sun

Sani Sanskrit for Saturn

Sanskrit The ancient language of India

Sayana Zodiac Tropical Zodiac based on symbolic position of the constellations of the zodiac

Septamsa One seventh of a zodiacal sign

Shad Bala The six sources — position, aspect, natural strength, motion, direction and time — from which a planet draws its strength

Shodasavarga Different sub-divisional charts

Simha Sanskrit for Leo

Spring Equinox See Vernal Equinox

Sukra Sanskrit for Venus

Summer Solstice The longest day of the year; 21 or 22 June; the first day of summer and the first degree of Cancer

Surya Sanskrit for Sun

Surya Siddhanta One of the Siddhantas, the five scientific astronomical treatises written around AD 400

Swakshetra Sign of planetary rulership

Thula Sanskrit for Libra

Tithi Indian lunar day which is measured by the length of time it takes for the Moon to travel 12°, $1/30$ of a lunar month or 360°

Trikona House Fifth or ninth house and considered to be auspicious

Uchcha Degree and sign of planetary exaltation

Upachaya House Third, sixth, tenth or eleventh house and considered inauspicious

Varga Short for Shodasavarga

Vargottama A position of planetary strength which occurs when the planet's zodiacal sign is identical to its corresponding Navamsa sign

Vedas The series of religious books comprising sacred hymns and poems which map out myths, legends and tenets of Hinduism

Vernal or Spring Equinox Also called the equinoctial point and is the point at which the celestial equator intersects with the ecliptic; Occurring on 21 March, it indicates the first day of spring, the first degree of Aries and is a day when there is an equal amount of daylight and nighttime hours

Vimshoddhari Dasa Totalling 120 years, this system maps out the planetary periods and sub-periods which define a person's life

Vrischika Sanskrit for Scorpio

Vrishaba Sanskrit for Taurus

Winter Solstice The shortest day of the year; 21 or 22 December; the first day of winter and the first degree of Capricorn

Yuga One of four planetary eras which, when added together, make up the Maha Yuga, literally meaning 'great year'

APPENDIX

The following mail-order services provide computerized Hindu Astrological calculations in addition to providing Western Astrological charts.

Astro Computing Services, PO Box 16430, San Diego, CA 92116-0430, USA. 1-800-888-9983.

James Braha, Astro-Logos, PO Box 1961, Hollywood, FL 33022-1961, USA. 1-305-922-6726. (Analysis of Hindu Charts via telephone and cassette.)

The following companies sell astrological software programs which compute Hindu Astrological calculations

Matrix Software, 315 Marion, Big Rapids, Michigan 49307, USA. Sales: 1-800-PLANETS. Support: 1-616-796-2483. Fax: 1-616-796-3060.

Matrix UK, c/o Martin Davis, PO Box 9, Pitlochry, Perthshire PH9 0YD, Scotland. 03502-8616.

Astrocalc, 67 Peascroft Road, Hemel Hempstead, Herts HP3 8ER, UK.

Lord Ganesh, guardian of secret knowledge and astrology

INDEX

CHINESE ASTROLOGY
Interpreting the revelations of the Celestial Messengers
DEREK WALTERS

The Chinese have practised astrology for many thousands of years. They had compiled a systematic method of observing and interpreting the heavens long before contact had been made with the Western world.

CHINESE ASTROLOGY is the first comprehensive study of this fascinating subject to be made available in a Western language. The author traces the history of Chinese astrology from its earliest records to the present and explains the principles on which the art is founded. The subject is brought to life by the inclusion of a number of actual Chinese horoscopes from different periods. Among the many astrological texts which are quoted is the complete two-thousand year old treatise written by the Grand Astrologer, Ssu Ma Ch'ien.

Derek Walters is Europe's foremost authority on Chinese Astrology, respected not only for his thorough academic knowledge of the subject, but also as an actual practitioner of Chinese Divination. He writes frequently for a leading astrological magazine, and has appeared on British radio and television.

PSYCHOLOGICAL ASTROLOGY

Astrological symbolism and the human psyche

KAREN HAMAKER-ZONDAG

Astrology is an ancient art, but its truths are timeless. The validity of its claims are slowly being realized through the application of contemporary disciplines.

This book is part of that process and examines the traditional wisdom of astrology in the light of Jungian psychology, revealing the horoscopes as an accurate picture of our psychic structure and a key to self-knowledge and personal growth.

Beginning with a lucid analysis of Jung's terminology – including archetypes, the collective unconscious and the theory of synchronicity – PSYCHOLOGICAL ASTROLOGY goes on to explore in depth the striking correspondence between Jung's theory of psychological types and the traditional astrological elements.

Karen Hamaker-Zondag has been fascinated by astrology for many years. Her studies of Jung have led her to equate his revolutionary concepts with astrological theory, and her book makes an important contribution to the study of both astrology and human behaviour.

SYNASTRY
A complete guide to the astrology of relationships
PENNY THORNTON

Synastry is a complex but precise method of charting the inter-play and development of human relationships through astro-logical analysis. In synastry, birth charts are compared in order to bring out the fundamental interactions between two people and stimulate greater understanding of how they relate to each other on all levels.

In this comprehensive introduction the basic principles of chart comparison are explained and are illustrated by in-depth case studies – including a detailed critical analysis and composite charts of the Prince and Princess of Wales.

'Clear, substantive and emanates from the heart . . . Sparkling prose is backed up by solid astrological principle . . . Suitable for all levels of astrologers, it is highly recommended.' – *The Astrological Journal.*

'An excellent addition to the library of any astrologer in-terested in learning to use astrology as a tool for increased awareness and growth.' – *Barbara Somerfield, Director, National Astrological Society, USA*

'A work of considerable insight and value.' – *Australian Astrologer's Journal*

Penny Thornton, a former dancer with the Royal Ballet, is a consultant astrologer specializing in synastry and a member of the Council of the Astrological Association. As well as teaching, lecturing and broadcasting on astrology she holds counselling sessions and workshops in London and Surrey.

HOW TO INTERPRET A BIRTH CHART
A guide to the analysis and synthesis of astrological charts
MARTIN FREEMAN

Having constructed the birth chart as accurately as possible, the astrologer then has to interpret what is laid out in it – a mass of complex and often conflicting information.

This introductory guide provides the student with a solid grounding in natal analysis and interpretation, but more importantly it offers invaluable advice on the difficult art of chart synthesis – the technique of pulling together the pieces of the astrological jigsaw to form a coherent picture that so often eludes the beginner.

'Martin Freeman introduces some delightful new "keynotes" and the phrases describing the attributes of the signs have an inspirational quality which stimulates the imagination beyond the bald keywords of earlier textbooks.' – *Astrological Journal*

'An excellent book on the basic factors used in chart interpretation . . . contains many words of wisdom to the novice astrologer.' – *Faculty of Astrological Studies Newsletter*

Martin Freeman works as an astrological consultant and separately as an analytical psychotherapist in London. He has been actively involved in the Astrological Association in the UK and was President of the Faculty of Astrological Studies from 1979 to 1986.

CYCLES OF DESTINY
Understanding return charts
RONALD C. DAVISON

The result of years of painstaking research and the last great work of the late Ronald Davison, CYCLES OF DESTINY is the long-awaited companion volume to THE TECHNIQUE OF PREDICTION.

Davison shows, step-by-step, how to calculate returns, horoscopes generated when planets return to the exact positions they occupied at birth. He examines both postnatal and antenatal solar return charts, as well as a further 10 different types including ascensional, precessional, converse and lunation returns. He demonstrates their efficacy using case studies, as well as showing how the various returns can be linked together, giving closer and closer focus on a particular moment at which the major events in a life are unmistakably indicated.

On the basis of his findings, Davison reflects deeply on free will, on the ethics of prediction and on the nature of time itself. He also comments on the part of fortune in the return chart and produces evidence in support of the prenatal epoch method of establishing the exact time of birth.

Ronald Davison became President of the Astrological Lodge in 1952, an office he held for 30 years, and also produced the respected journal Astrology *from 1959 until just a year before his death in January 1985. After he retired from the Civil Service in 1974 he kept in frequent contact with leading European astrologers and went on several lecture tours of the USA where he was very well received, making him one of the few real astrologers whose work and reputation was genuinely world-wide.*